LEADERSHIP
AND
SOCIAL CHANGE

LEADERSHIP
AND
SOCIAL CHANGE

Edited by
William R. Lassey

UNIVERSITY ASSOCIATES
Publishers and Consultants
P.O. Box 615, Iowa City, Iowa 52240

ISBN 0-88390-054-8
Copyright © 1971 by University Associates

First Printing, December, 1971
Second Printing, March, 1973

UNIVERSITY ASSOCIATES is an educational organization engaged in human relations training, research, consulting, publication, and both pre-service and in-service education. The organization consists of university-affiliated educational consultants and experienced facilitators in human relations and leadership training.

In addition to offering general laboratory experiences, University Associates designs and carries out programs on a contractual basis for various organizations. These programs fall under the following areas of specialization: Human Relations Training, Leadership Development, Organization Development, Community Development, and Educational Research.

PREFACE

A published textbook which sufficiently synthesized leadership research to make it reasonably comprehensible for student or adult groups has so far not been available. Consequently I have searched for several years to find appropriate reading materials for a course on "The Sociology of Leadership" and for practical reference readings for leadership development workshops offered by Montana State University. This book represents the culmination of the "search" for a useful set of the best materials available on leadership concepts and research.

A number of individuals deserve credit for assistance in preparation of the readings in book form. My immediate superiors at Montana State University, Roy Huffman, Vice President for Research, Ernest Ahrendes, Coordinator of Extension and Community Services, and Del Samson, Head of the Department of Sociology, have each provided encouragement and freedom in pursuit of the project.

My colleagues in the Center for Planning and Development, Anne S. Williams and Howard Huffman graciously assumed part of my administrative and research responsibilities so that I might have time to prepare the manuscript.

Students in the courses and participants in leadership workshops were most helpful in evaluating the utility of the readings for their own better preparation as budding or developing leaders. This book is dedicated to them and to future students of the subject.

My sincere thanks are offered to Mrs. Shirley Wyckman, not only for the almost infinite variety of detailed work she undertook in preparation of the manuscript and her devotion to perfection in completing the task, but for her patience with a sometimes temperamental and always absentminded professor.

The authors and publishers who consented to the reprinting of articles deserve appreciation for their willingness to trust their contributions to a new volume. Bill Pfeiffer, Executive

Director of University Associates Press, provided encouragement, support, and advised me on the requirements for a complete and useful volume.

Finally, my family—wife, Mickey and daughters, Dione and Maureen—found me occasionally absent in body and often absent in mind, because of attention to this work; my grateful love and appreciation is here acknowledged for their patience and devotion.

William R. Lassey
Bozeman, Montana
August 20, 1971

TABLE
OF
CONTENTS

xi

INTRODUCTION

The readings and original contributions contained in this book were selected for two primary reasons: (1) to provide the reader with an overview of some of the most thoroughly tested concepts about leadership behavior, consequences of such behavior, and application of the concepts to leadership situations and (2) to present a point of view about participative or democratic strategies of leadership.

The second objective arises from a conviction that leadership and management research evidence is heavily supportive of the participative model; leadership which attempts to maximize individual initiative, intrinsic or self-generated motivation, and autonomy of those led is more likely to be effective in task accomplishment than leadership which imposes control over individuals in an authoritarian and centralized fashion. Productivity of organizations, effectiveness of communities in meeting social needs of citizens, and other leadership situations will be enhanced by maximizing potential for involvement of persons who will be affected by any decisions made. The participative process works better than any alternative process, but because we have failed to adequately understand how "democracy" can be applied in many circumstances, we have subverted democratic values in favor of more authoritarian systems. This has been particularly true in large bureaucracies or complex organizational systems.

Behavioral science research in organizations and communities has helped to redefine and clarify the leadership process and has almost invariably tended to support the utility of participative strategies in meeting basic human psychological and social requirements. In an extended time perspective man seems to function better and be more productive when treated as though he can make useful contributions to decisions that affect him, regardless of the organizational setting.

The selection of readings in this book is therefore by no

means random; they were carefully chosen to represent research results from the several disciplines which appear to have made the greatest contributions to understanding of leadership: psychology, sociology, management science, communication science, and political science. The emphasis is on applied research results; that is, leadership theory is treated in each selection, but always with a primary concern for the practical consequences of the theory for specific leadership situations.

Although, many of the readings speak of the leader as "manager" in a formal business organizational setting, the principles or concepts discussed in each case have applications on a much broader basis. This is so in large part because organizations of various sizes and descriptions provide the primary setting for man to function as leader or follower. Soundly based research findings in one organization will often have direct application to other circumstances. Thus, many of the principles generated by behavioral scientists in business organizations with a "profit" motive have important implications for governmental, political or voluntary organizations with very different explicit goals. The principles are based on the social and psychological characteristics of the human species, rather than the particular circumstance in which man functions.

The Rational and Emotional Dimensions of Man

The recent advances in understanding of leadership have arisen from investigations of two inter-related characteristics of human beings: consideration of both the *rational* and *emotional* parts of man are crucial to the appreciation of why some leaders are effective while others are not. Unless leaders operate on the basis of how men feel *as well as* how they visibly act or react, they cannot hope to be followed with confidence by those without leadership status. This leads to the conception of two principle leadership functions which appear as central elements within most of the readings in this book. *Task* functions are those which focus primarily on getting particular jobs done, whether they be managing a government bureaucracy, selling products for profit, managing the sale of services for a fee, organizing a community for construction of a swimming pool, or other tasks. *Maintenance* functions have to do with meeting the emotional needs of the individuals and groups while they are involved in the task accomplishment process. Although most leaders may consider themselves primarily concerned with task, it is eminently clear that maintenance functions are central to the long range effectiveness of an organized effort. A leader must not lose sight of the primary goals (tasks) of the organization, but he dare not ignore the primary needs of the human beings involved in seeking those goals if he hopes to attain some consistent level of productivity. There is increasing evidence that maintenance (or motivation) skills of leaders have *more* to do with maximizing organized productivity of men or women at work than technical competence in accomplishing a given task.

For men to perform at a level approaching their maximum potential, they must be treated as integrated human beings who want to accomplish specific goals while maintaining an emotionally satisfying role in the goal achievement process. This seems to be true regardless of the leadership context.

Organization of the Readings

The readings are not intended to be useful only if read sequentially. Each contribution is essentially a self-contained presentation of basic leadership concepts or research results. Nevertheless, it might be helpful to readers unfamiliar with leadership studies to read Parts I and II, BASIC CONCEPTS and COMMUNICATION AND LEADERSHIP before the sections on ORGANIZATIONAL CHANGE AND LEADERSHIP, COMMUNITY CHANGE AND LEADERSHIP and THE STUDY OF LEADERSHIP, since these sections apply many of the basic concepts and research results to practical situations.

Although the book is divided into sections, many readers with primary interest in community leadership may find the selections on "communication" or "organization" as useful and applicable as the section labeled "community change and leadership." This is only to emphasize the inter-related nature of the concepts and research results and their application to general leadership approaches regardless of the context.

The various sub-divisions of the book are preceded by a brief introduction which summarizes each selection within that section, while emphasizing some of the major issues discussed by each author.

PART I
BASIC CONCEPTS

PART I
BASIC CONCEPTS

Although it is inappropriate to suppose that leadership and social change can be neatly divided into mutually exclusive subdivisions, some separation of selections by leadership context is helpful to the organization of thought. The first part is therefore devoted to contributions which can be termed basic in the sense that they would seem to apply regardless of the context.

Thus the first selection, "Dimensions of Leadership," emphasizes definitions, functions, authority, power, and styles of leadership. Each of these topics is treated in greater depth in later selections of Part I and, with respect to research studies or specific leadership situations, in Parts II, III, IV and V.

The role of the leader as helper is introduced in a selection by Jack R. Gibb, one of the most pre-eminent students of leadership. Gibb analyzes the role of leaders in assisting the growth and productivity of those for whom the leader has responsibility. He emphasizes the kind of leadership orientations and behaviors which will most likely motivate human beings to make the maximum contribution toward organizational or group goals, while also realizing individual goals and needs.

Although the next selection, by McGregor, analyzes leadership in management terminology, his concepts are basic to a wide range of leadership situations. The book from which the selection is taken, *The Human Side of Enterprise,* is considered one of the classics in application of behavioral science knowledge to large business organizations. He emphasizes the key point that leadership is basically a "relationship" between the person assigned to leadership responsibility or who emerges as a leader and those with whom he must collaborate in achieving prescribed or collaboratively selected goals. He recommends that a heterogeneous mix of talented individuals is likely to provide the best potential for creative and effective leadership in any leadership situation where succession to positions

3

of higher influence is not predetermined.

The article by Tannenbaum and Schmidt is another classic conceptualization of key issues in leadership; it has had widespread influence on the better understanding of authoritarian as opposed to democratic styles of leadership. Numerous more recent studies have failed to counter the basic analytical framework developed by the authors. They emphasize that the style of leadership depends on the degree of "authoritarianism" which characterizes the leadership situation. To attempt a completely democratic (shared) leadership style in a context where a more authoritarian style is the norm would be to invite disharmony and eventual ineffectiveness. Nevertheless, their conclusion is clear: participative leadership is, if the situation permits, the more productive style. The leader must decide, on the basis of his sophisticated understanding of the situation, which style is most appropriate; his effectiveness will depend more on appreciation of the forces in himself, in his subordinates, and in the circumstances of their interaction, than on the specific task or tasks to which they are devoted.

The final selection in this section is a complex conceptualization of the psychological and social factors which contribute to three levels of leader-group effectiveness: attempted, successful and effective leadership. It is only partially tested as a theory, but it helps substantially to clarify the multiplicity of factors which must be considered in the complex interaction of leader and group as they attempt to achieve a maximum level of goal attainment.

DIMENSIONS OF LEADERSHIP
by William R. Lassey

A definition of leadership adapted from Tannenbaum, Weschler and Massarik[1] is appropriate as an initial framework: *Leadership is interpersonal influence exercised through the process of communication toward the attainment of a specified*

[1] Tannenbaum, Robert; Irving Weschler, and Fred Massarik. *Leadership and Organization: A Behavioral Science Approach.* N.Y.: McGraw Hill Book Co., 1961.

goal or goals. However, in recent years researchers in the behavioral sciences have become increasingly certain that we could not understand the nature of leadership by examining only the behavior of the designated "leader." Actions of the persons "led" are also key factors affecting leader behavior, as is the structure and environment of the group or organizational "situation" or "environment"; that is, the *type* of leader or leadership required depends upon the situation.

Functional Dimensions of Leadership

Two sets of functions have been identified, the performance of which at appropriate times are necessary in order for a group or organization to achieve its goal: *task functions* must be executed in selecting and carrying out the defined goal or goals; *maintenance functions* are required to strengthen and maintain group or organizational viability. A good football team must be skilled in blocking and tackling and in performing complex offensive and defensive play patterns (task functions), but team "spirit," cooperation, interdependence and member satisfaction (maintenance functions) must also exist at a high level if the team is to be successful. The following list contains some of the most important functions.

TASK FUNCTIONS[2]

Initiating activity: proposing solutions, suggesting new ideas, new definitions of the problem, new attacks on problems or new organization of material.

Information seeking: asking for clarification of suggestions, requesting additional information or facts.

Information giving: offering facts or generalizations, relating one's own experience to group problems, to illustrate points.

Opinion giving: stating an opinion or belief concerning a suggestion or one of several suggestions, particularly concerning its value rather than its factual basis.

Elaborating: clarifying, giving examples or developing meanings, trying to envision how a proposal might work out if adopted.

Coordinating: showing relationships among various ideas or suggestions, trying to pull ideas and suggestions together,

[2] For greater elaboration on these functions, see Warren G. Bennis and Herbert A. Shepherd, "Group Observation," in W. G. Bennis, Kenneth D. Benne and Robert Chin (eds.), *The Planning of Change*, New York: Holt, Rinehart and Winston, Inc. 1961, pp. 743-756.

trying to draw together activities of various subgroups or members.

Summarizing: pulling together related ideas or suggestions, restating suggestions after the group has discussed them.

Testing feasibility: making application of suggestions to real situations, examining practicality and workability of ideas, pre-evaluating decisions.

Evaluating: submitting group decisions or accomplishments to comparison with group standards, measuring accomplishments against goals.

Diagnosing: determining sources of difficulties, appropriate steps to take next, the main blocks to progress.

MAINTENANCE FUNCTIONS

Encouraging: being friendly, warm, responsive to others, praising others and their ideas, agreeing with and accepting contributions of others.

Gate-keeping: trying to make it possible for another member to make a contribution to the group by saying, "We haven't heard anything from Jim yet," or suggesting limited talking time for everyone so that all will have a chance to be heard.

Standard setting: expressing standards for the group to use in choosing its content or procedures or in evaluating its decisions, reminding the group to avoid decisions which conflict with group standards.

Following: going along with decisions of the group, somewhat passively accepting ideas of others, serving as audience during group discussion and decision making.

Expressing group feeling: summarizing what group feeling is sensed to be, describing reactions of the group to ideas or solutions.

Evaluating: submitting group decisions or accomplishments to comparison with group standards, measuring accomplishments against goals.

Consensus testing: tentatively asking for group opinions in order to find out if the group is nearing consensus on a decision, sending up trial balloons to test group opinions.

Harmonizing: mediating, conciliating differences in points of view, making compromise solutions.

Tension reducing: draining off negative feelings by jesting or pouring oil on troubled waters, putting a tense situation in wider context.

TYPES OF NONFUNCTIONAL BEHAVIOR

From time to time—more often perhaps than anyone likes to admit—people behave in nonfunctional ways that do not help and sometimes actually harm the group or organization and the work it is trying to do. Some of the more common types of nonfunctional behaviors are described below:

Aggression: working for status by criticizing or blaming others, showing hostility against the group or some individual, deflating the ego or status of others.

Blocking: interfering with the progress of the group by going off on a tangent, citing personal experiences unrelated to the problem, arguing too much on a point, rejecting ideas without consideration.

Self-confessing: using the group as a sounding board, expressing personal, nongroup oriented feelings or points of view.

Competing: vying with others to produce the best ideas, talk the most, play the most roles, gain favor with the leader.

Seeking sympathy: trying to induce other group members to by sympathetic to one's problems or misfortunes, deploring one's own ideas to gain support.

Special pleading: introducing or supporting suggestions related to one's own pat concerns or philosophies, lobbying.

Horsing around: clowning, joking, mimicking, disrupting the work of the group.

Recognition seeking: attempting to call attention to one's self by loud or excessive talking, extreme ideas, unusual behavior.

Withdrawing: acting indifferent or passive, resorting to excessive formality, day dreaming, doodling, whispering to others, wandering from the subject.

Nonfunctional behavior usually results when individual needs are not being met by the group. The occurrence of such behavior is a sign that the maintenance functions are inadequate.

Authority and Power Dimensions[3]

There are at least four possibilities for acquisition of authority and power:

1. *By force*—The leader usurps the power because he is stronger, braver or more clever than the rest of the

---

[3] Much of the material in this section is adapted from a presentation by Burns B. Crookston at the Intermountain Laboratory for Group Development, Cedar City, Utah, 1961.

group.
2. *By default*—Nobody in the group wants power or authority.
3. *By inheritance*—Succession to power; continuing organization with built-in delegation of power to successive leaders.
4. *By delegation*—The group gives power and authority to the leader.

The leader, once vested with authority and power, necessarily takes on greater "psychological size" than other members of the group.

The leader also becomes psychologically larger for other reasons:

1. *Member attitudes toward authority*—These are conditioned by life experiences, beginning with the mother, then the father, and later the teacher and other people who control childhood behavior or set and enforce limits because they have the power to reward and punish; those who control a child's life are usually physically and psychologically larger. Childhood feelings and attitudes toward authority are projected upon leaders of groups to which the individual belongs later in his life.
2. *Member needs for security*—Some group or organizational members are glad to have the leader psychologically larger. They have needs for protection or are fearful of taking responsibility for themselves. Thus the bigger the leader is psychologically, the greater is his perceived protective role, and the higher is his afforded status.

The psychologically larger leader encounters three basic types of reactions from the group: (1) *Dependency*—submissiveness or willingness to go along with the leader's proposals. (See figure below).

(2) *Counterdependency*—reactive, opposing, resisting behavior of two types: (a) Individual opposition or (b) organized

opposition often typified by labor-management or student-faculty relationships. (See figures below).

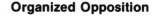

Individual Opposition   **Organized Opposition**

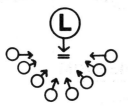   

Dependent reactions are related to member needs for security. They want to be dependent on the leader and are glad he will make the decisions for the group.

Counterdependent reactions are often related to member attitudes toward authority. Authority figures have controlled, rewarded, or punished the member all his life. He shows his resentment by fighting, rejecting and punishing the authority. By this means the member feels that perhaps he can gain stature.

Most groups and organizations contain both dependent and counterdependent members. Also a single group may change from being predominantly dependent to counterdependent. Both reactions may exist in most of us—a kind of ambivalence toward powerful leaders. We would like their direction and protection, and yet we also somewhat fear and hate their power over us.

(3) *Interdependence*—Once the group member has solved his authority problem, he is able to perceive the leader in a more realistic psychological dimension. The difference in psychological size between the member and the leader becomes much smaller when the member no longer has to react emotionally to the leader. Thus he becomes interdependent in his relationship with the leader.

With the growing complexity of organizations and societies, the status leader no doubt continues to be required, but the leader can help to decrease the authority problem.

1. He can clearly recognize the degree of his authority and the freedom of the group. Different kinds of leader behavior are related to the balance of power between leader and group.
2. Clearly define areas of leader authority and group freedom.

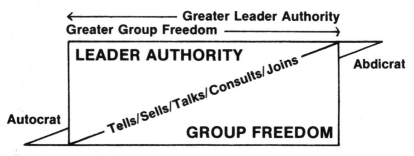

Greater use of leader authority tends to depend on:
1. Low trust or confidence in the group.
2. Fear of losing power.
3. Fear of peer or supervisor disapproval.
4. A value system arising from an authoritarian background.

Less use of authority tends to depend on:
1. High trust and confidence in the group.
2. Confidence in self.
3. Security in relationships with peers and supervisors.
4. A value system arising from a democratic background.

Styles of Leadership

Familiar leadership styles include: (1) autocratic, (2) democratic, and (3) laissez faire. *Autocratically* led groups tend to be obedient to the commands of the leader. Considerable tension and individualistic feeling is often evident. Such groups tend to demonstrate little inner strength; they may be apathetic and uncooperative in the absence of their leader, and may be unable to continue work.

Democratically led groups tend to be cooperative, keen about their task, show little tension, show a pronounced "we" feeling, and do not threaten each other. When the leader leaves they tend to continue on their own momentum. The group tends to have noticeable inner strength.

The *laissez faire* group may hardly function at all. It is often rife with individualistic feelings, and little may be accomplished in achieving the task. However, they may show considerable development and greater effectiveness over time after discovering how to function as a team.[4]

---

[4] See Ralph White and Ronald Lippit, "Leader Behavior and Member Reaction in Three Social Climates," pp. 585-611 in D. Cartwright and A. Zander, *Group Dynamics: Research and Theory*, Harper and Row, 1960.

Six differences may be noted:

1. Democratic leadership usually results in a more satisfying, efficient leadership than laissez faire.
2. A democratic climate can also be efficient.
3. An autocratic style creates hostility and aggressiveness among its members.
4. Discontent which does not appear on the surface often occurs in the autocratic groups.
5. There tends to be more dependency and less individuality in the autocratic as compared to the democratic group.
6. There is more orientation to the needs of the group and more acceptance of each other in the democratic group.

This discussion of basic concepts is expanded considerably and is more fully documented in later selections, particularly in the readings that immediately follow.

IS HELP HELPFUL?*
(or, A Key Role of Leadership)

by Jack R. Gibb

People in the service professions often see themselves as primarily engaged in the job of helping others. Helping becomes both the personal style of life and a core activity that gives meaning and purpose to the life of the professional. The youth worker, the camp director, the counselor, the consultant, the therapist, the teacher, the lawyer—each is a helper.

Helping is a central social process. The den mother, the committee chairman, the parent, the personal friend, the board member, the dance sponsor—each is a helper.

Help, however, is not always helpful. The recipient of the proffered help may not see it as useful. The offering may not lead to greater satisfaction or to better performance. Even less often does the helping process meet a more rigorous criterion— lead to continued growth on the part of the participants.

* Reprinted by permission from ASSOCIATION FORUM AND SECTION JOURNALS of the Association of Secretaries of the YMCA; Personnel Services, National Council of' YMCA's.

To begin with, a person may have varied motivations for offering help. He may wish to improve performance of a subordinate, reduce his own guilt, may wish to demonstrate his superior skill or knowledge, induce indebtedness, control others, establish dependency, punish others, or simply meet a job prescription. These conscious or partially conscious motivations are so intermingled in any act of help that it is impossible for either the helper or the recipient to sort them out.

Depending upon his own needs and upon the way he sees the motives of the helper, the recipient will have varied reactions. He may feel helpless and dependent, or jealous of the helper who has the strength or resources to be in the helper role. He may feel indebted, or pressured to conform to the perceived demands or beliefs of the helper.

We have all noticed that in certain cases the recipient of the help becomes more helpless and dependent, less able to make his own decisions or initiate his own actions, less self-sufficient, more apathetic and passive, less willing to take risks, more concerned about propriety and conformity, and less creative and venturesome. We have also seen circumstances in which following help, recipients become more creative, less dependent upon helpers, more willing to make risk decisions, more highly motivated to tackle tough problems, less concerned about conformity, and more effective at working independently or inter-dependently. Help may or may not lead to personal growth and organizational health.

Under certain conditions both the giver and the receiver grow and develop. In general people tend to grow when there is reciprocal dependence—inter-dependence, joint determination of goals, real communication in depth, and reciprocal trust. To the degree that these conditions are absent, people fail to grow.

From the standpoint of the organization, help must meet two criteria: the job or program must be done effectively, and the individual members must grow and develop. These two criteria tend to merge. The program and the organization are effective only as the participants grow. The same conditions that lead to organizational health lead to personal growth. The following table presents a theory of the helping relationship. Seven parallel sets of orientations are presented. One set of conditions maximize help and a parallel set of conditions minimize help.

Reciprocal trust. People accept help from those they trust. When the relationship is one of acceptance and trust, offers of help are appreciated, listened to, seen as potentially helpful, and often acted upon. The receiver accepts help from one whose perceived motives are congenial to him. He tends to reject offers from people whose offering is seen as a guise for attempts to control, punish, correct, or gain power. "Help" is most helpful when given in an atmosphere in which people have reciprocal feelings of confidence, warmth, and acceptance. When one feels that his worth as a person is valued he is able to place himself in psychological readiness to receive aid.

THE HELPING RELATIONSHIP

Orientations that help	Orientations that hinder
1. Reciprocal trust (confidence, warmth, acceptance)	1. Distrust (fear, punitiveness, defensiveness)
2. Cooperative learning (inquiry, exploration, quest)	2. Teaching (training, advice giving, indoctrinating)
3. Mutual growth (becoming, actualizing, fulfilling)	3. Evaluating (fixing, correcting, providing a remedy)
4. Reciprocal openness (spontaneity, candor, honesty)	4. Strategy (planning *for,* maneuvering, gamesmanship)
5. Shared problem solving (defining, producing alternatives, testing)	5. Modeling (demonstration, information giving, guiding)
6. Autonomy (freedom, interdependency, equality)	6. Coaching (molding, steering, controlling)
7. Experimentation (play, innovation, provisional try)	7. Patterning (standard, static, fixed)

Distrust. When people fear and distrust each other, even well-intended help is resisted, resented, or seen as unhelpful. Offers of help are sometimes given in service of motivations that are unacceptable to the receiver. That is, one offers help in order to place the other person in a dependent position, elicit expressions of gratitude, assert one's superiority, or punish him. In distrust the recipient's guard is up. He is likely to project his distrusts into the helper and to resist or resent the help.

One often gives help to camouflage or assuage his desire to change another person—change his character, habits, or misconceptions. The desire to change another person is essentially hostile. At a deep level, one who genuinely accepts another person does not wish to change him. A person who is accepted is allowed to be, become, determine his own goals and follow them at his own pace. The person who genuinely wishes to help offers the help that the recipient wishes. Genuine help is not foisted upon the receiver. Neither the punisher nor the child really believes that the punishment is given "for the good of the child."

Punishment or censure may be given with a conscious desire to help but usually is accompanied by a deep component of retaliation, or by a desire to hurt, control, or assert superiority. The giver often speaks of his act as "helpful" in order to rationalize to himself and to the receiver acts that are done for other motivations.

Cooperative learning. People are helpful to each other when they are engaged in a cooperative quest for learning. The learning atmosphere is one of joint inquiry and exploration. Needs for help and impulses to give help arise out of the demands of the common cooperative task. Help is thus reciprocal. The helper and helpee roles are interchangeable. Each participant has the intent to learn and feels he can learn from the partners and from the common task. The boss and the subordinate, the teacher and the student, the professional worker and the youth—all are most helpful when each member of the pair sees the relationship as a quest with potential learning for each. An effective project team is guided by the task and not by the teacher. It is motivated by the shared potential for learning.

Teaching. When one participant in a project sets out to teach, train, advise, persuade, or indoctrinate the other members or is seen as wanting to do so, the learning of each member is reduced. People cannot be taught. People must learn. People cannot be trained. They grow and develop. The most deeply helpful relationship is one of common inquiry and quest, a relationship between co-learners and co-managers in which each is equally dependent upon the other for significant help and in which each sees and accepts this relationship.

Mutual growth. The most permanent and significant help

occurs in a relationship in which both members are continually growing, becoming and seeking fulfillment. Each member participates in a mutual assessment of progress, accepts this reality of growth, and participates in a way that will maximize the growth of both participants. In a fundamental sense one can only help himself. The helper can only participate with another in an effort to create a climate in which growth can occur.

Evaluating. Growth is often hindered when one member of the helping team sets out to appraise or remedy the defects in the other member. Help is most effective when it is seen as a force moving toward growth rather than as effort to remove gaps, remedy defects or bring another person up to a standard criterion. The limits of growth of any person are extremely difficult to foresee or to assess. The potential for growth is consistently underestimated by both participants in helping relationship.

Reciprocal openness. One of the essential conditions for effective human learning is the opportunity for feedback of knowledge of progress. Feedback is essential in acquiring skills, knowledge, and attitudes. In the areas where professional help is most commonly sought or given, the essential progress in learning and growth is blocked most often by the failure to obtain adequate data on people's feelings and perceptions of each other. In order to do effective work one must know how others feel and how they see things. In the usual situations in which professional helpers find themselves, there are many pressures which camouflage or distort the relevant data necessary for efficient work and best learning. Many factors reduce the availability of the relevant data: differential status, differential perceived power, and fears that one can hurt or be hurt.

Strategy. When some part of the helping process is closed or unavailable to all participants, people are likely to become anxious, resentful, or resistant. Neither participant in the helping process can "use" the other for his own needs. The helping process is most effective when one plans with another, not for another. One is not helped when he is maneuvered into some action which he does not understand. Gamesmanship and gimmicks are antithetical to the helping process.

Shared problem solving. The productive helping relationship focuses upon the problem to be solved. Problem solving involves a joint determination of the problem, continual redefinition of the problem as successive insights are gained, joint focus upon possible alternative solutions, joint exploration of the data, and continual reality testing of the alternatives. The expertness and resources of each person are shared. The aspect of the behavior about which help is given is seen as a shared problem—not as a defect to be remedied or as something to be solved by the helper as consultant.

Modeling. A common image of the helping relationship is one where the helper offers a model for the advisee to follow. The expert gives a demonstration of how the recipient may solve his problems. The problem is defined by the expert. Diagnosis is made by the expert. The expert is challenged to offer additional alternatives to the solution of the problem and perhaps even to test the solutions. The process is uni-directional. The limitations of modeling are many. Dependency is increased. The pupil seldom gives better than the model. The worker tries to conform to the image of the supervisor. Growth is limited.

Autonomy. The ideal relationship for helping is an interdependent one in which each person sees the other as both helper and recipient in an exchange among equals. It is essential that each participant preserve his freedom and maintain his autonomous responsibility for guiding himself toward autonomous responsibility for guiding himself toward his own learnings, growth, and problem solving. The helper must work himself out of the helping job. The supervisor, youth worker, and counselor must become decreasingly necessary to the people being helped. Psychological weaning, however painful to both helper and recipient, must continue if help is to be truly helpful.

Coaching. The coach molds, steers, or controls the behavior of the recipient, much as a tennis coach or physical education director molds the behavior of the athlete or skill-directed recipient of help. This is another uni-directional process in which the coach is assumed to have special diagnostic and observational powers which he applies in a skilled way to the behavior of the recipient, who puts himself in the hands of the coach. The recipient of help is encouraged to maintain respectful dependency upon the coach, to not challenge his coaching or expertness, to put implicit trust in his abilities and powers, and to receive from the coach motivational or inspirational guidance. Both coach and pupil suffer under this pattern. Each may gain in skill. Neither grows as a person.

Experimentation. Tentativeness and innovative experimentation are characteristic of the most productive helping relationship. There is a sense of play, excitement, and fun in the common exploratory quest for new solutions to continually changing problems. The helping process is viewed as a series of provisional trials. Each participant joins in the game and adds to the general excitement. Errors can be made—and are perhaps expected. Help is a search. Finding creative solutions to newly defined problems is a game—full of zest and intrinsic drives that keep the game going.

Patterning. Help is limited when the process is seen as an attempt on the part of one person to help another meet a prescribed standard, come up to a criterion, or reach a goal specified in advance. Helping is a creative synthesis of growth and a continual search for new forms.

"Help" is not always helpful—but it can be. Both the helper and the recipient can grow and learn when help is given in a relationship of trust, joint inquiry, openness, and interdependence. Growth-centered helping processes lead to healthy groups and effective organizations.

AN ANALYSIS OF LEADERSHIP*
by Douglas McGregor

Are successful managers born or "made"? Does success as a manager rest on the possession of a certain core of abilities and traits, or are there many combinations of characteristics which can result in successful industrial leadership? Is managerial leadership—or its potential—a property of the individual, or is it a term for describing a relationship between people? Will the managerial job twenty years from now require the same basic abilities and personality traits as it does today?

The previous chapters of this volume suggest tentative answers to these questions. Knowledge gained from research in the social sciences sheds additional light on these and other questions relevant to leadership in industry. It does not provide final, definitive answers. There is much yet to be learned. But the accumulated evidence points with high probability toward

* From *The Human Side of Enterprise*, by Douglas McGregor. Copyright © 1960 by McGraw-Hill Inc. Used by permission of McGraw Hill Book Company.

certain ones among a number of possible assumptions.
Prior to the 1930s it was widely believed that leadership
was a property of the individual, that a limited number of people were uniquely endowed with abilities and traits which made
it possible for them to become leaders. Moreover, these abilities
and traits were believed to be inherited rather than acquired.

As a consequence of these beliefs, research studies in this
field were directed toward the identification of the universal
characteristics of leadership so that potential leaders might
be more readily identified. A large number of studies were published—many based on armchair theorizing, but some utilizing
biographical or other empirical data.

Examination of this literature reveals an imposing number
of supposedly essential characteristics of the successful leader
—over a hundred, in fact, even after elimination of obvious dup-
lication and overlap of terms. The search still continues in some
quarters. Every few months a new list appears based on the
latest analysis. And each new list differs in some respects from
the earlier ones.

However, social science research in this field since the
1930s has taken new directions. Some social scientists have become interested in studying the behavior as well as the personal
characteristics of leaders. As a result, some quite different
ideas about the nature of leadership have emerged.

The research in this field in the last twenty years has been
prolific. A recent summary cites 111 references, of which six
were published prior to 1930. As a result of such work, a number of generalizations about leadership may be stated with reasonable certainty. Among these, the following are particularly
significant for management.

Generalizations from Recent Research

It is quite unlikely that there is a single basic pattern of
abilities and personality traits characteristic of all leaders.
The personality characteristics of the leader are not unimportant, but those which are essential differ considerably depending upon the circumstances. The requirements for successful
political leadership are different from those for industrial
management or military or educational leadership. Failure is
as frequent as success in transfers of leaders from one type of
social institution to another. The reasons are perhaps evident
in the light of the discussion in earlier chapters of this volume.

Even within a single institution such as industry, different circumstances require different leadership characteristics. Comparisons of successful industrial leaders in different historical periods, in different cultures, in different industries, or even in different companies have made this fairly obvious. The leadership requirements of a young, struggling company, for example, are quite different from those of a large, well-established firm. Within the individual company different functions (sales, finance, production) demand rather different abilities and skills of leadership. Managers who are successful in one function are sometimes, but by no means always, successful in another. The same is true of leadership at different organizational levels. Every successful foreman would not make a successful president (or vice versa!). Yet each may be an effective leader.

On the other hand, leaders who differ notably in abilities and traits are sometimes equally successful when they succeed each other in a given situation. Within rather wide limits, weaknesses in certain characteristics can be compensated by strength in others. This is particularly evident in partnerships and executive teams in which leadership functions are, in fact, *shared*. The very idea of the team implies different and supplementary patterns of abilities among the members.

Many characteristics which have been alleged to be essential to the leader turn out not to differentiate the successful leader from unsuccessful ones. In fact, some of these—integrity, ambition, judgment, for example—are to be found not merely in the leader, but in any successful member of an organization.

Finally, among the characteristics essential for leadership are skills and attitudes which can be acquired or modified extensively through learning. These include competence in planning and initiating action, in problem solving, in keeping communication channels open and functioning effectively, in accepting responsibility, and in the skills of social interaction. Such skills are not inherited, nor is their acquisition dependent on the possession of any unique pattern of inborn characteristics.

It is, of course, true that the few outstanding leaders in any field have been unusually gifted people, but these preeminent leaders differ widely among themselves in their strengths and weaknesses. They do not possess a pattern of leadership characteristics in common. The evidence to date does not prove conclusively that there is no basic universal core of personal qualifications for leadership. However, few of the social scientists who have worked extensively during recent years in this field would regard this as a promising possibility for further work. On the contrary, the research during the past two decades has shown that we must look beyond the personal qualifications of the leader if we wish to understand what leadership is.

Leadership is a Relationship

There are at least four major variables now known to be involved in leadership: (1) the characteristics of the leader; (2) the attitudes, needs, and other personal characteristics of the followers; (3) characteristics of the organization, such as its purpose, its structure, the nature of the tasks to be performed; and (4) the social, economic, and political milieu. The personal characteristics required for effective performance as a leader vary, depending on the other factors.

This is an important research finding. *It means that leadership is not a property of the individual, but a complex relationship among these variables.* The old argument over whether the leader makes history or history makes the leader is resolved by this conception. Both assertions are true within limits.

The relationship between the leader and the situation is essentially circular. Organization structure and policy, for example, are established by top management. Once established, they set limits on the leadership patterns which will be acceptable within the company. However, influences from above (a change in top management with an accompanying change in philosophy), from below (following recognition of a union and adjustment to collective bargaining, for example), or from outside (social legislation, changes in the market, etc.) bring about changes in these organizational relationships. Some of this may lead to a redefinition of acceptable leadership patterns. The changes which occurred in the leadership of the Ford Motor Company after Henry Ford I retired provide a dramatic illustration.

The same thing is true of the influence of the broader milieu. The social values, the economic and political conditions, the general standard of living, the level of education of the population, and other factors characteristic of the late 1800s had much to do with the kinds of people who were successful as industrial leaders during that era. Those men in turn helped to shape the nature of the industrial environment. Their influence affected the character of our society profoundly.

Today, industry requires a very different type of industrial leader than it did in 1900. Similarly, today's leaders are helping to shape industrial organizations which tomorrow will require people quite different from themselves in key positions. An important point with respect to these situational influences on leadership is that they operate selectively—in subtle and unnoticed as well as in obvious ways—to reward conformity with acceptable patterns of behavior and to punish deviance from these. The differing situations from company to company, and from unit to unit within a company, each have their selective consequences. The observable managerial "types" in certain companies are illustrative of this phenomenon. One consequence of this selectivity is the tendency to "weed out" deviant individuals, some of whom might nevertheless become effective, perhaps outstanding, leaders.

Even if there is no single universal pattern of characteristics of the leader, it is conceivable at least that there might be certain universal characteristics *of the relationship* between the leader and the other situational factors which are essential for optimum organized human effort in all situations. This is doubtful. Consider, for example, the relationship of an industrial manager with a group of native employees in an under-developed country on the one hand, and with a group of United States workmen who are members of a well-established international union on the other. Moreover, even if research finally indicates that there are such universal requirements of the relationship, there will still be more than one way of achieving them. For example, if "mutual confidence" between the leader and the led is a universal requirement, it is obvious that there are many ways of developing and maintaining this confidence.

We have already considered some of the significant conditions for the success of certain relationships involving interdependence in industrial organizations today. To achieve these conditions, the supervisor requires skills and attitudes, *but these can be acquired by people who differ widely in their inborn traits and abilities.* In fact, one of the important lessons from research and experience in this field is that the attempt to train supervisors to adopt a single leadership "style" yields poorer results than encouraging them to create the essential conditions *in their individual ways* and with due regard for their own particular situations. Note also in this connection how organization structure and management philosophy may either encourage or inhibit the supervisor in establishing these conditions.

It does not follow from these considerations that *any* individual can become a successful leader in a given situation. It *does* follow that successful leadership is not dependent on the possession of a single universal pattern of inborn traits and abilities. It seems likely that leadership potential (considering the tremendous variety of situations for which leadership is required) is broadly rather than narrowly distributed in the population.

Research findings to date suggest, then, that it is more fruitful to consider leadership as a relationship between the leader and the situation than as a universal pattern of characteristics possessed by certain people. The differences in requirements for successful leadership in different situations are more striking than the similarities. Moreover, research studies emphasize the importance of leadership skills and attitudes which can be acquired and are, therefore, not inborn characteristics of the individual.

It has often happened in the physical sciences that what was once believed to be an inherent property of objects—gravity, for example, or electrical "magnetism," or mass—has turned out to be a complex relationship between internal and external factors. The same thing happens in the social sciences, and leadership is but one example.

Implications for Management

What is the practical relevance for management of these findings of social science research in the field of leadership? First, if we accept the point of view that leadership consists of a relationship between the leader, his followers, the organization, and the social milieu, and if we recognize that these situational factors are subject to substantial changes with time, we must recognize that we cannot predict the personal characteristics of the managerial resources that an organization will require a decade or two hence. Even if we can list the positions to be filled, we cannot define very adequately the essential characteristics of the people who will be needed in those situations at that time. *One of management's major tasks, therefore, is to provide a heterogeneous supply of human resources from which individuals can be selected to fill a variety of specific but unpredictable needs.*

This is a blow to those who have hoped that the outcome of research would be to provide them with methods by which they could select today the top management of tomorrow. It is a boon to those who have feared the consequences of the "crown prince" approach to management development. It carries other practical implications of some importance.

With the modern emphasis on career employment and promotion from within, management must pay more than casual attention to its recruitment practices. It would seem logical that this process should tap a variety of sources: liberal arts as well as technical graduates, small colleges as well as big universities, institutions in different geographic regions, etc. It may be necessary, moreover, to look carefully at the criteria for selection of college recruits if heterogeneity is a goal. The college senior who graduates in the top 10 per cent of his class may come from a narrow segment of the range of potential leaders for industry. What of the student who has, perhaps for reasons unrelated to intellectual capacity, graduated in the middle of his class because he got A's in some subjects and C's and D's in others? What of the student whose academic achievement was only average because the education system never really challenged him?

As a matter of fact there is not much evidence that high academic achievement represents a necessary characteristic for industrial leadership. There may be a positive correlation, but it is not large enough to provide a basis for a recruitment policy. In fact, the current President of the United States would have been passed over at graduation by any management recruiter who relied on this correlation! It may be, on the contrary, that the *intellectual* capacity required for effective leadership in many industrial management positions is no greater than that required for graduation from a good college. Of course, there are positions requiring high intellectual capacity, but it does not follow that there is a one-to-one correlation between this characteristic and success as an industrial leader. (This question of intellectual capacity is, of course, only one reason why industry seeks the bulk of its potential managerial resources among college graduates today. There are other factors involved: confidence and social poise, skill acquired through participation in extracurricular activities, personal ambition and drive, etc. These, however, are relatively independent of class standing.)

It may be argued that intellectual *achievement,* as measured by consistently high grades in all subjects, is evidence of motivation and willingness to work. Perhaps it is—in the academic setting—but it is also evidence of willingness to conform to the quite arbitrary demands of the educational system. There is little reason for assuming that high motivation and hard work *in school* are the best predictors of motivation and effort in later life. There are a good many examples to the contrary.

A second implication from research findings about leadership is that a management development program should involve many people within the organization rather than a select few. The fact that some companies have been reasonably successful in developing a selected small group of managerial trainees may well be an artifact—an example of the operation of the "self-fulfilling prophecy." If these companies had been equally concerned to develop managerial talent within a much broader sample, they might have accomplished this purpose with no greater percentage of failures. And, if the generalizations above are sound, they would have had a richer, more valuable pool of leadership resources to draw on as a result.

Third, management should have as a goal the development of the unique capacities and potentialities of each individual rather than common objectives for all participants. This is a purpose which is honored on paper much more than in practice. It is difficult to achieve, particularly in the big company, but if we want heterogeneous leadership resources to meet the unpredictable needs of the future we certainly won't get them by subjecting all our managerial trainees to the same treatment.

Moreover, this process of developing heterogeneous resources must be continuous; it is never completed. Few human beings ever realize all of their potentialities for growth, even though some may reach a practical limit with respect to certain capacities. Each individual is unique, and it is this uniqueness we will constantly encourage and nourish if we are truly concerned to develop leaders for the industry of tomorrow.

Fourth, the promotion policies of the company should be so administered that these heterogeneous resources are actually considered when openings occur. There is little value in developing a wide range of talent if only a small and possibly limited segment of it constitutes the field of candidates when a particular position is being filled.

In view of the selective operation of situational variables referred to above, there may be legitimate questions concerning the value of an *exclusive* policy of "promotion from within." It is conceivable that in a large and reasonably decentralized company sufficient heterogeneity can be maintained by transfers of managerial talent between divisions, but it is probable that fairly strenuous efforts will be required to offset the normal tendency to create and maintain a "type," a homogeneous pattern of leadership within a given organization. Without such efforts competent individuals who don't "fit the pattern" are likely to be passed over or to leave because their talents are not rewarded. Many industrial organizations, for example, would not easily tolerate the strong individualism of a young Charles Kettering today.

Finally, if leadership is a function—a complex relation between leader and situation—we ought to be clear that every promising recruit is *not* a potential member of top management. Some people in some companies will become outstanding leaders as foremen, or as plant superintendents, or as professional specialists. Many of these would not be effective leaders in top management positions, at least under the circumstances prevailing in the company.

If we take seriously the implications of the research findings in this field, we will place high value on such people. We will seek to enable them to develop to the fullest their potentialities in the role they can fill best. And we will find ways to reward them which will persuade them that we consider outstanding leadership *at any level* to be a precious thing.

REFERENCES

Bennis, Warren G., "Leadership Theory and Administrative Behavior," *Administrative Science Quarterly*, vol. 4, no. 3, 1959.

Fortune Editors, The Executive Life. New York: Doubleday & Company, Inc., 1956.

Gibb, Cecil A., "Leadership," in Gardner Lindzey (ed.), *Handbook of Social Psychology*. Reading, Mass.: Addison-Wesley Publishing Company, 1954, vol. II.

Ginzberg, Eli, *What Makes an Executive*. New York: Columbia University Press, 1955.

Knickerbocker, Irving, "Leadership: A Conception and Some Implications," *Journal of Social Issues*, vol. 4, no. 3, 1948.

Selznick, Philip, *Leadership in Administration*. Evanston, Ill., Row, Peterson & Company, 1957.

HOW TO CHOOSE
A LEADERSHIP PATTERN*

by Robert Tannenbaum and
Warren H. Schmidt

*Should a leader be democratic or
autocratic in dealing with his
subordinates—or something in
between?*

"I put most problems into my group's hands and leave it
to them to carry the ball from there. I serve merely as a catalyst,
mirroring back the people's thoughts and feelings so that they
can better understand them."

"It's foolish to make decisions oneself on matters that affect
people. I always talk things over with my subordinates, but I
make it clear to them that I'm the one who has to have the final
say."

"Once I have decided on a course of action, I do my best to
sell my ideas to my employees."

"I'm being paid to lead. If I let a lot of other people make
the decisions I should be making, then I'm not worth my salt."

"I believe in getting things done. I can't waste time calling
meetings. Someone has to call the shots around here, and I
think it should be me."

Each of these statements represents a point of view about
"good leadership." Considerable experience, factual data, and
theoretical principles could be cited to support each statement,
even though they seem to be inconsistent when placed together.
Such contradictions point up the dilemma in which the modern
manager frequently finds himself.

NEW PROBLEM

The problem of how the modern manager can be "democratic" in his relations with subordinates and at the same time maintain the necessary authority and control in the organization for which he is responsible has come into focus increasingly in recent years. Earlier in the century this problem was not so acutely felt. The successful executive was generally pictured as possessing intelligence, imagination, initiative, the capacity to make rapid (and generally wise) decisions, and the ability to inspire subordinates. People tended to think of the world as being divided into "leaders" and "followers."

New Focus

Gradually, however, from the social sciences emerged the concept of "group dynamics" with its focus on *members* of the group rather than solely on the leader. Research efforts of social scientists underscored the importance of employee involvement and participation in decision making. Evidence began to challenge the efficiency of highly directive leadership, and increasing attention was paid to problems of motivation and human relations.

Through training laboratories in group development that sprang up across the country, many of the newer notions of leadership began to exert an impact. These training laboratories were carefully designed to give people a firsthand experience in full participation and decision making. The designated "leaders" deliberately attempted to reduce their own power and to make group members as responsible as possible for setting their own goals and methods within the laboratory experience.

It was perhaps inevitable that some of the people who attended the training laboratories regarded this kind of leadership as being truly "democratic" and went home with the determination to build fully participative decision making into their own organizations. Whenever their bosses made a decision without convening a staff meeting, they tended to perceive this as authoritarian behavior. The true symbol of democratic leadership to some was the meeting—and the less directed from the top, the more democratic it was.

Some of the more enthusiastic alumni of these training laboratories began to get the habit of categorizing leader behavior as "democratic" *or* "authoritarian." The boss who made too many decisions himself was thought of as an authoritarian, and his directive behavior was often attributed solely to his personality.

EXHIBIT I. CONTINUUM OF LEADERSHIP BEHAVIOR

Boss-   ←————————————————— Subordinate-
centered   centered
leadership ——————————————————→ leadership

Use of authority by the manager						Area of freedom for subordinates
∧	∧	∧	∧	∧	∧	∧
Manager makes decision and announces it.	Manager "sells" decision.	Manager presents ideas and invites questions.	Manager presents tentative decision subject to change.	Manager presents problem, gets suggestions, makes decision.	Manager defines limits; asks group to make decision.	Manager permits subordinates to function within limits defined by superior.

New Need

The net result of the research findings and of the human realtions training based upon them has been to call into question the stereotype of an effective leader. Consequently, the modern manager often finds himself in an uncomfortable state of mind.

Often he is not quite sure how to behave; there are times when he is torn between exerting "strong" leadership and "permissive" leadership. Sometimes new knowledge pushes him in one direction("I should really get the group to help make this decision"), but at the same time his experience pushes him in another direction ("I really understand the problem better than the group and therefore I should make the decision"). He is not sure when a group decision is really appropriate or when holding a staff meeting serves merely as a device for avoiding his own decision-making responsibility.

The purpose of our article is to suggest a framework which managers may find useful in grappling with this dilemma. First we shall look at the different patterns of leadership behavior that the manager can choose from in relating himself to his subordinates. Then we shall turn to some of the questions suggested by this range of patterns. For instance, how important is it for a manager's subordinates to know what type of leadership he is using in a situation? What factors should he consider in deciding on a leadership pattern? What difference do his long-run objectives make as compared to his immediate objectives?

RANGE OF BEHAVIOR

EXHIBIT I presents the continuum or range of possible leadership behavior available to a manager. Each type of action is related to the degree of authority used by the boss and to the amount of freedom available to his subordinates in reaching decisions. The actions seen on the extreme left characterize the manager who maintains a high degree of control while those seen on the extreme right characterize the manager who releases a high degree of control. Neither extreme is absolute; authority and freedom are never without their limitations.

Now let us look more closely at each of the behavior points occurring along this continuum:

The manager makes the decision and announces it.

In this case the boss identifies a problem, considers alternative solutions, chooses one of them, and then reports this decision to his subordinates for implementation. He may or may not give consideration to what he believes his subordinates will think or feel about his decision; in any case, he provides no opportunity for them to participate directly in the decision-making process. Coercion may or may not be used or implied.

The manager "sells" his decision.

Here the manager, as before, takes responsibility for identifying the problem and arriving at a decision. However, rather than simply announcing it, he takes the additional step of persuading his subordinates to accept it. In doing so, he recognizes the possibility of some resistance among those who will be faced with the decision, and seeks to reduce this resistance by indicating, for example, what the employees have to gain from his decision.

The manager presents his ideas, invites questions.

Here the boss who has arrived at a decision and who seeks acceptance of his ideas provides an opportunity for his subordinates to get a fuller explanation of his thinking and his intentions. After presenting the ideas, he invites questions so that his associates can better understand what he is trying to accomplish. This "give and take" also enables the manager and the subordinates to explore more fully the implications of the decision.

The manager presents a tentative decision subject to change.

This kind of behavior permits the subordinates to exert some influence on the decision. The initiative for identifying and diagnosing the problem remains with the boss. Before meeting with his staff, he has thought the problem through and arrived at a decision—but only a tentative one. Before finalizing it, he presents his proposed solution for the reaction of those who will be affected by it. He says in effect, "I'd like to hear what you have to say about this plan that I have developed. I'll appreciate your frank reactions, but will reserve for myself the final decision."

The manager presents the problem, gets suggestions, and then makes his decision.

Up to this point the boss has come before the group with a solution of his own. Not so in this case. The subordinates now get the first chance to suggest solutions. The manager's initial role involves identifying the problem. He might, for example, say something of this sort: "We are faced with a number of complaints from newspapers and the general public on our service policy. What is wrong here? What ideas do you have for coming to grips with this problem?"

The function of the group becomes one of increasing the manager's repertory of possible solutions to the problem. The purpose is to capitalize on the knowledge and experience of those who are on the "firing line." From the expanded list of alternatives developed by the manager and his subordinates, the manager then selects the solution that he regards as most promising.[1]

The manager defines the limits and requests the group to make a decision.

At this point the manager passes to the group (possibly in-

[1] For a fuller explanation of this approach, see Leo Moore, "Too Much Management, Too Little Change," *Harvard Business Review*, January-February 1956, p. 41.

cluding himself as a member) the right to make decisions. Before doing so, however, he defines the problem to be solved and the boundaries within which the decision must be made. An example might be the handling of a parking problem at a plant. The boss decided that this is something that should be worked on by the people involved, so he calls them together and points up the existence of the problem. Then he tells them:

"There is the open field just north of the main plant which has been designated for additional employee parking. We can build underground or surface multilevel facilities as long as the cost does not exceed $100,000.00. Within these limits we are free to work out whatever solution makes sense to us. After we decide on a specific plan, the company will spend the available money in whatever way we indicate."

The manager permits the group to make decisions within prescribed limits.

This represents an extreme degree of group freedom only occasionally encountered in formal organizations, as, for instance, in many research groups. Here the team of managers or engineers undertakes the identification and diagnosis of the problem, develops alternative procedures for solving it, and decides on one or more of these alternative solutions. The only limits directly imposed on the group by the organization are those specified by the superior of the team's boss. If the boss participates in the decision-making process, he attempts to do so with no more authority than any other member of the group. He commits himself in advance to assist in implementing whatever decision the group makes.

KEY QUESTIONS

As the continuum in EXHIBIT I demonstrates, there are a number of alternative ways in which a manager can relate himself to the group or individuals he is supervising. At the extreme left of the range, the emphasis is on the manager—on what *he* is interested in, how *he* sees things, how *he* feels about them. As we move toward the subordinate-centered end of the continuum, however, the focus is increasingly on the subordinates—on what *they* are interested in, how *they* look at things, how *they* feel about them.

When a business leadership is regarded in this way, a number of questions arise. Let us take four of especial importance:

Can a boss ever relinquish his responsibility by delegating it to someone else?

Our view is that the manager must expect to be held responsible by his superior for the quality of the decisions made, even though operationally these decisions may have been made on a group basis. He should, therefore, be ready to accept whatever risk is involved whenever he delegates decision-making power to his subordinates. Delegation is not a way of "passing the buck." Also, it should be emphasized that the amount of freedom the boss gives to his subordinates cannot be greater than the freedom which he himself has been given by his own superior.

Should the manager participate with his subordinates once he has delegated responsibility to them?

The manager should carefully think over this question and decide on his role prior to involving the subordinate group. He should ask if his presence will inhibit or facilitate the problem-solving process. There may be some instances when he should leave the group to let it solve the problem for itself. Typically, however, the boss has useful ideas to contribute, and should function as an additional member of the group. In the latter instance, it is important that he indicate clearly to the group that he sees himself in a *member* role rather than in an authority role.

How important is it for the group to recognize what kind of leadership behavior the boss is using?

It makes a great deal of difference. Many relationship problems between boss and subordinate occur because the boss fails to make clear how he plans to use his authority. If, for example, he actually intends to make a certain decision himself, but the subordinate group gets the impression that he has delegated this authority, considerable confusion and resentment are likely to follow. Problems may also occur when the boss uses a "democratic" facade to conceal the fact that he has already made a decision which he hopes the group will accept as its own. The attempt to "make them think it was their idea in the first place" is a risky one. We believe that it is highly important for the manager to be honest and clear in describing what authority he is keeping and what role he is asking his subordinates to assume in solving a particular problem.

Can you tell how "democratic" a manager is by the number of decisions his subordinates make?

The sheer *number* of decisions is not an accurate index of the amount of freedom that a subordinate group enjoys. More important is the *significance* of the decisions which the boss entrusts to his subordinates. Obviously a decision on how to arrange desks is of an entirely different order from a decision involving the introduction of new electronic data processing equipment. Even though the widest possible limits are given in dealing with the first issue, the group will sense no particular degree of responsibility. For a boss to permit the group to decide equipment policy, even within rather narrow limits, would reflect a greater degree of confidence in them on his part.

DECIDING HOW TO LEAD

Now let us turn from the types of leadership that are *practical* and *desirable*. What factors or forces should a manager consider in deciding how to manage? Three are of particular importance:

Forces in the manager.
Forces in the subordinates.
Forces in the situation.

We should like briefly to describe these elements and indicate how they might influence a manager's action in a decision-making situation.[2] The strength of each of them will, of course, vary from instance to instance, but the manager who is sensitive to them can better assess the problems which face him and determine which mode of leadership behavior is most appropriate for him.

Forces in the Manager

The manager's behavior in any given instance will be influenced greatly by the many forces operating within his own per-

[2] See also Robert Tannenbaum and Fred Massarik, "Participation by Subordinates in the Managerial Decision-Making Process," *Canadian Journal of Economics and Political Science*, August 1950, pp. 413-418.

sonality. He will, of course, perceive his leadership problems in
a unique way on the basis of his background, knowledge, and
experience. Among the important internal forces affecting him
will be the following:

(1) **His value system.** How strongly does he feel that individuals should have a share in making decisions which affect
them? Or, how convinced is he that the official who is paid to
assume responsibility should personally carry the burden of decision making? The strength of his convictions on questions like
these will tend to move the manager to one end or the other of
the continuum shown in EXHIBIT I. His behavior will also be
influenced by the relative importance that he attaches to organizational efficiency, personal growth of subordinates, and company profits.[3]

(2) **His confidence in his subordinates.** Managers differ
greatly in the amount of trust they have in other people generally, and this carries over to the particular employees they supervise at a given time. In viewing his particular group of subordinates, the manager is likely to consider their knowledge and
competence with respect to the problem. A central question he
might ask himself is: "Who is best qualified to deal with this
problem?" Often he may, justifiably or not, have more confidence in his own capabilities than in those of his subordinates.

(3) **His own leadership inclinations.** There are some managers who seem to function more comfortably and naturally
as highly directive leaders. Resolving problems and issuing orders come easily to them. Other managers seem to operate
more comfortably in a team role, where they are continually
sharing many of their functions with their subordinates.

(4) **His feelings of security in an uncertain situation.** The
manager who releases control over the decision-making process
thereby reduces the predictability of the outcome. Some managers have a greater need than others for predictability and stability in their environment. This "tolerance for ambiguity" is
being viewed increasingly by psychologists as a key variable in
a person's manner of dealing with problems.

The manager brings these and other highly personal variables to each situation he faces. If he can see them as forces
which, consciously or unconsciously, influence his behavior, he
can better understand what makes him prefer to act in a given

[3] See Chris Argyris, "Top Management Dilemma: Company Needs vs. Individual Development," *Personnel*, September 1955, pp. 123-134.

way. And understanding this, he can often make himself more effective.

Forces in the Subordinate

Before deciding how to lead a certain group, the manager will also want to consider a number of forces affecting his subordinates' behavior. He will want to remember that each employee, like himself, is influenced by many personality variables. In addition, each subordinate has a set of expectations about how the boss should act in relation to him (the phrase "expected behavior" is one we hear more and more often these days at discussions of leadership and teaching). The better the manager understands these factors, the more accurately he can determine what kind of behavior on his part will enable his subordinates to act more effectively.

Generally speaking, the manager can permit his subordinates greater freedom if the following essential conditions exist:

If the subordinates have relatively high needs for independence. (As we all know, people differ greatly in the amount of direction that they desire.)

If the subordinates have a readiness to assume responsibility for decision making. (Some see additional responsibility as a tribute to their ability; others see it as "passing the buck.")

If they have a relatively high tolerance for ambiguity. (Some employees prefer to have clear-cut directives given to them; others prefer a wider area of freedom.)

If they are interested in the problem and feel that it is important.

If they understand and identify with the goals of the organization.

If they have the necessary knowledge and experience to deal with the problem.

If they have learned to expect to share in decision making. (Persons who have come to expect strong leadership and are then suddenly confronted with the request to share more fully in decision making are often upset by this new experience. On the other hand, persons who have enjoyed a considerable amount of freedom resent the boss who begins to make all the decisions himself.)

The manager will probably tend to make fuller use of his own authority if the above conditions do *not* exist; at times there may be no realistic alternative to running a "one-man show." The restrictive effect of many of the forces will, of course, be greatly modified by the general feeling of confidence which subordinates have in the boss. Where they have learned to respect and trust him, he is free to vary his behavior. He will feel certain that he will not be perceived as an authoritarian boss on those occasions when he makes decisions by himself. Similarly, he will not be seen as using staff meetings to avoid his decision-making responsibility. In a climate of mutual confidence and respect, people tend to feel less threatened by deviations from normal practice, which in turn makes possible a higher degree of flexibility in the whole relationship.

Forces in the Situation

In addition to the forces which exist in the manager himself and in his subordinates, certain characteristics of the general situation will also affect the manager's behavior. Among the more critical environmental pressures that surround him are those which stem from the organization, the work group, the nature of the problem, and the pressures of time. Let us look briefly at each of these:

Type of Organization. Like individuals, organizations have values and traditions which inevitably influence the behavior of the people who work in them. The manager who is a newcomer to a company quickly discovers that certain kinds of behavior are approved while others are not. He also discovers that to deviate radically from what is generally accepted is likely to create problems for him.

These values and traditions are communicated in many ways—through job descriptions, policy pronouncements, and public statements by top executives. Some organizations, for example, hold to the notion that the desirable executive is one who is dynamic, imaginative, decisive, and persuasive. Other organizations put more emphasis upon the importance of the executive's ability to work effectively with people—his human relations skills. The fact that his superiors have a defined concept of what the good executive should be will very likely push the manager toward one end or the other of the behavioral range.

In addition to the above, the amount of employee participation is influenced by such variables as the size of the working units, their geographical distribution, and the degree of inter- and intra-organizational security required to attain company goals. For example, the wide geographical dispersion of an organization may preclude a practical system of participative decision making, even though this would otherwise be desirable. Similarly, the size of the working units or the need for keeping plans confidential may make it necessary for the boss to exercise more control than would otherwise be the case. Factors like these may limit considerably the manager's ability to function flexibly on the continuum.

Group Effectiveness. Before turning decision-making responsibility over to a subordinate group, the boss should consider how effectively its members work together as a unit.

One of the relevant factors here is the experience the group has had in working together. It can generally be expected that a group which has functioned for some time will have developed habits of cooperation and thus be able to tackle a problem more effectively than a new group. It can also be expected that a group of people with similar backgrounds and interests will work more quickly and easily than people with dissimilar backgrounds, because the communication problems are likely to be less complex.

The degree of confidence that the members have in their ability to solve problems as a group is also a key consideration. Finally, such group variables as cohesiveness, permissiveness, mutual acceptance, and commonality of purpose will exert subtle but powerful influence on the group's functioning.

The Problem Itself. The nature of the problem may determine what degree of authority should be delegated by the manager to his subordinates. Obviously he will ask himself whether they have the kind of knowledge which is needed. It is possible to do them a real disservice by assigning a problem that their experience does not equip them to handle.

Since the problems faced in large or growing industries increasingly require knowledge of specialists from many different fields, it might be inferred that the more complex a problem, the more anxious a manager will be to get some assistance in solving it. However, this is not always the case. There will be times when the very complexity of the problem calls for one person to work it out. For example, if the manager has most of the background and factual data relevant to a given issue, it may be easier for him to think it through himself than to take the time to fill in his staff on all the pertinent background information.

The key question to ask, of course, is: "Have I heard the ideas of everyone who has the necessary knowledge to make a significant contribution to the solution of this problem?"

The Pressure of Time. This is perhaps the most clearly felt pressure on the manager (in spite of the fact that it may sometimes be imagined). The more that he feels the need for an immediate decision, the more difficult it is to involve other people. In organizations which are in a constant state of "crisis" and "crash programing" one is likely to find managers personally using a high degree of authority with relatively little delegation to subordinates. When the time pressure is less intense, however, it becomes much more possible to bring subordinates in on the decision-making process.

These, then, are the principal forces that impinge on the manager in any given instance and that tend to determine his tactical behavior in relation to his subordinates. In each case his behavior ideally will be that which makes possible the most effective attainment of his immediate goal within the limits facing him.

LONG-RUN STRATEGY

As the manager works with his organization on the problems that come up day by day, his choice of a leadership pattern is usually limited. He must take account of the forces just described and, within the restrictions they impose on him, do the best that he can. But as he looks ahead months or even years, he can shift his thinking from tactics to large-scale strategy. No longer need he be fettered by all of the forces mentioned, for he can view many of them as variables over which he has some control. He can, for example, gain new insights or skills for himself, supply training for individual subordinates, and provide participative experiences for his employee group.

In trying to bring about a change in these variables, however, he is faced with a challenging question: At which point along the continuum *should* he act?

Attaining Objectives

The answer depends largely on what he wants to accomplish. Let us suppose that he is interested in the same objectives that most modern managers seek to attain when they can shift their attention from the pressure of immediate assignments:

1. To raise the level of employee motivation.
2. To increase the readiness of subordinates to accept change.
3. To improve the quality of all managerial decisions.
4. To develop teamwork and morale.
5. To further the individual development of employees.

In recent years the manager has been deluged with a flow of advice on how best to achieve these longer-run objectives. It is little wonder that he is often both bewildered and annoyed. However, there are some guidelines which he can usefully follow in making a decision.

Most research and much of the experience of recent years give a strong factual basis to the theory that a fairly high degree of subordinate-centered behavior is associated with the accomplishment of the five purposes mentioned.[4] This does not mean that a manager should always leave all decisions to his assistants. To provide the individual or the group with greater freedom than they are ready for at any given time may very well tend to generate anxieties and therefore inhibit rather than facilitate the attainment of desired objectives. But this should not keep the manager from making a continuing effort to confront his subordinates with the challenge of freedom.

CONCLUSION

In summary, there are two implications in the basic thesis that we have been developing. The first is that the successful leader is one who is keenly aware of those forces which are most relevant to his behavior at any given time. He accurately understands himself, the individuals and group he is dealing with, and the company and broader social environment in which he operates. And certainly he is able to assess the present readiness for growth of his subordinates.

But this sensitivity or understanding is not enough, which brings us to the second implication. The successful leader is one who is able to behave appropriately in the light of these percep-

---

[4] For example, see Warren H. Schmidt and Paul C. Buchanan, *Techniques that Produce Teamwork* (New London, Arthur C. Croft Publication, 1954); and Morris S. Viteles, *Motivation and Morale in Industry* (New York, W. W. Norton & Company, Inc., 1953).

tions. If direction is in order, he is able to direct; if considerable participative freedom is called for, he is able to provide such freedom.

Thus, the successful manager of men can be primarily characterized neither as a strong leader nor as a permissive one. Rather, he is one who maintains a high batting average in accurately assessing the forces that determine what his most appropriate behavior at any given time should be and in actually being able to behave accordingly. Being both insightful and flexible, he is less likely to see the problems of leadership as a dilemma.

SOME OBSERVATIONS ABOUT A GENERAL THEORY OF LEADERSHIP*

by Bernard M. Bass

Studying Behavior in Groups

The productive capacity of modern man and his machines, and the increased complexity of organized activity, have increased our awareness of the significance of understanding, predicting, and controlling interpersonal behavior—although the matter has been of interest to man throughout history. To understand human behavior, we must develop methods and principles for studying behavior in groups, for a large proportion of human activity takes place within groups. The universality of interpersonal phenomena is attributed to the prolonged biological dependence of the mammalian, particularly the human child, on his parents.

The study of interpersonal behavior is complicated by the elusiveness of its effects and the fact that individuals belong to several groups at the same time. Until recently, theory about social behavior was mainly speculative and seldom subjected to experimental test. Now, a variety of rigorous "small" theories

* Reprinted from Bernard M. Bass, *Leadership, Psychology and Organizational Behavior,* Harper and Row, 1960. Copyright © 1960 by Bernard M. Bass, By Permission of Harper & Row, Publishers.

are being developed about leadership, compliance, evaluation, and other interpersonal phenomena. This volume has been an attempt to formulate a more comprehensive theory about group behavior and is likely to suffer in rigorousness and precision because of the scope of activities encompassed. However, the theory is stated in experimentally testable terms.

The importance of the group, the situation, and the individual members are relative matters. We can increase or decrease the significance of each at will. We need to develop ways of studying and describing the interacting effects of all three. We think we should begin with concepts rooted in individual behavior.

Nature and Purpose of Theory

The purpose of a theory is to promote understanding. Theory provides the concepts and definitions which abstract the important elements in the observable phenomena we are interested in describing. Operations proceed on two planes: the empirical and the rational. The constructs of the rational plane are connected to the observables of the empirical plane by operational definitions. Propositions are deduced from the postulated relationships among the constructs. They are also induced from examining the empirical relationships among the observables. Validating the propositions by both means increases our confidence that we understand the phenomena. Yet, while the observable relationships are likely to withstand much further change (although they may become more precise), the rationale accounting for the relationship is likely to be modified and replaced by a newer and better model.

Group Effectiveness

A group is defined as a collection of individuals whose existence as a collection is rewarding to the individuals (or enables them to avoid punishment). A group does not necessarily perceive itself as such. The members do not have to share common goals. Nor are interaction, interlocking roles, and shared ways of behavior implied in the definition, although these are common characteristics of many groups.

The extent to which a group actually rewards its members is the group's effectiveness. The extent to which members anticipate such reinforcement is the attractiveness of the group. In natural groups, goals and goal attainment are likely to be multidimensional. The source of reward may be the task or the interaction among members, or both. Rewards may be *relevant* or *irrelevant, immediate* or *delayed, partial* or *total.* Generally, task effectiveness accompanies interaction effectiveness, although situations can be described where only the task or only the interaction is positively reinforcing. It is particularly important to know whether the goal attainment producing effectiveness is relevant to the members. Mere productivity indices may be irrelevant to workers. Group goal attainment will modify subsequent behavior to the extent it is relevant to the members of the group. While goals may be immediate or distant, it is probable that immediate rather than ultimate effectiveness is more significant for understanding interaction among individuals.

Group Attractiveness

A group is more attractive the greater the rewards which may be earned by membership in the group and the greater the subjective expectancy that these rewards will be obtained through membership. Attraction to a group may be modified, therefore, by changing the amount or intensity of rewards for members and by changing expectations about obtaining the rewards. The clearer are the rewards of the group, the more attractive will the group be. Similarly, the more members share the same goals obtainable through cooperative effort, the more they will be attracted to each other.

Individuals are attracted to groups because groups tend to be more rewarding than isolated activity. The more rewarding or effective are the groups, the more members will be attracted to them. The more attracted to the groups, the more members will attempt to behave in a way to maintain or increase the effectiveness of the groups.

Leaders and Leadership

Interaction occurs when one member's behavior stimulates another whose resultant change (or lack of change) in behavior in turn stimulates the first member. Formal interactions occur between occupants of positions, while informal ones occur between persons regardless of their positions. The formal organization is a consistent pattern of formal interactions. The corresponding pattern of consistent informal interactions, the informal organization, arises in response to changing problems not solved by the more formal rigid organization. For example, it may arise because of failure in formal communications. But, in doing so, it may aid rather than conflict with the formal organization, depending on other factors.

The large numbers of types of leaders described by earlier investigators fall into a few categories. Some have equated leadership with status, the importance of position. Others have equated leadership with esteem, the value of persons regardless of their positions. Still others have singled out certain behaviors and called those behaviors leadership.

The definition used in our theory is similar to those earlier ones defining leadership as influence on others in a group. Leadership is the observed effort of one member to change other members' behavior by altering the motivation of the other members or by changing their habits. If the leadership is successful, what is observed is a change in the member accepting the leadership. Changing behavior by disturbing the central nervous system is arbitrarily excluded, but psychotherapy and teaching are included within the meaning of leadership.

Members who lead may also do other things. The foreman may keep inventory records as well as exhibit leadership. But being a foreman is not identical with being a leader.

Related to leadership, yet different in meaning, are behavioral contagion, influence, and followership. But following is not necessarily the opposite of leading; sometimes one may lead by following.

The observed change in the behavior of the follower results from the alteration of his motivation, or from initiating of structure by the leader. Motivation is changed by changing the expectations of reward or punishment. The mass persuader leads through this type of activity. In the formal organization, leaders vary from motivating others with promise of reward, support, affection, and consideration to threats of punishment, burdensome demands, and deflation of the self-esteem of subordinates. This variation in consideration is unidimensional and accounts for much of described leader behavior in industry and military organizations.

Leadership also is accomplished by initiating structure— making others more able to overcome the obstacles thwarting goal attainment. Activities include instructing, supervising, informing, ordering, and deciding. Again a single factor describes how leaders in formal organizations vary in such initiation.

Conceiving leadership in this way permits an easier integration of theories concerning the perception, learning, and behavior of the individual in a nonsocial (isolated) situation with theory emerging from research on perception, learning, and behavior of individuals in groups.

Measurement and Evaluation of Leadership

Our understanding of leadership will depend on how we measure and evaluate it. Earlier investigators using wisdom research, case history analyses, nomination, ratings, and categorization did not attempt to distinguish between attempted, successful, and effective leadership. But a dynamic analysis of the leadership process requires differentiation. Nonobjective assessment methods are not likely to as readily provide the necessary discrimination because of the halo error in ratings and other difficulties of discrimination.

An objective method of assessing attempted leadership is to measure the amount of time a subject participates in an initially leaderless discussion. The reliability of this and related measures of participation is high and accounts for much of the observed and evaluated differences in leadership among discussants.

One possible objective approach to assessing successful leadership is to present a group with a problem whose solution requires ranking the alternative answers to the problem. Each member is asked to report privately his own initial opinion. Then the members interact—usually in discussion. They reach another decision or decisions, as a group or as individuals. Who has influenced whom is gauged from the changes in correlations among the various members' rankings from before to after they interact.

Effective leadership is exhibited by successful leaders of groups which become effective as a consequence of the leadership. Measurement requires assessing the effectiveness of the groups led as well as the success of the leadership.

Leadership and Group Effectiveness

Changes occur in the behavior of members of a group in order to increase the rewards for performance. While such changes can be initiated by individual isolated trial and error or other personal means, it is assumed that they more often are the product of interaction, since evidence indicates that (1) more changes occur when interaction is possible; (2) the changes occur faster; (3) interaction brings rewards not possible in isolation; and (4) isolated individuals are likely to reduce the variability of their behavior or withdraw from the environment if it is not a stimulating one.

If group effectiveness depends on the occurrence of interaction, it also depends on the occurrence of attempted and successful leadership, since leadership is interaction. The more difficult are the problems facing the group and blocking goal attainment or the less able the membership to cope with their problems and reach their goals, the more the leadership is necessary and likely to be attempted and successful. But if the difficulties are too great, members' expectations of failure may make the group sufficiently unattractive to cause the members to withdraw from it, rather than attempt to solve the problems or attempt and succeed as leaders.

Motivation to Attempt Leadership

Individuals differ in personality and personal goals, and in whether they are task-oriented, self-oriented or interaction-oriented. This results in further individual differences in tendency to attempt leadership. Also, energetic persons, regardless of other conditions, are more likely to attempt more leadership than those less active generally. Similarly, persons with strong needs to achieve are more likely to attempt leadership than those without such needs. Again, members more attracted to the group expecting more rewards for goal attainment, will be more likely to attempt leadership than those lower in attraction to the group.

Idealized types of task-, interaction-, and self-oriented members can be conceived, although naturally most persons will exhibit some of all three tendencies, depending to some extent on the situation. Task-oriented members are most attracted to the group by expectations of task success and its rewards. They are reinforced primarily by task effectiveness. Others are similarly more concerned with interaction and interaction effectiveness. Still other members are primarily attracted to a group as a source of esteem, status, or direct reward to themselves regardless of task and interaction effectiveness. An analysis of a particular group's goals and those of its members often is required to determine whether the various members are self-, task-, or interaction-oriented. A member high personally in need achievement may exhibit interaction orientation at a social gathering, and task orientation in a work group. Orientation changes with the aging of a group in existence over long periods of time. Members tend to be attracted to each other initially to complete some tasks they cannot handle alone. Then the groups tend to move from task orientation to a concern with interaction as an end in itself. Finally, self-orientation comes to the fore prior to the disintegration of the groups.

The self-oriented leader is more concerned with his success as a leader than the task or interaction effectiveness of his leadership. Therefore, the self-oriented leader is usually detrimental to group effectiveness. He is less likely to change his behavior to meet changing group needs. He may even try to divert the group from one goal to another. But the self-oriented member is less likely to persist in the face of failure to lead others.

The task-oriented leader will attempt leadership only when the group is attractive because of its tasks and the rewards for task success. He will more readily cease attempting leadership if his successes are ineffective.

The interaction-oriented leader will avoid attempting leadership likely to disrupt current patterns of interaction. He will attempt leadership mainly when interaction difficulties present themselves and he sees himself as able to cope with them.

Ability and Persuasive Leadership

One member can persuade another if he has demonstrated his ability to solve the other member's problems. In persuasive leadership, the leader serves as a secondary reinforcer of the behavior of the follower.

A variety of generalized aptitudes and more specific proficiencies are associated with observed success as a leader. In a wide variety of situations, the more fluent, intelligent, original, and adaptable member is more likely to succeed as a leader. The member more empathic or sensitive to the needs of his group is more likely to succeed as leader. Proficiency in the activities of the group also characterizes successful leaders. Again, ability derived from a member's position can also produce successful leadership.

But the would-be leader cannot be too much more able than those he leads to succeed maximally as a leader. Moreover, his ability must be relevant or significant for solving the problems of the groups he expects to lead.

Development and Transfer of Ability to Lead

It is assumed that positive transfer, the facilitation of new performance by earlier behavior, is greater the more similar the new and old performances. But negative transfer will occur if the new situation is seen as similar and is responded to as if it is similar when it is actually different from the old. Both positive and negative transfer are common in social development.

It follows from these assumptions that the leader successful and effective earlier will succeed and be effective to a maximum in a new situation the more it resembles the earlier one and is perceived as similar. The earlier-effective leader will attempt less leadership in the new situation if he sees it as different. He will be least effective in the new situation if it is seen as similar to the earlier one but is not.

The leader successful and ineffective earlier will attempt less leadership in a new situation seen as similar. If others see it as similar, he will be less successful in influencing them.

An unsuccessful leader of an earlier situation will attempt less leadership in a new one if he sees the new one as similar to the earlier situation. If he does attempt leadership and the other members see the situation as similar, he will be less likely to succeed.

One is more likely to attempt leadership in a new situation if he attempted it in an earlier one seen as similar.

Most of these and related deductions have not been tested as yet, but various studies can be arranged to lend empirical support to some of the propositions. For example, consistency of leadership displayed by individuals in early and later leaderless discussions decreases insofar as the later discussions are among differently composed groups, about different problems, and further away in time from the earlier discussions. Similarly, there is a much higher correlation between leadership displayed in junior high school and high school by students than among students in elementary school reexamined in high school.

Considerable additional evidence supports the generality of transfer across changing situations, but the evidence does not indicate how the consistency or generality is affected by the similarity or differences between situations. The observed generality suggests the utility of situational tests, such as the leaderless group discussion, for assessing future leadership potential in "real-life" situations.

But, while illustrations of negative transfer from industry

and government can be cited, no experimental evidence has been uncovered.

The transfer phenomena suggest that the interaction experiences of children and adolescents with their parents, siblings, peers, and other adults play an important role in the development of leadership potential. The ability of biographical information blanks to forecast future leadership success and the biographical analyses of "great men" suggest the utility of further exploration of the links between childhood and adult leadership behavior.

From studies of the social development of the child, a number of factors are likely to affect the future success of the adult as a leader, particularly if the conditions persist into and through adolescence. These include the early pattern of interaction with the mother, and later the father and teacher; family factors such as birth order and number; parental attitudes toward children; and adolescent opportunities for social learning.

Management Development

There have been almost no specific tests contrasting the efficacy of various methods of executive training as now practiced in industry. The leadership training apparently aims to (1) increase the ability to solve the problems of those to be led; (2) reinforce success as a leader by giving opportunities to attempt leadership and to see the effects of the attempts; and (3) to increase motivation to attempt leadership.

It is probable that those programs attempting to increase proficiencies rather than to modify aptitudes or personality traits are more likely to succeed. Particularly important is the need for the superiors of the trainees to provide active support and acceptance of what is to be learned.

Training may include coaching by superiors; guided experience; understudy training; management apprenticeships; job rotation; counseling by professional consultants; and project assignments. Use may be made of problem-solving discussions, case history analyses, and role playing, in addition to many formal and informal class and course procedures.

Power and Coercive Leadership

While a member with ability can successfully persuade others to follow him, a member with power can coerce others to follow. His power may derive from his person or his position. A powerful person can directly reinforce the behavior of others by granting or denying rewards or punishments to the others, depending on their behavior. A person has power over others if he controls what the others want. If the other members are not motivated to gain these goals, the control does not yield power. The stronger the motivation, the greater the resulting power. Coercion occurs when members publicly but not privately comply with the suggestions or direction of another member. But the inhibition of their own preferences results in dissatisfaction and frustration, which in turn may lead to a variety of attempts to reduce the frustration. Coercion may produce hostility among the coerced. Or the less powerful members may withdraw from the situation. Or they may overreact, resulting in a loss in task effectiveness. Or they may compensate by forming a new informal organization to counter the frustrating effects of being coerced.

Power provides successful coercive leadership but it is not as likely to be effective as far as the coerced members are concerned.

Ability, Power, and Permissive Leadership

To lead successfully and permissively, a member must have the power to impose restrictions on what other members are permitted to do, and he must have the ability to know when such restrictions are necessary and when he would do better to avoid such impositions. While power used to coerce will produce hostility, withdrawal, apathy, "forced" behavior toward irrelevant goals, the same power, coupled with ability, can be used permissively. Permissiveness is less likely to result in hostility and withdrawal since the goals selected by those led permissively are likely to be relevant to them.

Group decision-making is usually involved in permissive leadership. As such, the permissive leader can avoid using his power to coerce (except when necessary to impose some restrictions on the interacting members). Instead, he can make use of the power of the group and the members' acceptance of the group as more able than themselves as individuals.

Membership in groups facilitates compliance with suggestions. The tendency to conform to majority opinion, to the norms established by the group, to modal behavior, seems to be a universal phenomenon. Such compliance is found in adolescent cliques, in conformity to cultural values, in military discipline,

in the typical work group, in delinquent gangs, and in the laboratory. The more attractive a group, the more rewards expected
from it, the more power it will have over its members, and the
more members will conform to group standards. Conformity
will be greater the more certain or clear are the standards, and
when the group is made more important to its members. Conformity is greater among the less confident members, the more
acquiescent members, and those closer initially to the majority
position.

A great deal of evidence suggests that permissive leadership, group decision-making, and permission to interact prior
to reaching such decisions produce more effective groups and
more satisfied members. Exceptions are likely to occur when
members are under severe stress or are of low ability.

Status and Leadership

Status is the worth or value to the organization of the occupant of a position, regardless of who the occupant is personally.
Status provides the power to coerce, the ability to persuade as
well as the power and ability to be a permissive leader, but
status is not leadership.

Status can be gauged from the rank or echelon of an occupant's position in an organization. Also, various methods of job
evaluation can be used to determine the worth of the various
positions making up the formal organization. Special sociometric
analyses also can be employed.

Status is usually accompanied by visible symbols of position
and worth. Sometimes, however, the symbols remain after
the status has disappeared. While habitual compliance to the
symbols may be maintained, the loss of status and of the power
and ability accompanying it results in a loss in likelihood of success as a leader.

Considerable experimental evidence and related research
support the theorem that the higher one's status, the more likely
he is to succeed as a leader among those of lower status. This
generalization applies equally well to status and leadership in
societies, in formal industrial and military organizations as well
as to impromptu initially leaderless group discussions. But the
control accompanying status must be of what is potentially rewarding to those of lower status. Otherwise, the status will
yield control, but not power, resulting in less leadership success.

Esteem and Leadership

Esteem is the worth of an individual to his group, regardless of his position. Esteem contributes to subsequent status, and heightened status tends to increase one's esteem. Esteem depends to some extent on what abilities are relevant to goal attainment by the group; to what the group values. Esteem is not popularity, although they tend to be related, particularly when the group is mainly concerned with pleasant interactions.

Esteem is measured by some form of merit rating by superiors, peers, or subordinates in formal organizations, or by one's associates in informal organizations. Or it can be estimated by outside observers. Sociometric ratings by peers tend to be consistent over considerable periods of time, particularly for more mature subjects.

Esteemed members tend to be more able, more likely to conform, better adjusted, seemingly more similar in attitudes and attributes to the average member and more like other esteemed members.

The esteemed member can successfully coerce others by means of his personal power or he can successfully persuade them because of his apparently greater ability. Since continued coercion is likely to produce a loss of esteem, permissive or persuasive leadership must be emphasized by an esteemed member in order for him to maintain his esteem.

Esteem has been found associated with success in leading initially leaderless group discussions, with success in military leadership, and with success in leading other children. The effects can be reproduced in the laboratory.

Mutual esteem is positively associated with the attractiveness of a group. Since attractiveness contributes to effectiveness, mutual esteem likewise is related to group effectiveness. In the same way, conformity in groups is likely to be greater when mutual esteem is high.

Self-esteem presages attempted leadership. Self-esteem increases with success and in turn reduces tendencies to conform or acquiesce. Self-accorded status operates in a similar way.

Conflict

Leadership may be rejected despite the ability or power behind it because of a variety of conflicts.

Events preceding the attempted leadership, or taking place concurrently, may result in the failure of what would have been successful leadership. The attempted leadership may require excessive energy expenditure not commensurate with promised rewards for compliance; it may demand unacceptable distribution of rewards; it may threaten loss of esteem or status. In all of these cases, despite the power or ability promoting success, the attempted leadership may be rejected. Or followers may resort to pseudosolutions, such as rationalization for acceptance, withdrawal, and displaced aggression, rather than reject power figures openly.

The would-be leader is often the "man-in-the-middle" caught between the demands of his superiors and the desires of his subordinates. A variety of resolutions of his dilemma have been adopted, some regarded as tactful, others as hypocritical. Many comment on the need of a leader caught in such conditions to wear a mask, to be a good actor.

If one's self-esteem is higher than the esteem he is accorded by other members, he is likely to attempt more leadership and succeed less than a member whose esteem matches his high self-esteem. Status and self-accorded status follow the same proposition, but self-esteem is more likely to be overestimated than is self-accorded status.

Since status or esteem produces success as a leader, if the high-status member is not esteemed or vice versa, conflict is likely. Status-esteem incongruencies lead to a variety of conflicts, if the high-status and the high-esteem members differ in their respective ideas and goals. Ways of mitigating status-esteem incongruence include ensuring the promotion of the esteemed, increasing or maintaining the esteem of those promoted to higher status, and increasing the agreement about aims of the formal and informal organizations.

Ability-esteem or ability-status incongruence not only bring conflict, but also group ineffectiveness. If the powerful member lacks ability, he may succeed as a leader but is less likely to be effective than the powerful member with ability to solve the group's problems. Again, one solution avoiding this difficulty is to ensure promoting the most able members. Another is for lower-status members to mask their abilities, avoiding conflict, but not fostering group effectiveness.

Interaction Potential

Interaction potential is the tendency of any pair of a group to interact. As interaction potential increases between two individuals, we observe an increase in:

1. The probability of their interacting in a given amount of time.
2. Rate or frequency of interaction between the pair.
3. Speed of initiation of an interaction between the pair.
4. Duration of interaction between the pair.
5. The total amount of interaction in a group composed of many small pairs.

A pair of individuals are more likely to interact if they are:

1. Members of a small rather than a large group.
2. Geographically and socially close.
3. Connected by a communication channel free of "noise" or blockage, free to contact each other rather than lacking in opportunity for contact and meeting.
4. Intimate and familiar and experienced with each other rather than distant and unfamiliar.
5. Mutually esteemed.
6. Attracted to each other.
7. Similar in abilities and attitudes rather than different.
8. More mature than young children.
9. More in contact with reality, energetic and outward-oriented.

Other factors that increase interaction potential may include alcohol, boredom, third parties, interaction primacy, the importance of message, the amount of situational stimulation, the time available to interact, and the amount of coordination required for completion of the task.

Interaction Potential and Group Effectiveness

If groups tend to move toward greater effectiveness and if most changes in groups are by means of interaction, then it follows that increased effectiveness accompanies increased interaction among members. Large, distant, disconnected, unfamiliar, and heterogeneous groups of members will be less likely to reach a given state of effectiveness compared to small, proximate, connected, intimate, homogeneous groups. We must qualify this generalization as we consider each variable separately. However, the qualifications themselves logically follow from the differences that exist among such diverse variables as size, propinquity, connectedness, and so on and some of their unique effects on behavior in groups, above and beyond considerations of interaction potential. Thus, increased homogeneity in attitudes is accompanied by increased willingness to express hostility openly as well as increased interaction potential.

Overcoming Ineffectiveness
Due to Lack of Interaction Potential

A variety of techniques and modifications are introduced into group activities in order to counteract the effects of initially low interaction potential.

Some raise effectiveness by raising interaction potential directly, while others raise interaction potential indirectly or attack effectiveness rather than interaction potential as such. The processes or techniques include establishing formal organization and increasing the differentiation of members in status (which, in turn, may create new difficulties for the group); increasing the training of assigned leaders; increasing the educational level or degree of understanding of the members of the group activities; establishing and reinforcing reliable common sources of information for all members; increasing the rapidity and frequency of transmittal or information; and splintering the group.

More direct methods include increasing propinquity mechanically; restricting size arbitrarily; increasing familiarity; promoting feelings of homogeneity; increasing mutual esteem; and developing new communication procedures.

Historical developments of civilized societies to some extent may be described in terms of changing interaction potential and its effects.

Leadership During Emergencies

When members must cope with danger, sudden threat, any attempts to aid them in removing themselves from the obvious possibilities will be welcomed. Attempts to lead are more likely to be accepted more readily than if no crises were present. Such attempts are also more likely to be immediately effective.

Since speed of interaction is likely to be effective, groups with greater interaction potential are likely to be more immediately effective when faced with emergencies. Small, intimate, proximate, communicative groups are more likely to be effective in crises. Or stratified groups with highly trained leaders and members are more likely to be able to cope with sudden crises.

Since stress increases with increasing motivation, and since attractiveness also increases with motivation, attractive groups are likely to experience more stress when thwarted from obtaining their goals than unattractive groups.

PART II
LEADERSHIP
AND COMMUNICATION

INTRODUCTION:
COMMUNICATION
AND LEADERSHIP[1]

Human communication is a complicated phenomenon. The complexities of motivation and behavior of the sender meet the equal complexities of perception and motivation of the receiver. A variety of impressions or messages are sent or received in any effort toward communication, and frequently considerable non-verbal, as well as verbal, interaction among the persons involved is necessary for effective communication to take place.

It is important in examining face-to-face communication in the leader-follower context to recognize some of the basic forces affecting the individuals involved. If mutual understanding is poor within a group, there is no effective way of working together; if there is no agreed-upon procedure, or if competition between members or with the leader is present, little work will be accomplished.

An important issue in understanding the complexities of a leadership situation is to realize that a variety of group and individual purposes is always present. Frequently it is helpful to recognize that there is a level of surface tasks and a level of hidden tasks or purposes. A variety of hidden individual and group purposes, feelings and needs, while not openly recognized as the concern of the group, are nevertheless just as effective in determining what happens in the group as is the surface task.

It is in the midst of this complex of factors that communication takes place.

As noted above, communication is obviously not by words alone. Tone of voice, choice of words, bodily posture all communicate a variety of messages. Two persons may say, "Good morning" to each other and convey a number of messages. One "Good morning" may indicate supplication, awareness of sub-

[1] Much of this section is adapted from material printed in the Reading Book, *Laboratories in Human Relations Training*, NTL Institute for Applied Behavioral Science (mimeograph), revised, 1969, and is extensively revised and edited by William R. Lassey.

ordinate status, or anxiety as to how the greeting will be received. The other may convey condescension, awareness of power of position, rejection, or hostility.

Ingredients in Communication

Communication results from complex motivational systems on the part of both parties. Therefore it is important to recognize certain factors of motivation and behavior, as well as a number of other variables associated with any interpersonal confrontation. The following diagram illustrates some of these variables in simplified form:[2]

A MODEL OF SOME OF THE INGREDIENTS
IN COMMUNICATION

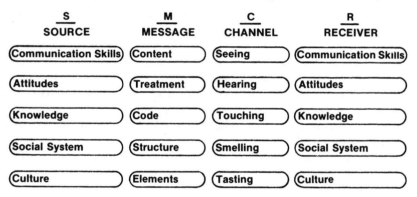

S	M	C	R
SOURCE	**MESSAGE**	**CHANNEL**	**RECEIVER**
Communication Skills	Content	Seeing	Communication Skills
Attitudes	Treatment	Hearing	Attitudes
Knowledge	Code	Touching	Knowledge
Social System	Structure	Smelling	Social System
Culture	Elements	Tasting	Culture

Frequently we seek a single, simple cause to understand the behavior and communication of the other, when, in reality, a variety of causes are inevitably present. In fact, behavior results from many different forces operating in a number of directions in the total life space in which we exist.

There are not only a variety of complex motivations on the part of the communicator and a variety of messages communicated by him at each moment, but the receiver of the communications "hears" the communication with an equally complex perceptual system. Each of us has a perceptual screen or filter through which we perceive the behavior of others. We "hear" what we want to hear, either laudatory or critical. Thus the complexity of both sending and receiving make communi-

[2] Adapted from David K. Berlo, *The Process of Communication*, Holt, Rinehart and Winston, 1960. Berlo describes and explains the model in detail.

cation a difficult human act. Of the messages the individual may transmit, many of which he is unaware, he cannot know which are received by the other, or whether the perceptual screen of the other distorts the message he attempted to convey.

Each of us is concerned with developing and maintaining our self-image. Communications that are "heard" as threatening our image of ourselves and the image we wish others to have are responded to by defensive or aggressive reactions, even though the sender was not consciously aware that he was threatening the self-image of the other. As a result neither listens to the other or responds to the image from which the other speaks. Each talks past the other.

Behavioral Communication

Behavior results from perception of our own needs to relate to other people and from what we perceive about the actions of others. There are a few typical forms of behavior all of us engage in from time to time. Frequently we are not aware of the extent to which our pattern of behavior affects others.

Fighting with others tends to appear in several guises: in humor, in debate and argument, in semantic quibbling, in strategy and counter-strategy. With social growth people tend to refine ways of fighting and to compete in various subtle forms of humor and debate. Debate tends to lead to polarization and counter-debate and is the convenient structure for socialized fighting.

We all have needs to *control* and *influence* others. Advertising, propaganda, guidance, education, persuasion, management, manipulation are variously colored ways of describing our efforts to control the lives of others: to get them to do something that is good for us or what we think is good for them. When we give advice, offer up another group member as a candidate for a group role, or "bring out a silent member," we are trying to control the individuals' behavior.

We all have needs at times to *punish* others or feel good when others are punished and have various and sundry subtle ways of disguising our needs to hurt others. Setting up a leader for the kill, talking through another's remark, using a remark for "innocent" humor, encouraging a silent member to talk: all are methods which may be motivated by needs to punish, and may be so perceived.

It is necessary for all of us to *withdraw* at times. We may

become umpire to get out of the game, volunteer for an observer
or secretarial role, sulk, listen, daydream, or take other ways of
getting out of active verbal interaction with others. Withdrawal
may be seen as resentment, ignorance, apathy or veiled attack.

Most of us need at times to *seek support*, need occasional
or frequent reassurance that others respect us, love us, or accept
us. Some of us try to keep others at a comfortably effective distance (withdrawal), while others seek to maintain intimacy with
a wide variety of people.

Few of us are as *accepting* of people as we might well be.
Liking a person is not necessarily accepting him. Accepting
someone does not necessarily mean liking him. Accepting a person means essentially recognizing him as another human being
with strong needs, feelings, purposes and one who should be
listened to and understood so that effective relations can be
established. Acceptance of a person should be the prelude to
listening and endeavoring to be helpful.

It is difficult to really *listen*. Most of us listen only partially
to the other. Consequently we make assumptions about communication that are often inadequate. Listening requires con-
centration to perceive the various communication levels present
and the various feelings and needs within the individual.

The most important requirement is to be more *aware* of
our own behavior and its consequences on others. We can then
find more effective ways of relating to people.

Communication Process

Communication can be thought of as a step-by-step process.

1. The individual has some feelings about himself (his self-
   image) and has a set of attitudes toward the others with
   whom he wishes to interact.

2. These feelings and attitudes become intentions toward
   the others. For example, if he feels that his ideas are
   wanted and appreciated and if he would like to make a
   contribution, we can predict that he will have the intention of making positive contributions in a group situation.

3. These intentions cause the individual to initiate some
   behavior toward the others in the group. His behavior is
   governed by

      a. his intentions, and
      b. his past responses to behavior from the other people. We might think of this whole phase of the process as leading up to BEHAVIOR OUTPUT.
4. The behavior then passes through a perceptual screen which exists in the others. This screen includes value systems of the individuals who are receiving the behavior output, each individual's expectations of how he should behave in this situation, and experience with how he has behaved in similar situations.
5. The behavior is then evaluated by the others in terms of these expectations.
6. As a result of this evaluation, the members of the group develop some intentions toward the individual.
7. These intentions serve to generate behavior output from the group members directed at the individual,
8. This behavior goes back through the original sender's screen: that is, his feelings about himself and his attitudes (the ones he started with). He receives feedback which either supports or modifies his expectations.

This apparently abstract and complex process can perhaps be simplified through an illustration. Let us suppose we are talking about member "X" in a group. He is a secure person, sees himself as effective in his relations with others, and feels warmly toward others. His intentions, based on this combination of feelings and attitudes, are to express his ideas, to cooperate, and to be quite active in a group. His "behavior output" then is active and friendly.

This behavior output is perceived by others as warm, friendly, competent, cooperative. Given these perceptions of member "X," the intentions of other members toward him are friendly, respect his opinions, seek his ideas, and generally accept his influence attempts.

These intentions show themselves in the behavior of other members toward him.

He perceives the behavior of other members through his "screen," telling him that he is liked and accepted and that he is satisfying his needs to be respected and influential. In other words, the feedback confirms his initial image. So he continues to produce similar types of intentions and behavior.

This person is likely to maintain high status in a group and hold a position of leadership.

Perhaps of more interest to us is what happens with people who don't have this initial image. For example, if a person sees himself as quite inadequate, and they see him this way also, his intentions are likely to be cautious, which will produce very low "behavior output."

This low behavior output may well be perceived by others as somewhat neutral, neither friendly nor unfriendly, and therefore tends to produce very little behavior toward him. Such an individual is likely to read this as a confirmation of his own low evaluation of himself, tending to reinforce his behavior pattern of withdrawal.

A third illustration: a person feels he is quite adequate, but that others tend to be unfriendly and competitive toward him. This produces intentions to keep them from blocking him, and to compete or to get his way in spite of their attitudes. Expressed in behavior, such a person is likely to be very active. He probably initiates many ideas and probably reacts critically to others.

When this behavior is received, it probably makes others feel irritated and makes them tend to reject his ideas even when they are good. This produces intentions to either reject or resist him. The behavior toward him then is either to ignore him or to fight him. He perceives this behavior as a confirmation of his initial attitudes, and so the circle starts again.

To effect change in such a situation, there are several alternative ways of initiating action:

A. We can help the individual take a longer look at his own feelings about himself and his own attitudes. Perhaps his initial image (that others distrust him) is the place where some help can be given.

B. Another starting point or leverage point for changing the situation would be at the point of the individual's behavior. By helping a person explore his own behavior and perhaps giving him some new feedback, he might be helped to consciously attempt new behavior.

C. Help the people who are reacting to an individual explore the basis for their own reactions and evaluations. Perhaps they are jumping to conclusions and pre-evaluating, which means they are probably not listening to his contributions. If this could be changed, perhaps the whole process would be improved.

D. Establish some change in the behavior of others toward

the individual so that the feedback he gets helps him to correct his own images and behavior.

The leader who wishes to improve his interaction with his staff and organization needs to be aware of his own behavior systems as well as the behavior of others; that is, he needs to understand the processes within himself and the situation which will influence his potential for exerting positive and productive influence.
ence.

The Analysis of Leadership and Communication

Boulding illustrates eloquently the relationships between our "image" of reality and communication processes in the selection immediately following. His book, entitled *The Image*, is a classic conceptualization of the relevance of communication to all human endeavor, particularly leadership activity. This approach illuminates in very personalized fashion the importance of communication to the individual view of reality which governs his behavior. The meaning of a message is the change or effect it has on the "image" of the recipient, which may be almost totally at variance with the "intended" meaning of the person constructing the message. Boulding emphasizes the importance of values or value scales as "perhaps the most important elements determining the effects of messages . . ." This will have much to do with the willingness of an individual to change as he is presented with new knowledge, because new knowledge must be integrated with the existing knowledge structure if it is to have an impact, while maintaining internal psychological consistency.

The selection by Burke, entitled "Interpersonal Communication" is much more specific, attempting to provide practical guidance to anyone seeking greater effectiveness at the interpersonal level. He discusses key issues in sending and receiving messages, particularly in spoken form, which will facilitate clarity of understanding and accuracy in transmission of meaning. He particularly emphasizes the importance of careful listening and suggests how this may be facilitated by "active" listening or "empathy." One means to accomplish this is through specific attention to non-verbal behavior: facial expressions, gestures, and other expressions of emotion or meaning. If listening is effective Burke suggests that risk is involved: the risk of being changed as a consequence of careful attention to the frame of reference and intentions of your partner or partners in the communication process.

The final selection in Part II, by Gibb, applies communication concepts to the dynamics of leadership in educational and organizational situations. He contrasts leadership styles—defensive or authoritarian versus participative or democratic—and discusses how "style" relates to the communication tendencies of individuals characterized by these two extremes in approach. Obviously there are many intermediate approaches on the authoritarian-democratic continuum. Gibb particularly emphasizes the role of the reward system as a key element in communication and motivational processes. The defensive-authoritarian leader tends to emphasize high control over the behavior of subordinates by careful attention to manipulation of information flow. This leads to efforts by subordinates to circumvent the control startegy by distorting the upward flow of information and hence absorbs energy that might otherwise be devoted to task accomplishment. The reward system is used throughout the growth process of individuals, from childhood to maturity, as a device for structuring behavior. Gibb suggests that the defensive approach to reward has unfortunate ramifications for human growth because it tends to re-enforce authoritarian tendencies which permeate society and obstruct maximization of human and organizational potential.

He emphasizes a major point that has powerful implications for leadership behavior: Gibb suggests that in the participative leadership style communication becomes a true "process" rather than a "program." Effective communication happens more as a natural part of the leadership style rather than as a carefully constructed effort to persuade or manipulate subordinates. An atmosphere of openness and honesty on the part of individuals in positions of leadership serves as a model for similar behavior by subordinates. There is an atmosphere of trust which tends to decrease distortion of messages and facilitates understanding between all parties in the group or organizational setting. Valid, direct, authentic and open communication results, which supports inter-dependent, high-trust, self-determining and open behavior by both leaders and followers.

COMMUNICATION
AND "THE IMAGE"*

by Kenneth Boulding

As I sit at my desk, I know where I am. I see before me a window; beyond that some trees; beyond that the red roofs of the campus of Stanford University; beyond them the trees and the roof tops which mark the town of Palo Alto; beyond them the bare golden hills of the Hamilton Range. I know, however, more than I see. Behind me, although I am not looking that direction, I know there is a window, and beyond that the little campus of the Center for the Advanced Study in the Behavioral Sciences; beyond that the Coast Range; beyond that the Pacific Ocean. Looking ahead of me again, I know that beyond the mountains that close my present horizon, there is a broad valley; beyond that a still higher range of mountains; beyond that other mountains, range upon range, until we come to the Rockies; beyond that the Great Plains and the Mississippi; beyond that the Atlantic Ocean, beyond that is Europe; beyond that is Asia. I know, furthermore, that if I go far enough I will come back to where I am now, In other words, I have a picture of the earth as round. I visualize it as a globe. I am a little hazy on some of the details. I am not quite sure, for instance, whether Tanganyika is north or south of Nyasaland. I probably could not draw a very good map of Indonesia, but I have a fair idea where everything is located on the face of this globe. Looking further, I visualize the globe as a small speck circling around a bright star which is the sun, in the company of many other similar specks, the planets. Looking still further, I see our star the sun as a member of millions upon millions of others in the Galaxy. Looking still further, I visualize the Galaxy as one of millions upon millions of others in the universe.

I am not only located in space, I am located in time. I know

* Reprinted with permission from Kenneth Boulding, *The Image*, Ann Arbor: University of Michigan Press, 1960, Chapter 1. © Copyright by the University of Michigan Press.

that I came to California about a year ago, and I am leaving it in about three weeks. I know that I have lived in a number of different places at different times. I know that about ten years ago a great war came to an end, that about forty years ago another great war came to an end. Certain dates are meaningful: 1776, 1620, 1066. I have a picture in my mind of the formation of the earth, of the long history of geological time, of the brief history of man. The great civilizations pass before my mental screen. Many of the images are vague, but Greece follows Crete, Rome follows Assyria.

I am not only located in space and time, I am located in a field of personal relations. I not only know where and when I am, I know to some extent who I am. I am a professor at a great state university. This means that in September I shall go into a classroom and expect to find some students in it and begin to talk to them, and nobody will be surprised. I expect, what is perhaps even more agreeable, that regular salary checks will arrive from the university. I expect that when I open my mouth on certain occasions people will listen. I know, furthermore, that I am a husband and a father, that there are people who will respond to me affectionately and to whom I will respond in like manner. I know, also, that I have friends, that there are houses here, there, and everywhere into which I may go and I will be welcomed and recognized and received as a guest. I belong to many societies. There are places into which I go, and it will be recognized that I am expected to behave in a certain manner. I may sit down to worship, I may make a speech, I may listen to a concert, I may do all sorts of things.

I am not only located in space and in time and in personal relationships, I am also located in the world of nature, in a world of how things operate. I know that when I get into my car there are some things I must do to start it; some things I must do to back out of the parking lot; some things I must do to drive home. I know that if I jump off a high place I will probably hurt myself. I know that there are some things that would probably not be good for me to eat or to drink. I know certain precautions that are advisable to take to maintain good health. I know that if I lean too far backward in my chair as I sit here at my desk, I will probably fall over. I live, in other words, in a world of reasonably stable relationship, a world of "ifs" and "thens," of "if I do this, then that will happen."

Finally, I am located in the midst of a world of subtle intimations and emotions. I am sometimes elated, sometimes a little depressed, sometimes happy, sometimes sad, sometimes inspired, sometimes pedantic. I am open to subtle intimations of a presence beyond the world of space and time and sense. What I have been talking about is knowledge. Knowledge, perhaps, is not a good word for this. Perhaps one would rather say my Image of the world. Knowledge has an implication of validity, of truth. What I am talking about is what I believe to be true: my subjective knowledge. It is this Image that largely governs my behavior. In about an hour I shall rise, leave my office, go to a car, drive down to my home, play with the children, have supper, perhaps read a book, go to bed. I can predict this behavior with a fair degree of accuracy because of the knowledge which I have: the knowledge that I have a home not far away, to which I am accustomed to go. The prediction, of course, may not be fulfilled. There may be an earthquake, I may have an accident with the car on the way home, I may get home to find that my family has been suddenly called away. A hundred and one things may happen. As each event occurs, however, it alters my knowledge structure or my image. And as it alters my image, I behave accordingly. *The first proposition of this work, therefore, is that behavior depends on the image.*

What, however, determines the image? This is the central question of this work. It is not a question which can be answered by it. Nevertheless, such answers as I shall give will be quite fundamental to the understanding of how both life and society really operate. One thing is clear. The image is built up as a result of all past experience of the possessor of the image. Part of the image is the history of the image itself. At one stage the image, I suppose, consists of little else than an undifferentiated blur and movement. From the moment of birth, if not before, there is a constant stream of messages entering the organism from the senses. At first these may merely be undifferentiated lights and noises. As the child grows, however, they gradually become distinguished into people and objects. He begins to perceive himself as an object in the midst of a world of objects. The conscious image has begun. In infancy the world is a house and, perhaps, a few streets or a park. As the child grows his image of the world expands. He sees himself in a town, a country, on a planet. He finds himself in an increasingly complex web of personal relationships. Every time a message reaches him his image is likely to be changed in some degree by it, and as his image is changed his behavior patterns will be changed likewise.

We must distinguish carefully between the image and the messages that reach it. The messages consist of information in the sense that they are structured experiences. *The meaning of a message is the change which it produces in the image.*

When a message hits an image one of three things can happen. In the first place, the image may remain unaffected. If we think of the image as a rather loose structure, something like a molecule, we may imagine that the message is going straight through without hitting it. The great majority of messages is of this kind. I am receiving messages all the time, for instance, from my eyes and my ears as I sit at my desk, but these messages are ignored by me. There is, for instance, a noise of carpenters working. I know, however, that a building is being built nearby and the fact that I now hear this noise does not add to this image. Indeed, I do not hear the noise at all if I am not listening for it, as I have become so accustomed to it. If the noise stops, however, I notice it. This information changes my image of the universe. I realize that it is now five o'clock, and it is time for me to go home. The message has called my attention, as it were, to my position in time, and I have re-evaluated this position. This is the second possible effect or impact of a message on an image. It may change the image in some rather regular and well-defined way that might be described as simple addition. Suppose, for instance, to revert to an earlier illustration, I look at an atlas and find out exactly the relation of Nyasaland to Tanganyika. I will have added to my knowledge, or my image; I will not, however, have very fundamentally revised it. I still picture the world much as I had pictured it before. Something that was a little vague before is now clearer.

There is, however, a third type of change of the image which might be described as a revolutionary change. Sometimes a message hits some sort of nucleus or supporting structure in the image, and the whole thing changes in a quite radical way. A spectacular instance of such a change is conversion. A man, for instance, may think himself a pretty good fellow and then may hear a preacher who convinces him that, in fact, his life is worthless and shallow, as he is at present living it. The words of the preacher cause a radical reformulation of the man's image of himself in the world, and his behavior changes accordingly. The psychologist may say, of course, that these changes are smaller than they appear, that there is a great mass of the unconscious which does not change, and that the relatively small change in behavior which so often follows intellectual conversion is a testimony to this fact. Nevertheless, the phenomenon of reorganization of the image is an important one, and it occurs to all of us and in ways that are much less spectacular than conversion. The sudden and dramatic nature of these reorganizations is perhaps a result of the fact that our image is in itself resistant to change. When it receives messages which conflict with it, its first impulse is to reject them as in some sense untrue. Suppose, for instance, that somebody tells us something which is inconsistent with our picture of a certain person. Our first impulse is to reject the proffered information as false. As we continue to receive messages which contradict our image, however, we begin to have doubts, and then one day we receive a message which overthrows our previous image and we revise it completely. The person, for instance, whom we saw as a trusted friend is now seen to be a hypocrite and a deceiver.

Occasionally, things that we see, or read, or hear, revise our conceptions of space and time, or of relationships. I have recently read, for instance, Vasiliev's *History of the Byzantine Empire*. As a result of reading this book I have considerably revised my image of at least a thousand years of history. I had not given the matter a great deal of thought before, but I suppose if I had been questioned on my view of the period, I would have said that Rome fell in the fifth century and that it was succeeded by a little-known empire centering in Constantinople and a confused medley of tribes, invasions, and successor states. I now see that Rome did not fall, that in a sense it merely faded away, that the history of the Roman Empire and of Byzantium is continuous, and that from the time of its greatest extent the Roman Empire lost one piece after another until only Constantinople was left; and then in 1453 that went. There are books, some of them rather bad books, after which the world is never quite the same again. Veblen, one can never quite see a a university campus or an elaborate house in just the same light as before. In a similar vein, David Riesman's division of humanity into inner-directed and other-directed people is no doubt open to serious criticism by the methodologists. Nevertheless, after reading Riesman one has a rather new view of the universe and one looks in one's friends and acquaintances for signs of inner-direction or other-direction.

One should perhaps add a fourth possible impact of the messages on the image. The image has a certain dimension, or quality, of certainty or uncertainty, probability or improbability, clarity or vagueness. Our image of the world is not uniformly certain, uniformly probable, or uniformly clear. Messages, therefore, may have the effect not only of adding to or of reorganizing the image. They may also have the effect of clarifying it, that is, of making something which previously was regarded as less certain more certain, or something which was previously seen in a vague way, clearer.

Messages may also have the contrary effect. They may introduce doubt or uncertainty into the image. For instance, the noise of carpenters has just stopped, but my watch tells me it is about four-thirty. This has thrown a certain amount of confusion into my mental image. I was under the impression that the carpenters stopped work at five o'clock. Here is a message which contradicts that impression. What am I to believe? Unfortunately, there are two possible ways of integrating the message. I shall not know for certain which is the right one, however, until I have an opportunity of comparing my watch with a timepiece or with some other source of time which I regard as being more reliable.

The impact of messages on the certainty of the image is of great importance in the interpretation of human behavior. Images of the future must beheld with a degree of uncertainty, and as time passes and as the images become closer to the present, the messages that we receive inevitably modify them, both as to content and as to certainty.

The subjective knowledge structure of image of any individual or organization consists not only of images of "fact" but also images of "value." We shall subject the concept of a "fact" to severe scrutiny in the course of the discussion. In the meantime, however, it is clear that there is a certain difference between the image which I have of physical objects in space and time and the valuations which I put on these objects or on the events which concern them. It is clear that there is a certain difference between, shall we say, my image of Stanford University existing at a certain point in space and time, and my image of the value of Stanford University. If I say "Stanford University is in California," this is rather different from the statement "Stanford University is a good university, or is a better university than X, or a worse university than Y." The latter statements concern my image of values, and although I shall argue that the process by which we obtain an image of values is not very different from the process whereby we obtain an image of fact, there is clearly a certain difference between them.

The image of value is concerned with the *rating* of the various parts of our image of the world, according to some scale of betterness or worseness. We, all of us, possess one or more of these scales. It is what the economists call a welfare function. It does not extend over the whole universe. We do not now, for instance, generally regard Jupiter as a better planet than Saturn. Over that part of the universe which is closest to ourselves, however, we all erect these scales of valuation. Moreover, we change these scales of valuation in response to messages received much as we change our image of the world around us. It is almost certain that most people possess not merely one scale of valuation but many scales for different purposes. For instance, we may say A is better than B for me but worse for the country, or it is better for the country but worse for the world at large. The notion of a hierarchy of scales is very important in determining the effect of messages on the scales themselves.

One of the most important propositions of this theory is that the value scales of any individual or organization are perhaps the most important elements determining the effect of the messages he receives on his image of the world. If a message is perceived that is neither good nor bad it may have little or no effect on the image. If it is perceived as bad or hostile to the image which is held, there will be resistance to accepting it. This resistance is not usually infinite. An often repeated message or a message which comes with unusual force or authority is able to penetrate the resistance and will be able to alter the image. A devout Moslem, for instance, whose whole life has been built around the observance of the precepts of the Koran will resist vigorously any message which tends to throw doubt on the authority of his sacred work. The resistance may take the form of simply ignoring the message, or it may take the form of emotive response: anger, hostility, indignation. In the same way, a "devout" psychologist will resist strongly any evidence presented in favor of extrasensory perception, because to accept it would overthrow his whole image of the universe. If the resistances are very strong, it may take very strong, or often repeated messages to penetrate them, and when they are penetrated, the effect is a realignment or reorganization of the whole knowledge structure.

On the other hand, messages which are favorable to the existing image of the world are received easily and even though they may make minor modifications of the knowledge structure, there will not be any fundamental reorganization. Such messages either will make no impact on the knowledge structure or their impact will be one of rather simple addition or accretion. Such messages may also have the effect of increasing the stability, that is to say, the resistance to unfavorable messages, which the knowledge structure or image possesses.

The stability or resistance to change of a knowledge structure also depends on its internal consistency and arrangement. There seems to be some kind of principle of minimization of internal strain at work which makes some images stable and others unstable for purely internal reasons. In the same way, some crystals or molecules are more stable than others because of the minimization of internal strain. It must be emphasized that it is not merely logical consistency which gives rise to internal cohesiveness of a knowledge structure, although this is an important element. There are important qualities of a nonlogical nature which also give rise to stability. The structure may, for instance, have certain aesthetic relationships among the parts. It may represent or justify a way of life or have certain consequences which are highly regarded in the value system, and so on. Even in mathematics, which is of all knowledge structures the one whose internal consistency is most due to logic, is not devoid of these nonlogical elements. In the acceptance of mathematical arguments by mathematicians there are important criteria of elegance, beauty, and simplicity which contribute toward the stability of these structures.

Even at the level of simple or supposedly simple sense perception we are increasingly discovering that the message which comes through the senses is itself mediated through a value system. We do not perceive our sense data raw; they are mediated through a highly learned process of interpretation and acceptance. When an object apparently increases in size on the retina of the eye, we interpret this not as an increase in size but as movement. Indeed, we only get along in the world because we consistently and persistently disbelieve the plain evidence of our senses. The stick in water is not bent; the movie is not a succession of still pictures; and so on.

What this means is that for any individual organism or or-

ganization, there are no such things as "facts." There are only
messages filtered through a changeable value system. This
statement may sound rather startling. It is inherent, however, in
the view which I have been propounding. This does not mean,
however, that the image of the world possessed by an individual
is a purely private matter or that all knowledge is simply subjective knowledge, in the sense in which I have used the word.
Part of our image of the world is the belief that this image is
shared by other people like ourselves who also are part of our
image of the world. In common daily intercourse we all behave
as if we possess roughly the same image of the world. If a group
of people are in a room together, their behavior clearly shows
that they all think they are in the same room. It is this shared
image which is "public" knowledge as opposed to "private"
knowledge. It follows, however, from the argument above that
if a group of people are to share the same image of the world,
or to put it more exactly, if the various images of the world
which they have are to be roughly identical, and if this group of
people are exposed to much the same set of messages in building up images of the world, the value systems of all individuals
must be approximately the same.

The problem is made still more complicated by the fact that
a group of individuals does not merely share messages which
come to them from "nature." They also initiate and receive
messages themselves. This is the characteristic which distinguishes man from the lower organisms—the art of conversation
or discourse. The human organism is capable not only of having
an image of the world, but of talking about it. This is the ex-
traordinary gift of language. A group of dogs in a pack pursuing
a stray cat clearly share an image of the world in the sense that
each is aware to some degree of the situation which they are all
in, and is likewise aware of his neighbors. When the chase is
over, however, they do not, as far as we know, sit around and
talk about it and say, "Wasn't that a fine chase?" or, "Isn't it
too bad the cat got away?" or even, "Next time you ought to go
that way and I'll go this way and we can corner it." It is discourse or conversation which makes the human image public
in a way that the image of no lower animal can possibly be. The
term, "universe of discourse" has been used to describe the
growth and development of common images in conversation
and linguistic intercourse. There are, of course, many such
universes of discourse, and although it is a little awkward to

speak of many universes, the term is well enough accepted so that we may let it stay.

Where there is no universe of discourse, where the image possessed by the organism is purely private and cannot be communicated to anyone else, we say that the person is mad (to use a somewhat old-fashioned term). It must not be forgotten, however, that the discourse must be received as well as given, and that whether it is received or not depends upon the válue system of the recipient. This means that insanity is defined differently from one culture to another because of these differences in value systems and that the schizophrenic of one culture may well be the shaman or the prophet of another.

Up to now I have sidestepped and I will continue to sidestep the great philosophical arguments of epistemology, I have talked about the image. I have maintained that images can be public as well as private, but I have not discussed the question as to whether images are *true* and how we know whether they are true. Most epistemological systems seek some philosopher's stone by which statements may be tested in order to determine their "truth," that is, their correspondence to outside reality. I do not claim to have any such philosopher's stone, not even the touchstone of science. I have, of course, a great respect for science and scientific method—for careful observation, for planned experience, for the testing of hypotheses and for as much objectivity as semirational beings like ourselves can hope to achieve. In my theoretical system, however, the scientific method merely stands as one among many of the methods whereby images change and develop. The development of images is part of the culture or the subculture in which they are developed, and it depends upon all the elements of that culture or subculture. Science is a subculture among subcultures. It can claim to be useful. It may claim rather more dubiously to be good. It cannot claim to give validity.

In summation, then, my theory might well be called an organic theory of knowledge. Its most fundamental proposition is that knowledge is what somebody or something knows, and that without a knower, knowledge is an absurdity. Moreover, I argue that the growth of knowledge is the growth of an "organic" structure. I am not suggesting here that knowledge is simply an arrangement of neuronal circuits or brain cells, or something of that kind. On the question of the relation between the physical and chemical structure of an organism and its knowledge structure, I am quite prepared to be agnostic. It is, of course, an article of faith among physical scientists that there must be somewhere a one-to-one correspondence between the structures of the physical body and the structures of knowledge. Up to now, there is nothing like empirical proof or even very good evidence for this hypothesis. Indeed, what we know about the brain suggests that it is an extraordinarily unspecialized and, in a sense, unstructured object; and that if there is a physical and chemical structure corresponding to the knowledge structure, it must be a kind which at present we do not understand. It may be, indeed, that the correspondence between physical structure and mental structure is something that we will never be able to determine because of a sort of "Heisenberg principle" in the investigation of these matters. If the act of observation destroys the thing observed, it is clear that there is a fundamental obstacle to the growth of knowledge in that direction.

All these considerations, however, are not fundamental to my position. We do not have to conceive of the knowledge structure as a physico-chemical structure in order to use it in our theoretical construct. It can be inferred from the behavior of the organism just as we constantly infer the images of the world which are possessed by those around us from the messages which they transmit to us. When I say that knowledge is an organic structure, I mean that it follows principles of growth and develoment similar to those with which we are familiar in complex organizations and organisms. In every organism or organization there are both internal and external factors affecting growth. Growth takes place through a kind of metabolism. Even in the case of knowledge structure, we have a certain intake and output of messages. In the knowledge structure, however, there are important violations of the laws of conservation. The accumulation of knowledge is not merely the difference between messages taken in and messages given out. It is not like a reservoir; it is rather an organization which grows through an active internal organizing principle much as the gene is a principle or entity organizing the growth of bodily structures. The gene, even in the physico-chemical sense may be thought of as an inward teacher imposing its own form and "will" on the less formed matter around it. In the growth of images, also, we may suppose similar models. Knowledge grows also because of inward teachers as well as outward messages. As every good teacher knows, the business of teaching is not that of penetrating the student's defenses with the violence or loudness of the teacher's messages. It is, rather, that of co-operating with the student's own inward teacher whereby the student's image may grow in conformity with that of his outward teacher. The existence of public knowledge depends, therefore, on certain basic similarities among men. It is literally because we are of one "blood," that is, genetic constitution, that we are able to communicate with each other. We cannot talk to the ants or bees; we cannot hold conversations with them, although in a very real sense they communicate to us. It is the purpose of this work, therefore, to discuss the growth of images, both private and public, in individuals, in organizations, in society at large, and even with some trepidation, among the lower forms of life. Only thus can we develop a really adequate theory of behavior.

INTERPERSONAL COMMUNICATION*

by Warner Burke

Communication, by definition, involves at least two individuals, the sender and the receiver. Consider yourself, first of all, as the sender of some message. There are certain filters or barriers (internal) which determine whether or not the message is actually transmitted. These barriers may be categorized as follows: (1) Assumptions about yourself—Do I really have something to offer? Am I safe to offer suggestions? Do I really want to share the information? Will others really understand? How will the communication affect my self-esteem? (2) Attitudes about the message itself—Is the information valuable? Do I see the information correctly, or understand it well enough to describe it to others? (3) Sensing the receiver's reaction—Do I become aware of whether or not the receiver is actually understanding? Or in other words, can I "sense" from certain cues or reactions by the receiver whether or not we are communicating?

* Taken from Selected Readings Series Nine, *Behavioral Science and the Manager's Role*, edited by William B. Eddy, W. Warner Burke, Vladimir A. Dupre, Oron South, NTL Institute for Applied Behavioral Science, 1969.

Now consider yourself as the receiver. As a receiver you may filter or not hear certain aspects (or any aspect for that matter) of a message. Why? Because the message may seem unimportant or too difficult. Moreover, you may be selective in your attention. For example, you may feel that the sender is being redundant, so you quit listening after the first few words. You may be preoccupied with something else. Or your filtering or lack of attention may be due to your past experience with the sender. You may feel that "this guy has never made a point in his life and never will!"

Many times the receiver never makes use of his "third ear." That is, trying to be sensitive to nonverbal communication. The sender's eyes, gestures, and sometimes his overall posture communicate messages that the insensitive listener never receives.

There may be barriers that exist between the sender and the receiver, e.g., cultural differences. Environmental conditions may also cause barriers, e.g., poor acoustics. More common, however, are the differences in frames of reference. For example, there may not be a common understanding of purpose in a certain communication. You may ask me how I'm feeling today. To you the phrase, "How ya doing?" is nothing more than a greeting. However, I may think that you really want to know and I may tell you—possibly at length.

Now that some of the problems in interpersonal communication have been mentioned, let us delve somewhat deeper into this process of transferring a message from the brain and emotion of one person to the brain and emotion of another human being.

Sending the Message

In communicating a message effectively to another person, there are several obvious factors which are beneficial. Such things as correct pronunciation, lack of distracting brogue, dialect, or accent, or a pleasant resonance in one's voice usually facilitate the sending of a message.

Assuming the sender of a message really has a desire to be heard and understood and not just speak for the sake of speaking, he wants some assurance that he has communicated. The key to effective communication on the part of the speaker, then, is to obtain some feedback, of one form or another, from his listener(s). Some bright persons who really have something to say are ineffective speakers, be it lecturing or speaking to someone at a cocktail party, because they are unable to tell or care whether their listener(s) is understanding, or they do not make any effort to check on their effectiveness as a communicator. For example, many lecturers in a classroom situation are often unaware of when a listener is sound asleep. Unless there is interaction of some type between the speaker and his listener, the speaker is susceptible to "losing" his listener. Often the speaker must take the initiative in order to receive any feedback regarding the effectiveness of his communication. When speaking before a large group, I often resort to the simple act of requesting my audience to shake their head "yes" if they understand what I have just said, or "no" if they did not understand. Even though this technique is simple, I usually get considerable feedback quickly and I know immediately what I must do at that point to make my speech more effective or whether to continue on with my next point.

Even when talking to just one other person the speaker must often take the initiative, in an interactive sense, to determine whether his message is being understood. Even though I sometimes take the risk of "bugging" my listener, I often stop and ask him if he understands what I mean, or I occasionally ask him to tell me what he thinks I meant in my message.

There is a fairly small percentage of people who speak articulately and clearly enough to be understood most of the time. Most of us have to work at it, especially when we are attempting to communicate a message which is fairly abstract or when we want to tell something which is quite personal or highly emotional. In sending the message effectively, we must do two things simultaneously, (1) work at finding the appropriate words and emotion to express what we want to say, and (2) continually look for cues from the listener to get some feedback even if we must ask our listener for some.

Receiving the Message

In considering interpersonal communication, we might, at first thought, think that listening is the easier of the two functions in the process. If we assume, however, that the listener really wants to understand what the speaker is saying, then the process is not all that easy. The basic problem that the listener faces is that he is capable of thinking faster than the speaker can talk. In their *Harvard Business Review* article, Nichols and Stevens state that the average rate of speech for most Americans is about 125 words per minute. Most of our thinking processes involve words, and our brains can handle many more words per minute than 125. As Nichols and Stevens point out, what this means is that, when we listen, our brains receive words at a very slow rate compared with the brain's capabilities.

As you have experienced many times, you know that you can listen to what someone is saying and think about something else at the same time. As the "cocktail party" phenomenon illustrates, the human brain is truly remarkable in its ability to process a considerable amount of input simultaneously. Sometimes, at a cocktail party, I want to hear not only what the person in my small gathering is saying, but also what that lovely creature is talking about in the group about six feet away. If the overall noise level is not too loud, I can hear and understand both conversations.

The problem with listening, then, is that we have "spare" time in our thinking processes. How we use that spare time determines the extent of our listening effectiveness. It is easy for us to be distracted in listening, especially if the speaker talks slowly or haltingly or if he says something that stimulates another thought. For example, suppose you are listening to a friend who is telling you about a problem he is having in his department. In the process of describing the problem, he mentions a person whom you know, whereupon you start thinking about the person at length. Later, when your friend asks you what you would do about his problem, you're apt to respond, "what problem?"

Thus, a fundamental problem the listener must consider in the communicative process is the fact that his brain is capable of responding to a speaker at several different levels simultaneously. Naturally, this can be an asset to the listener rather than a problem. For example the listener can attend to non-verbal cues the speaker gives, e.g., facial expression, gesture, or tone of voice, as well as listen to the words themselves.

Besides a highly active brain, an effective listener has another factor to consider in the communicative process. This factor involves the process of trying to perceive what the speaker is saying from his point of view.

A Barrier and a Gateway

According to Carl Rogers, a leading psychotherapist and psychotherapy researcher, the major barrier to effective communication is the tendency to evaluate. That is, the barrier to mutual interpersonal communication is our very natural tendency to judge, to evaluate, to approve or disapprove the statement or opinion of the other person or group. Suppose someone says to you, "I didn't like what the lecturer had to say." Your typical response will be either agreement or disagreement. In other words, your primary reaction is to evaluate the statement from your point of view, from your own frame of reference.

Although the inclination to make evaluations is common, it is usually heightened in those situations where feelings and emotions are deeply involved. Thus, the stronger our feelings, the more likely it is that there will be no mutual element in the communication. There will be only two ideas, two feelings, two judgments, missing each other in the heat of the psychological battle.

If having a tendency to evaluate is the major barrier to communication, then the logical gateway to communication is to become an active listener, to listen with understanding. Don't let this simple statement fool you. Listening with understanding means to see the expressed idea and attitude from the other person's point of view, to see how it feels to him, to achieve his frame of reference concerning his subject. One word that summarizes this process of listening with understanding is "empathy."

In psychotherapy, for example, Carl Rogers and his associates have found from research that empathetic understanding—understanding with a person not about him—is such an effective approach that it can bring about major changes in personality.

Suppose that in your next committee meeting you were to conduct an experiment which would test the quality of each committee member's understanding. Institute this rule: "Each person can speak up for himself only after he has first related the ideas and feelings of the previous speaker accurately and to that speaker's satisfaction." This would mean that before presenting your own point of view, it would be necessary for you to achieve the other speaker's frame of reference—to understand his thoughts and feelings so well that you could summarize them for him.

Can you imagine what this kind of approach might mean if it were projected into larger areas, such as congressional debates or labor-management disputes? What would happen if labor, without necessarily agreeing, could accurately state management's point of view in a way that management could accept; and management, without necessarily approving labor's stand, could state labor's case in a way that labor agreed was accurate? It would mean that real communication was established, and conditions would be more conducive for reaching a workable solution.

Toward More Effective Listening

Some steps the listener can take to improve interpersonal communication have been stated. To summarize and be more explicit, let us consider these steps.

1. Effective listening must be an active process. To make certain that you are understanding what the speaker is saying, you, as the listener must interact with him. One way to do this is to paraphrase or summarize for the speaker what you think he has said.

2. Attending to nonverbal behavior that the speaker is communicating along with his verbal expression usually helps to understand the oral message more clearly. Often a facial expression or gesture will "tell" you that the speaker feels more strongly about his subject than his words would communicate.

3. The effective listener does not try to memorize every word or fact the speaker communicates, but, rather, he listens for the main thought or idea. Since your brain is such a highly effective processor of information, spending your listening time in more than just hearing the words of the speaker can lead to more effective listening. That is, while listening to the words, you can also be searching for the main idea of the message. Furthermore, you can attempt to find the frame of reference for the speaker's message as well as look at what he is saying from his perspective. This empathetic process also includes your attempting to experience the same feeling about the subject as the speaker.

These three steps toward more effective listening seem fairly simple and obvious. But the fact remains that we don't practice these steps very often. Why don't we?

According to Carl Rogers, it takes courage. If you really understand another person in this way, if you are willing to enter his private world and see the way life appears to him without any attempt to make evaluative judgments, you run the risk of being changed yourself. This risk of being changed is one of the most frightening prospects many of us face.

Moreover, when we need to utilize these steps the most, we are likely to use them the least, that is, when the situation involves a considerable amount of emotion. For example, when we listen to a message that contradicts our most deeply held prejudices, opinions, or convictions, our brain becomes stimulated by many factors other than what the speaker is telling us. When we are arguing with someone, especially about something that is "near and dear" to us, what are we typically doing when the other person is making his point? It's certainly not listening empathetically! We're probably planning a rebuttal to what he is saying, or we're formulating a question which will embarrass the speaker. We may, of course, simply be "tuning him out." How often have you been arguing with someone for 30 minutes or so, and you make what you consider to be a major point for your point of view, and your "opponent" responds by saying, "But that's what I said 30 minutes ago!"

When emotions are strongest, then, it is most difficult to achieve the frame of reference of the other person or group. Yet it is then that empathy is most needed if communication is to be established. A third party, for example, who is able to lay aside his own feelings and evaluation, can assist greatly by listening with understanding to each person or group and clarifying the views and attitudes each holds.

When the parties to a dispute realize that they are being understood, that someone sees how the situation seems to them, the statements grow less exaggerated and less defensive, and it is no longer necessary to maintain the attitude, "I am 100% right and you are 100% wrong."

Summary

Effective communication, at least among human beings, is not a one-way street. It involves an interaction between the speaker and the listener. The responsibility for this interaction is assumed by both parties. You as the speaker can solicit feedback and adjust your message accordingly. As a listener, you can summarize for the speaker what you think he has said and continually practice the empathetic process.

One of the joys of life, at least for me, is to know that I have been heard and understood correctly and to know that someone cares enough to try to understand what I have said. I also get a great deal of satisfaction from seeing this same enjoyment on the face of a speaker when he knows I have understood him.

DYNAMICS OF LEADERSHIP AND COMMUNICATION*

by Jack R. Gibb

People must be led. People perform best under leaders who are creative, imaginative and aggressive—under leaders who lead. It is the responsibility of the leader to marshall the forces of the organization, to stimulate effort, to capture the imagination, to inspire people, to coordinate efforts, and to serve as a model of sustained effort.

The leader should keep an appropriate social distance, show no favorites, control his emotions, command respect, and be objective and fair. He must know what he is doing and where he wants to go. He must set clear goals for himself and for the group or institution, and then communicate these goals well to all members of the organization. He must listen for advice and counsel before making decisions. But it is his responsibility to make decisions and to set up mechanisms for seeing that the decisions are implemented. After weighing the facts and seeking expert counsel, he must make policy and rules, set reasonable boundaries, and see that these are administered with justice and wisdom, even compassion.

The leader should reward good performance and learn effective ways of showing appreciation. He must be equally ready to give negative criticism where warranted and to appraise performance frequently, fairly, and unequivocally. He must command strong discipline, not only because people respect a strong leader, but because strength and firmness communicate care and concern. Good leadership requires good followship. People tend to follow good leaders. Leaders are born. Methods of election and selection are thus very important. Finding the right chairman or president is the critical variable

* Reprinted from *Current Issues in Higher Education, 1967, In Search of Leaders.* Washington: American Association for Higher Education, National Education Association, p. 55.

in the success of a program or an institution. The quality of an organization is often judged by the perceived quality of the leadership.

The above is an oversimplified statement of one view of leadership theory and practice. A similarly oversimplified statement of an alternative viewpoint follows.

People grow, produce, and learn best when they set their own goals, choose activities that they see as related to these goals, and have a wide range of freedom of choice in all parts of their lives. Under most conditions persons are highly motivated, like to take responsibilities, can be trusted to put out a great deal of effort toward organizational goals, are creative and imaginative, and tend to want to cooperate with others.

Leadership is only one of several significant variables in the life of the group or the institution. Leaders can be helpful and often are. The most effective leader is one who acts as a catalyst, a consultant, and a resource to the group. His job is to help the group to grow, to emerge, and to become more free. He serves the group best when he is a whole person, is direct, real, open, spontaneous, permissive, emotional, and highly personal. The leader at his best is an effective member. He acts in such a way as to facilitate group strength, individual responsibility, diversity, nonconformity, and aggressiveness. The leader is thus not necessary to the group and quickly becomes replaceable, dispensable, and independent. The good leader tends not to lead. He permits, feels, acts, relates, fights, talks—acts human as do other members of the group and the institution. The leader is present, available, and with the group as a person, not as a role.

We find many shades and variations of each of these two over-simplified statements of the theory and practice of leadership in our society. Several years of consulting and research in representative organizations make it very clear to me that attitudes toward leadership tend to cluster around these two poles. This bifurcation has analogues in current educational theory, politics, religion, philosophy, and administration.

Defensive Leadership

The first view, described variously as authoritarian, paternalistic, or conservative, I classify as defensive because dynamically the view defends the administrator against his own fears and distrusts and against perceived or anticipated attack from the outside. This authoritarian or defensive view is particularly appropriate to some viable aspects of the culture we live in: to organizational forms inherited from the medieval church and military; to a life of vertical hierarchy, prescribed role responsibilities, and delegated authority; to a highly competitive economic and educational system; to the current dominant values of efficiency, excellence, productivity, task performance, and perfectionism; to the impersonality, alienation, loneliness, impotence, and indifference in our people; to a world of automation, programming, data processing, and engineering; to a forensic, persuasive, public relations, and marketing mode of interpersonal commerce; to a world continually at war, threatened by war, or preparing for war; in short, to a world of machines. It is not accidental that all around the country when administrators administer the ultimate forensic weapon in arguing against participative forms of leadership they say, "but it would never work in the military or on the production line."

Actually, research indicates that this point is probably not true, but in any event the image of the leaders of our educational and governmental institutions using as a reference point for administrative theory the demands of the military organization and the production line is at least disconcerting.

It seems to me equally clear that defensive leadership is highly inappropriate and perhaps even fundamentally dissonant with another viable side of the world we live in: with education for growth, intimacy, authenticity, humanness, and creativity; with the Judeo-Christian ethics of love, honesty, intimacy, faith, cheek-turning, and brotherhood; with a climate for research, inquiry, scholarship, contemplation, and learning; with cooperation, group planning, team building, and various successful forms of group effort; with the new emerging models of industrial organization and manufacturing productivity; with what might be thought of as the behavioral science approach to organizational change; with the world of ambiguity, feeling, conflict, sorrow, creativity, and diversity; with many new and exciting developments in education, architecture, the creative arts, economics, management, and all phases of modern life; in short, with the world of human beings, with people.

I have deliberately drawn sharp and oversimplified distinctions in a problem area which is very complex and legitimately polemic. It is essential today that those who are administra-

tively responsible for the colleges and universities of America
see clearly this conflict and its implications for all facets of
American Life. It is my observation that much of the dysfunctional disturbance that the papers report daily from the college
campuses is created as unintended but inevitable effects of defensive leadership practices among administrators of American
colleges.

Let us look at the dynamics of defensive leadership. The
major dynamic of the defensive model is fear and distrust.
Observations indicate that people who have mild or more
serious fears tend to do several things: distrust the people being
led; filter the data that are given to the followers and develop
strategies for such filtering and programming of data dissemi-
nation; attempt to control and manipulate the motivations of
the followers; and attempt to control their behavior. The inci-
dence and degree of low trust, strategic, persuasional, and
controlling behavior varies directly with the amount of fear.
Most of us who are leaders or are placed in leadership roles
have varying degrees of fear about our own adequacy, how we
are seen by others, the effectiveness of our leadership strategies, the effects of rebellion, the anxieties about insubordina-
tion and other unfollowerlike behavior. I guess that our major
fear has to do with anxiety about being followed!

The behavior of leaders tends to camouflage, perhaps even
to themselves, the underlying fears which support the strategic,
manipulative, and controlling behavior. For images of fear on
assuming leadership roles one has but to think of the new
teachers in the schoolroom, the new mother bringing back her
first baby from the hospital, the new lieutenant guiding a patrol
into action, or the newly appointed administrative official
handling a student riot. The fears that we all have are quelled
and softened by various adaptive, self-deceptive, and facade-
building mechanisms for presenting ourselves to ourselves and
to others.

Some educational leaders are today more fearful than ever.
In reaction to student strikes, riots, demonstrations, and protests, as well as to the more normal vicissitudes of campus life,
college and university leaders utilize defensive practices that
generate unintended byproducts of fear, distrust, hostility, and
counter-defensive behavior. The classical models of leadership
are time and again proved to be ineffective. Why does defensive
leadership arise and persist among educational leaders?

A reciprocal or circular process seems to be operating. Normal fears of life are exacerbated by the ambiguity, high control, and threat of the group or organization. However necessary this ambiguity and control is thought to be, it serves to create fears and hostilities which in turn call forth still more restrictive ambiguity and controlling behavior. This reciprocal fear-distrust cycle sustains the defensive behavior of leadership. The fears accompany and reinforce feelings of inadequacy and self-rejection in leaders and other members of the group or organization.

But the fears, hostilities, and distrusts are so successfully camouflaged in the social defenses that the casual observer might well think the above description of educational life to be strangely out of touch with reality as he sees it. Certainly it is not the conscious intent of educational leaders to create such a state of affairs.

Why is it then that we get in the university so many unintended effects? These unintended effects seem to result from a kind of self-fulfilling prophecy: low-trust, high-fear theories, when put into practice, actually generate distrust and fears that not only confirm the assumptions underlying the theories, but also provide emotional support and strong motivation to continue the low-trust, high-fear behavior. An interactive and self-preserving cycle is thus set in motion, supported in depth by latent fear-distrust and by rationalized theories which appear to be confirmed. Leadership behavior, thus supported, is exceedingly difficult to change.

Behind the facade of paternalism, politeness, one-big-happy-family-living, heartiness, and the accompanying soft-sell influence and velvet-glove control lie defensive relationships that pervade the colleges. Defensive leadership is characterized by low trust, data distortion, persuasion, and high control. These four aspects of defensive leadership are parallel to four basic dimensions of all group or social behavior: the feeling climate, the flow of data within the system, the formation of goals, and the emergence of control.

The key to defensive leadership is a state of low trust. The defensive leader assumes that the average person cannot be trusted, he is essentially lazy and irresponsible, action must be taken to inspire and motivate him, and he requires supervision and control. The defensive leader can counteract his feelings of inferiority by assuming that his subordinates are less than they actually are; and he can service his hostile feelings by keeping the subordinate in demeaning, dependent, and inferior roles in relation to himself and to leadership as a class.

The defensive leader or administrator rationalizes the service of his needs by developing formal or informal leader theories which both justify and camouflage his fears and hostilities. An essential step in theory and practice is to manipulate the flow of information and communication within the organization. Information sent down from the top is often deliberately "corrected" to increase morale, to allay fears, to put the best administrative foot forward and to justify administrative action. "Correction" is achieved by consciously or unconsciously filtering and distorting information to present a good image, to encourage positive thinking, or to build loyalty.

Strategies are devised to improve the administrative image: a worker's name is remembered to make him feel good; a birthday file is kept to demonstrate that the administrator feels the subordinate is important enough to warrant a birthday card. The "good" administrator is especially careful to smile acceptingly at those members of the "family" team towards whom he has temporary or sustained feelings of animosity. Interpersonal cues are thus manipulated and distorted to present a facade of warmth, friendliness, or cohesiveness.

The defensive leader is continually challenged to create new prods, rewards, and gimmicks as the old ones become ineffective. Thus the responsibility for sustaining motivations is thrust upon the administrator or teacher rather than upon the student. The inherent impetus to derive self-satisfaction and self-respect through accomplishment for its own sake becomes atrophied and lost. Self-satisfaction becomes dysfunctional as an incentive system.

The Reward System

The person who is being motivated by others through extrinsic rewards tends either to resist being influenced or to come under the control of the rewarder. He is motivated, not to achieve something, but to gain the approval of the teacher or administrator, to hunt for his satisfactions in status, grade, and social approval rather than to look for his satisfactions within, in terms of self-respect, self-approval, and the achievement of personal goals.

Thus the roots of dependence and apathy lie in the reward

system, for the person who learns to find his values from without is always at the mercy of other persuaders—teachers, companions, demogogues, groups, or other sources of approval and authority. He becomes dependent, passive, and susceptible to all sorts of external controls.

The reward system may in others foster resistance and rebellion, resentment, cynicism, and a variety of negative and competitive feelings. People who work under competition learn to be competitive, and the extrinsic rewards do not satisfy the deep needs for self-satisfaction and self-respect which are gained by achieving our personal goals as unique individuals.

Both dependency and resistance require controls, and the defensive leader expends a considerable amount of energy devising a variety of controls both for the people and for the processes of the enterprise. The more fearful and anxious he is, the more he feels caught in recurring emergencies and the greater is his need to control. Regulations are put on car-parking, coffee break duration, channels of reporting, library schedules, methods of work, habits of dress, use of safety devices, more and more complex filing systems, rigid report systems—until all aspects of living in the organization are controlled.

The conscious and official reasons given for the controls usually relate to organization and productive efficiency, but the underlying impulses often spring from, or are reinforced by, the leader's personal needs for rigid order or needs to demonstrate his superiority and strength, express hostility, exercise power, justify his position ("What else would I do if I didn't plan these controls?"), reinforce hierarchy, force people to be orderly or confirming, and keep them in line.

Control systems become functionally autonomous—traditional and conventional elements of the organizational system—and often outlive any practical utility. Indeed, people seem to sense that many regulations actually serve personal needs for punishment or power and bear little relation to the actual needs of the organization itself. In looking at organizations we have often found that many controls are universally violated in the system by common consent. In fact, there is clear indication—and often conscious awareness—that some controls are so dysfunctional that if everyone obeyed them the system would come to a grinding halt.

These defensive techniques of leadership produce certain predictable results. Fear and distrust beget fear and distrust. People who are distrustful tend to see untrustworthy behavior in others. If the relationship between an administrator and his subordinate is basically one of distrust, almost any action on either's part is perceived by the other as untrustworthy. Thus a cycle is created which nurtures self-corroborating leadership hypotheses.

This cycle is well illustrated in connection with communications. Any restriction of the flow of information and any closed strategy arouses energy devoted to circumventing the strategy and fosters counter-strategies that are at least as imaginative and often more effective than the original inducing strategy. A familiar example is the strategy of countering the top brass by distorting the upward-flowing data: feelings of hostility are camouflaged by deferential politeness; reports are "fixed up," records are doctored or "cooked" to fit administrative goals and directives. Such attempts are augmented by emergency and threat; the greater the fear and distrust, the greater the circumvention, counter-strategy, and counter-distortion.

Defensive leaders use various forms of persuasion to motivate subordinates toward the organization's goals, but often the results are either apathy and passivity or frenetic conformity. Persuasion is a form of control and begets resistance, which may take many subtle forms. Open and aggressive cold war between teachers and administrators, for instance, is an obvious form. More common—and less easy to deal with—is passive, often unconscious resistance such as apathy, apparent obtuseness, dependent demands for further and more minute instructions, bumbling, wheel-spinning, and a whole variety of inefficiencies that reduce creative work.

As we have seen, tight control leads to some form of dependency and its accompanying hostility; it may vary from the yes-man's deference and conformity to the no-man's rebellion against even the most reasonable and normal requests and rules. Deference and rebellion are cut from the same cloth. When unnecessary and arbitrary controls are imposed, or when normal controls are seen as unnecessary or arbitrary, as is the case when there is fear and distrust, then almost all members of the hierarchy become concerned with their feelings about authority. Most of us are ambivalent toward authority figures, and these mixed feelings are augmented in periods of stress and fear. In tightly controlled, disciplining, and disciplined organizations members demand clarity in rules and in boundary demarcations. But rules can never be made completely clear in practical work situations; boundaries are always permeable and inadequately defined. Thus the demands for further clarification are endless, and controls lead to further controls. We see how the cycle is set up: hostility and its inevitable counterpart, fear, are increased by the distrust, distortion, persuasion-reward, and control systems of defensive leadership; and the continuing cycle is reinforced at all stages, for as fear breeds distrust, distrust is rationalized and structured into theories which sanction distrustful leadership practices. The practices reinforce distrust; now the theorist is justified, and latent motivation to continue the cycle is itself reinforced.

Defensive leadership theories and practices permeate our society. We find them in the home, in school, and in the church, as well as in business organizations. Let us see, for instance, how the child-rearing patterns of our culture fit the picture described above. There are so many frightening things in the world that can harm helpless children. The fearful person can, with little effort, find a variety of frightening aspects in the environment of the child—anything from matches and electric outlets to busy roads and unacceptable playmates. Anxiety makes it easy to exaggerate the number of people ready to kidnap and even rape one's child; the fears of the parent embellish natural dangers and provide nourishment and comforting rationalization for defensive practices.

Communications must be managed for the good of the child. Because he might be worried or upset, emotional and financial discord must be camouflaged and a facade of security and serenity maintained. Children are inexperienced and immature, therefore they cannot be trusted to do things on their own. Moreover, since the natural interests of the child are likely to be frivolous, demeaning, or harmful, he should be carefully guided and persuaded to do what is right—to select appropriate playmates, read good books, and generally adopt goals set by the parental culture or aspirations. To protect the child from ubiquitous dangers and to set his feet on the proper path, parents readily learn to use bribes, praise, and deprivation as tools of coercion. And because children are initially dependent and helpless, it is easy for the fearful parent to prolong the period of dependency.

Schools reinforce these patterns. They receive children whose dependency has been created by defensive parental techniques, and they maintain the dependency by continuing these practices. Having been distrusted, children continue to be untrustworthy. The insecure teacher finds it necessary to maintain a protective facade; she rationalizes her behavior by making a number of low-trust, tight-control assumptions about the children under her tutelage. She builds a changing repertoire of tricks to keep them busy, orderly, neat, attentive, and—she hopes—motivated. Impressed by the awesome culture heritage she is charged to transmit, she feels it imperative that she instill in her pupils the goals, ideals, and rules of the culture. As bodies of knowledge become increasingly standardized, pressures towards indoctrination increase. By codifying rules, regulations, and standards, the teachers build internal control systems—in the classroom, and hopefully, in the children themselves. As part of the informal curriculum, children are taught facade-building; they are encouraged to put the best foot forward, to be polite, to be decorous, and to adopt the essentially hypocritical social graces of the dominant middle class.

An Alternative—Participative Leadership

What is the alternative to defensive leadership? This is not as easy to specify. The key to emergent leadership centers in a high degree of trust and confidence in people. Leaders who trust their colleagues and subordinates and have confidence in them tend to be open and frank, to be permissive in goal setting, and to be noncontrolling in personal style and leadership policy. People with a great deal of self-acceptance and personal security do trust others, do make trust assumptions about their motives and behavior. The self-adequate person tends to assume that others are also adequate and, other things being equal, that they will be responsible, loyal, appropriately work-oriented when work is to be performed, and adequate to carry out jobs that are commensurate with their levels of experience and growth.

Just as we saw that distrust arises from fear and hostility, so we can see that people with little fear and minimal needs to be hostile are ready to trust others. Of course, there is some risk in trusting others, in being open and freedom-giving.

People naturally tend to share their feelings and concerns with those whom they trust, and this is true at the simplest and most direct level of inter-personal relationships as well as at more complex levels of organizational communication. Thus a high-trust system may institute open planning meetings and evaluation meetings; public criteria for promotion; easily available information on salaries, cost figures, and budgets; and easy access to material in the files. There is comparatively little concern with public relations, with the corporate or family image, or with communications programs. Communication in such a system is a process rather than a program.

The participative leader is permissive in his relations with subordinates, for he assumes that as people grow they learn to assess their own aptitudes, discover their deep-lying interests, and develop their basic potentials. Therefore he gives his subordinates every opportunity to maximize self-determination and self-assessment, to verbalize their goals, to try new jobs or enlarge the scope of the work they are doing, and he trusts them to make mature judgments about job assignments. Where he is dealing with a work-team or a group, he lets the group make decisions about job allotments and work assignments.

This process of allowing people to be responsible for their own destinies, for setting their own targets, assessing their own development needs, searching out resources to aid in job accomplishment, and participating in setting organizational objectives is basic to high-trust leadership. Instead of using conventional defensive-leadership techniques of skilled persuasion to induce acceptance of leadership goals, the high-trust administration participates in cooperative determination of goals and in cooperative definition of production and staff problems. He knows that goal-information is a significant skill that must be learned, and that to develop such skill students and adults must exercise a variety of opportunities to make decisions, explore goals, and experiment with many kinds of activities.

The participative administrator joins in creating a climate in which he has no need to impose controls. He knows that in a healthy group controls emerge from group processes as the need is perceived. Then controls are mediated by group or organization objectives and by such relevant data as deadlines and target dates. People or groups who have set their own objectives and have clearly stated their own goals build internal tension-systems which maintain goal orientation and create appropriate boundaries.

Formal and written rules about such things as work space, library use, and stockroom neatness are less and less necessary when people are engaged in a common task with others whose feelings and perceptions they freely share; when there is trust and mutuality, people are inclined to respect the rights and con-

cerns of fellow members. This principle applies to large and
small systems alike—in either, the participative administrator
reduces as far as practicable all formal controls evidenced by
rules, regulations, written memoranda, signs, formal job speci-
fication sheets, rigid lines of responsibility and authority, and
the like.

The effects of participative leading are diametrically contrary to those of defensive leading. Love begets love. Respect
begets respect. Trust produces trust. People who are trusted
tend to trust themselves and to trust those in positions of responsibility. Moreover, the feeling that one is trusted encourages exploration, diversity, and innovation, for the person
spends little time and energy trying to prove himself. His time
and energy are freed to define and solve problems, accomplish
work, and create new dimensions of his job. A fearful person
uses a great deal of energy in defending himself against present
or anticipated threat or attack; a confident and self-assured person can direct his energy towards goals that are significant to
him as a person.

Again, openness begets openness. In the long run, at least,
one who freely shares data, whether of feelings or of figures,
reduces fear and distrust in himself and in others. Defensive
administrators build massive communication programs, not to
disseminate objective information but to mold attitudes, create
favorable and appropriate images, and influence people. Such
persuasional and distortive communication produces resistance. Direct and open flow of information, on the other hand,
serves to create an atmosphere which encourages people to
share information with those above as well as with those below.

In general, openness and information giving improves the
decision-making process, for experience in giving information
and expressing feelings enhances consensus; and the more
nearly a group can reach consensus on operational issues, the
higher the quality of the decision and the greater the group's
commitment to the program.

Moreover, participative goal-formation optimizes self-determination and self-assessment. Intrinsic motivations become
increasingly relevant and powerful. People explore their own
capacities and interests, and try to find or create work for themselves that is satisfying and fulfilling. They enlarge their own
jobs, asking for more responsibility and more creative and interesting work. Such work is fulfilling to the person, and ex-

trinsic rewards are secondary to satisfaction in accomplishing the task. Administrators find that people like to work; they "own" their jobs and feel great loyalty and responsibility toward the common goals of the group. People feel little need to escape from the work situation, and the "thank goodness it's Friday" clubs become less enticing. Concerns over salary and merit increases are symptomatic of defensive-leading pressures.

Participative administration creates interdependence and diminishes the problem of authority. For instance, work is allocated by consensus—people assess their abilities and select or create appropriate tasks. Where there is interdependence, conflict and disagreement are openly expressed and can thus be resolved and integrated into productive work. Where people feel they are workng together for a common goal, the organization of work can be flexible, diverse, and informal, with a minimum of written job boundaries and rigid role requirements. Channels of communication are free, open and spontaneous.

These concepts are a challenge to the university. The Ohio State studies, particularly, showed how far behind even the military and industry the university administration is in achieving some kind of more participative and less authoritarian administrative relationships. The headlines today are filled with conflicts. The university is in many ways more susceptible to the pressures which produce fear than is industry, government, or business. The university is at one and the same time vulnerable to attacks from public opinion and also historically inviolate. The products of the university are highly intangible, and it is difficult to apply vigorous controls to the product and to tell if the university is successful in the same way that a business or even the military is with its hard criteria for productivity, profit, or victory. Thus highly vulnerable, the university has preserved a historical isolation from social pressures; and administrative behavior is often medieval and out of touch with the vigorous demands of democratic growth. The university, strangely, is sometimes a citadel for autocratic administrative behavior.

The Ethics of Participation

I should say a word about the implications of this model for ethical behavior. In abstract, this model of leadership specifies a theory of ethics: That behavior is more ethical which is most trusting, most open, most self-determining, and most

interdependent. Thus one would look in the university setting
for unethical behavior in the areas of distrust, strategic filtering
of feelings and ideas (honesty), manipulative abridgement of
self-determination, and dependency-producing or rebellion-
producing high control behavior.

It seems to me that joint, interdependent, and shared planning is the central concept of the kind of participative, consul-
tative leadership that we are considering. Planning, to be
moral, in this framework, to be efficient, and to be growth-pro-
ducing must be organic to the institution, involve to an optimal
degree all of the participants, and must be done interdepen-
dently. It is easy to find illustrations on the university campus of
buildings in architectural styles that are unrelated to experimental learning theory, fund-raising methods that are planned
by a special group of people who are usually collecting funds in
ways that would be anathema to other members of the college
community, athletic programs that arise from financial need
rather than from educational policy, personnel practices that
are inherited unabashedly from business institutions, planning
as a fragmentary, emergency process engaged in by small
groups of people who are often out of touch with the university
as a community.

Our assumption is that the blocks to innovation and creativity are fear, poor communication, imposition of motivations,
and the dependency-rebellion syndrome of forces. People are
innovative and creative. The administration of innovation involves freeing the creativity that is always present. The administrative problem of innovation is to remove fear and increase
trust, to remove strategic and distortional blocks to open communication, to remove coercive, persuasional, and manipulative
efforts to pump motivation, and to remove the tight controls on
behavior that tend to channel creative efforts into circumvention, counter-strategy, and organizational survival rather than
into innovative and creative problem-solving.

Valid, direct, authentic, and open communication among
all segments of the organic institution is a central process of
effective leadership in the model we are examining. Effective
leadership grows with communication in depth. Effective
leadership is hampered by all forces which inhibit or restrain
communication in depth. If emergent or participative leadership were prevalent on the campus, communication programs
would become less and less necessary. Defensive administration breeds the conditions that require an increasing escalation

of massive communication programs to hopefully alleviate the conditions produced by the defensive leadership. We are attempting to become as a people and as a culture. We are in the process of discovering and creating models of interdependent, high-trust, self-determining, and open behavior. We are trying to create an interdependent, achieving, free, becoming culture. This has never been done in the world, and the strains of transition are awesome and somewhat frightening. But for those of us who are dedicated to the university as a way of life, the challenge to the college and university administrator and leader is clear. The challenge is there. The road is unclear. The goal is at one and at the same time preservation of certain concepts we hold dear and the achievement of a more free, a more open, a more self-determining, and a more human environment for learning and growth.

PART III
ORGANIZATIONAL CHANGE
AND LEADERSHIP

PART III
ORGANIZATIONAL CHANGE
AND LEADERSHIP

Organizations of wide variety and scope are the chief vehicles for accomplishing the work of the modern world. In times past it was possible for an individual to carve his niche in history through his own solitary efforts, but the complexity of modern society makes this increasingly difficult. The organization has become the chief characterizing force within the industrial nations; the effectiveness with which organizations function may be the distinguishing success factor in the competition for superiority between competing industries, government bureaucracies, and between countries.

Obsolescence of organizational approach is clearly a major obstacle to the effectiveness of local and state and federal government, small business, political parties, health and welfare services, and a wide variety of other important institutions. Unless mechanisms can be implemented to radically modernize and humanize organizations to meet future social, economic, political and technological needs, the danger of "future shock" overwhelming vast numbers of people is imminent.[1]

Leadership commitment, understanding and skill will obviously play a key role in the adaptation or development of organizations to meet the requirements of future society. McGregor argues, in the first selection of Part III, that organizations are obsolete in part because of false assumptions about how human beings function most effectively. He suggests that most organizations operate on the authoritarian model (or on the basis of "theory x" about human behavior), when in fact there is powerful evidence that the participative or democratic model (based on "theory y" assumptions about productive human functioning) is generally more effective in accomplish-

---

[1] See Alvin Toffler, *Future Shock*. New York: Random House, 1970.

ing organizational goals and in satisfying the emotional and human needs of individuals at all levels of the organization.

This is true in part because of the overwhelming tendency toward specialization both within and between organizations. As specialization develops, increasing skill and concentrated effort are applied to solving limited parts of problems or producing components of larger products. If an integrated solution to a problem is to be reached, or if a useful final product is to be produced, interdependence between specialized sub-groups with or between organizations must be attained. If an organization is to remain stable and continuously in process of adaptation to its specialized sub-units of highly specialized and highly skilled human resources, it must provide for mutually effective interdependence of its parts.

Among other implications, this means that the natural forces of competition and collaboration must be channeled constructively, rather than allowing unrestrained competition to produce havoc within or between organizations. Adequate "bonding" between sub-systems is therefore required, through mutual identification with larger organizational goals, communication and feedback, to assure mutual understanding of goals and the means to reach those goals and mutual concern for the maintenance of an atmosphere conducive to the meeting of the social-psychological needs of the human resources of the enterprise.

Behavioral science research provides powerful data to suggest that productivity does not long flourish in an atmosphere of distrust, suspicion, overtight control, disrespect, apathy or misunderstanding. It is to these issues that the series of selections in this section are addressed.

McGregor notes that most organizations have made impressive progress over the past thirty years, in the improvement of management practice and employee treatment. However, this has been accomplished without changing fundamental theories of management; organizations continue to operate on the authoritarian rather than the participative decision-making model, thus failing to take advantage of the creativity and potential contribution of all human resources within the organization.

The most significant contribution to leadership theory provided by McGregor is his elaboration of basic assumptions about human behavior and management of human resources, based on recent findings from social science theory. He calls these assumptions "theory y," and suggests how applications of the assumptions by managers or organizational leaders must be incorporated if they are to produce the radical changes in organizational approach called for by contemporary circumstances. The second selection by McGregor is an up-dated and elaborated extension of the "theory y" concept. He discusses in detail how the organizational leader views reality and how this view must adapt to new knowledge about human behavior and productivity. A theory of motivation is developed which takes account of the "theory y" assumptions. Implications for organizational management are discussed in detail.

McGregor gives particular attention to motivational systems which take advantage of intrinsic (internally generated) rewards as opposed to extrinsic (externally generated) rewards. He emphasizes that intrinsic reward is much more likely than extrinsic reward to engender commitment to high productivity and results from an identification of individual goals with organizational goals. This requires attention by the organization to both the rational and emotional needs of man. Both of these needs can best be met by involving men in satisfying group endeavors. The group should be the unit of organization, rather than the individual.

Bennis extends the same theme to call for a new concept of organizational leadership which he terms "post-bureaucratic." He argues that bureaucracy as we have known it is out-moded and does not fit the needs of contemporary reality. He further suggests that abundant examples of the new forms already exist as models to be studied and emulated.

Bennis points to convincing evidence that leadership of modern organization depends on new forms of knowledge and skill, not necessarily related to the primary tasks of the organization, but rather emphasizing interpersonal and organizational processes. This is the case because professionalization and higher educational levels have produced a new kind of employee who is motivated less by extrinsic rewards, such as money, and more by challenge, independence, further learning, and a professional career; the new employee is more committed to his profession than to any particular organization.

The consequence of converging changes will be a "team" or "participative" leadership concept, which attempts to take full advantage of the unique talents of each individual, while emphasizing how these competencies can function collaboratively. Leadership, Bennis asserts, must identify and support those individuals with a psychological and intellectual affinity for a number of languages and cultures who can serve as "linking pins" in bringing divergent interest groups and organizations together. Special departments or centers will be needed in most large organizations with the explicit assignment to constantly assess the state of the organization and design plans for adaptation to changing circumstances, all the while involving members of the organization sufficiently to gain commitment to required changes. The task of these new departments will be to adapt organizational sub-systems to fit the constantly changing circumstances and talents therein.

Blake and Mouton have developed a training program to incorporate within organizations many of the concepts discussed by McGregor and Bennis. The training revolves around a model which they call the "managerial grid"; the grid describes varying degrees of concern for people. The training program is designed to help build management skills that maximize concern for both production and people. The selection reprinted constitutes only a very brief introduction to the managerial grid concept but demonstrates some of the crucial issues which must be considered if personal goals are to be sufficiently identified with corporate objectives to maximize commitment to organizational success while also realizing personal goals.

The final article in this section is directed specifically to academic leadership, partially because colleges and universities should be providing a model of modern leadership approaches but in fact are often unfortunately traditional and organizationally obsolete. Because power is often lodged at the departmental level and departments tend to be oriented more to their own disciplinary goals rather than overall university goals, it is notoriously difficult to produce collaborative approaches to organizational modernization.

McConnell argues that democratic management is certainly an appropriate model, but this does not obviate the necessity for organizational leaders (academic administrators) to act decisively when the situation calls for overcoming uncertainty by deliberate decision. It is not possible to avoid the exercise of authority if the organization is to move forward. The administrator must avoid burying himself in detail, which might better be left to subordinates, so that he has time for the larger issues and decisions crucial to the long-range effectiveness of the institution. This requires delegation of most responsibilities to the level where competence exists to make decisions and where decisions must be implemented.

Leadership, as defined by McConnell, is more than mere "management." It requires constant re-examination of goals and means, so as to provide a basis for elimination of obsolete rules and organizational sub-systems. The leader should promote innovation, even at the risk of occasional error and instability. He should encourage diversity of ideas, experience, and approaches to educational process. Particularly, he should foster inter-disciplinary communication and encourage new cross-disciplinary groupings.

However, McConnell seems to contradict himself (while also disagreeing somewhat with McGregor and Bennis) when he insists that the top administrator must retain a final veto or decision power. He seems to suggest that team management must be limited by the final authority of someone with a higher knowledge of the appropriate answer; the authority figure with a strong hand is still required, even in the academic institution, particularly in the selection of other administrative personnel. He should only select administrators who are acceptable to their subordinates but should retain the authority to appoint.

These selections on organizational leadership form the heart of this volume, since they represent an application of leadership research to the institutions which seem increasingly crucial to the effective functioning of modern society. Unless we can learn to better organize, develop, manage and change the complex organizations of government, business, voluntary associations, educational institutions and a wide variety of other units of society, we will become hopelessly incapable of meeting the demands of the future.

THEORY Y: THE INTEGRATION OF INDIVIDUAL AND ORGANIZATIONAL GOALS*

by Douglas McGregor

To some, the preceding analysis will appear unduly harsh. Have we not made major modifications in the management of the human resources of industry during the past quarter century? Have we not recognized the importance of people and made vitally significant changes in managerial strategy as a consequence? Do the developments since the twenties in personnel administration and labor relations add up to nothing?

There is no question that important progress has been made in the past two or three decades. During this period the human side of enterprise has become a major preoccupation of management. A tremendous number of policies, programs, and practices which were virtually unknown thirty years ago have become common-place. The lot of the industrial employee— be he worker, professional, or executive—has improved to a degree which could hardly have been imagined by his counterpart of the nineteen twenties. Management has adopted generally a far more humanitarian set of values; it has successfully striven to give more equitable and more generous treatment to its employees. It has significantly reduced economic hardships, eliminated the more extreme forms of industrial warfare, provided a generally safe and pleasant working environment, *but it has done all these things without changing its fundamental theory of management.* There are exceptions here and there, and they are important; nevertheless, the assumptions of Theory X remain predominant throughout our economy.

Management was subjected to severe pressures during the Great Depression of the thirties. The wave of public antagonism, the open warfare accompanying the unionizations of the mass production industries, the general reaction against authoritarianism, the legislation of the New Deal produced a wide "pendulum swing." However, the changes in policy and practice which took place during that and the next decade were primarily adjustments to the increased power of organized labor and to the pressures of public opinion.

Some of the movement was away from "hard" and toward "soft" management, but it was short-lived, and for good reasons. It has become clear that many of the initial strategic interpretations accompanying the "human relations approach" were as naive as those which characterized the early stages of progressive education. We have now discovered that there is no answer in the simple removal of control—that abdication is not a workable alternative to authoritarianism. We have learned that there is no direct correlation between employee satisfaction and productivity. We recognize today that "industrial democracy" cannot consist in permitting everyone to decide everything, that industrial health does not flow automatically from the elimination of dissatisfaction, disagreement, or even open conflict. Peace is not synonymous with organizational health; socially responsible management is not co-extensive with permissive management.

Now that management has regained its earlier prestige and power, it has become obvious that the trend toward "soft" management was a temporary and relatively superficial reaction rather than a general modification of fundamental assumptions or basic strategy. Moreover, while the progress we have made in the past quarter century is substantial, it has reached the point of diminishing returns. The tactical possibilities within conventional managerial strategies have been pretty completely exploited, and significant new developments will be unlikely without major modifications in theory.

The Assumptions of Theory Y

There have been few dramatic break-throughs in social science theory like those which have occurred in the physical sciences during the past half century. Nevertheless, the accumulation of knowledge about human behavior in many specialized fields has made possible the formulation of a number of generalizations which provide a modest beginning for new theory with respect to the management of human resources.

1. The expenditure of physical and mental effort in work is as natural as play or rest. The average human being does not inherently dislike work. Depending upon controllable conditions, work may be a source of satisfaction (and will be voluntarily performed) or a source of punishment (and will be avoided if possible).

2. External control and the threat of punishment are not the only means for bringing about effort toward organizational objectives. Man will exercise self-direction and self-control in the service of objectives to which he is committed.

3. Commitment to objectives is a function of the rewards associated with their achievement. The most significant of such rewards, e.g., the satisfaction of ego and self-actualization needs, can be direct products of effort directed toward organizational objectives.

4. The average human being learns, under proper conditions, not only to accept but to seek responsibility. Avoidance of responsibility, lack of ambition, and emphasis on security are generally consequences of experience, not inherent human characteristics.

5. The capacity to exercise a relatively high degree of imagination, ingenuity, and creativity in the solution of organizational problems is widely, not narrowly, distributed in the population.

6. Under the conditions of modern industrial life, the intellectual potentialities of the average human being are only partially utilized.

These assumptions involve sharply different implications for managerial strategy than do those of Theory X. They are dynamic rather than static: They indicate the possibility of human growth and development; they stress the necessity for selective adaptation rather than for a single absolute form of control. They are not framed in terms of the least common denominator of the factory hand, but in terms of a resource which has substantial potentialities.

Above all, the assumptions of Theory Y point up the fact that the limits on human collaboration in the organizational setting are not limits of human nature but of management's ingenuity in discovering how to realize the potential represented by its human resources. Theory X offers management an easy rationalization for ineffective organizational performance: It is due to the nature of the human resources with which we must work. Theory Y, on the other hand, places the problems squarely in the lap of management. If employees are lazy, indifferent, unwilling to take responsibility, intransigent, uncreative, uncooperative, Theory Y implies that the causes lie in management's methods of organization and control.

The assumptions of Theory Y are not finally validated. Nevertheless, they are far more consistent with existing knowledge in the social sciences than are the assumptions of Theory X. They will undoubtedly be refined, elaborated, modified as further research accumulates, but they are unlikely to be completely contradicted.

On the surface, these assumptions may not seem particularly difficult to accept. Carrying their implications into practice, however, is not easy. They challenge a number of deeply ingrained managerial habits of thought and action.

The Principle of Integration

The central principle of organization which derives from Theory X is that of direction and control through the exercise of authority—what has been called "the scalar principle." The central principle which derives from Theory Y is that of integration: The creation of conditions such that the members of the organization can achieve their own goals *best* by directing their efforts toward the success of the enterprise. These two principles have profoundly different implications with respect to the task of managing human resources, but the scalar principle is so firmly built into managerial attitudes that the implications of the principle of integration are not easy to perceive.

Someone once said that fish discover water last. The "psychological environment" of industrial management—like water for fish—is so much a part of organizational life that we are unaware of it. Certain characteristics of our society, and of organizational life within it, are so completely established, so pervasive, that we cannot conceive of their being otherwise. As a result, a great many policies and practices and decisions and relationships could only be—it seems—what they are.

Among these pervasive characteristics of organizational life in the United States today is a managerial attitude (stemming from Theory X) toward membership in the industrial organization. It is assumed almost without question that organizational requirements take precedence over the needs of individual members. Basically, the employment agreement is that in return for the rewards which are offered, the individual will accept external direction and control. The very idea of integration and self-control is foreign to our way of thinking about the employment relationship. The tendency, therefore, is either to reject it out of hand (as socialistic, or anarchistic, or inconsistent with human nature) or to twist it unconsciously until it fits existing conceptions.

The concept of integration and self-control carries the implication that the organization will be more effective in achieving its economic objectives if adjustments are made, in significant ways, to the needs and goals of its members.

A district manager in a large, geographically decentralized company is notified that he is being promoted to a policy level position at headquarters. It is a big promotion with a large salary increase. His role in the organization will be a much more powerful one, and he will be associated with the major executives of the firm.

The headquarters group who selected him for this position have carefully considered a number of possible candidates. This man stands out among them in a way which makes him the natural choice. His performance has been under observation for some time, and there is little question that he possesses the necessary qualifications, not only for this opening but for an even higher position. There is genuine satisfaction that such an outstanding candidate is available.

The man is appalled. He doesn't want the job. His goal, as he expresses it, is to be the "best damned district manager in the company." He enjoys his direct associations with operating people in the field, and he doesn't want a policy level job. He and his wife enjoy the kind of life they have created in a small city, and they dislike actively both the living conditions and the social obligations of the headquarters city.

He expresses his feelings as strongly as he can, but his objections are brushed aside. The organization's needs are such that his refusal to accept the promotion would be unthinkable. His superiors say to themselves that of course when he has settled in to the new job, he will recognize that it was the right thing. And so he makes the move.

Two years later he is in an even higher position in the company's headquarters organization, and there is talk that he will probably be the executive vice-president before long. Privately he expresses considerable unhappiness and dissatisfaction. He (and his wife) would "give anything" to be back in the situation he left two years ago.

Within the context of the pervasive assumptions of Theory X, promotions and transfers in large numbers are made by unilateral decision. The requirements of the organization are given priority automatically and almost without question. If the individual's personal goals are considered at all, it is assumed that the rewards of salary and position will satisfy him. Should an individual actually refuse such a move without a compelling reason, such as health or a severe family crisis, he would be considered to have jeopardized his future because of this "selfish" attitude. It is rare indeed for management to give the individual the opportunity to be a genuine and active partner in such a decision, even though it may affect his most important personal goals. Yet the implications following from Theory Y are that the organization is likely to suffer if it ignores these personal needs and goals. In making unilateral decisions with respect to promotion, management is failing to utilize its human resources in the most effective way.

The principle of integration demands that both the organization's and the individual's needs be recognized. Of course, when there is a sincere joint effort to find it, an integrative solution which meets the needs of the individual *and* the organization is a frequent outcome. But not always—and this is the point at which Theory Y begins to appear unrealistic. It collides head on with pervasive attitudes associated with management by direction and control.

The assumptions of Theory Y imply that unless integration is achieved *the organization will suffer*. The objectives of the organization are *not* achieved best by the unilateral administration of promotions, because this form of management by direction and control will not create the commitment which would make available the full resources of those affected. The lesser motivation, the lesser resulting degree of self-direction and self-control are costs which, when added up for many instances over time, will more than offset the gains obtained by unilateral decisions "for the good of the organization."

One other example will perhaps clarify further the sharply different implications of Theory X and Theory Y.

It could be argued that management is already giving a great deal of attention to the principle of integration through its efforts in the field of economic education. Many millions of dollars and much ingenuity have been expended in attempts to persuade employees that their welfare is intimately connected with the success of the free enterprise system and of their own companies. The idea that they can achieve their own goals best by directing their effort toward the objectives of the organization has been explored and developed and communicated in every possible way. Is this not evidence that management is already committed to the principle of integration?

The answer is a definite no. These managerial efforts, with rare exceptions, reflect clearly the influence of the assumptions of Theory X. The central message is an exhortation to the industrial employee to work hard and follow orders in order to protect his job and his standard of living. Much has been achieved, it says, by our established way of running industry, and much more could be achieved if employees would adapt themselves *to management's definition* of what is required. Behind these exhortations lies the expectation that of course the requirements of the organization and its economic success must have priority over the needs of the individual.

Naturally, integration means working together for the success of the enterprise so we all may share in the resulting rewards. But management's implicit assumption is that working together means adjusting to the requirements of the organization *as management perceives them.* In terms of existing views, it seems inconceivable that individuals, seeking their own goals, would further the ends of the enterprise. On the contrary, this would lead to anarchy, chaos, irreconcilable conflicts of self-interest, lack of responsibility, inability to make decisions, and failure to carry out those that were made.

All these consequences, and other worse ones, *would* be inevitable unless conditions could be created such that the members of the organization perceived that they could achieve their own goals *best* by directing their efforts toward the success of the enterprise. If the assumptions of Theory Y are valid, the practical question is whether, and to what extent, such conditions can be created. To that question the balance of this volume is addressed.

The Application of Theory Y

In the physical sciences there are many theoretical phenomena which cannot be achieved in practice. Absolute zero and a perfect vacuum are examples. Others, such as nuclear power, jet aircraft, and human space flight, are recognized theoretically to be possible long before they become feasible. This fact does not make theory less useful. If it were not for our theoretical convictions, we would not even be attempting to develop the means for human flight into space today. In fact, were it not for the development of physical science theory during the past century and a half, we would still be depending upon the horse and buggy and the sailing vessel for transportation. Virtually all significant technological developments wait on the formulation of relevant theory.

Similarly, in the management of the human resources of industry, the assumptions and theories about human nature at any given time limit innovation. Possibilities are not recognized, innovating efforts are not undertaken, until theoretical conceptions lay a groundwork for them. Assumptions like those of Theory X permit us to conceive of certain possible way of organizing and directing human effort, *but not others*. Assumptions like those of Theory Y open up a range of possibilities for new managerial policies and practices. As in the case of the development of new physical science theory, some of these possibilities are not immediately feasible, and others may forever remain unattainable. They may be too costly, or it may be that we simply cannot discover how to create the necessary "hardware."

There is substantial evidence for the statement that the potentialities of the average human being are far above those which we typically realize in industry today. If our assumptions are like those of Theory X, we will not even recognize the existence of those potentialities and there will be no reason to devote time, effort, or money to discovering how to realize them. If, however, we accept assumptions like those of Theory Y, we will be challenged to innovate, to discover new ways of organizing and directing human effort, even though we recognize that the perfect organization, like the perfect vacuum, is practically out of reach.

We need not be overwhelmed by the dimensions of the managerial task implied by Theory Y. To be sure, a large mass production operation in which the workers have been organized by a militant and hostile union faces management with problems which appear at present to be insurmountable with respect to the application of the principle of integration. It may be decades before sufficient knowledge will have accumulated to make such an application feasible. Applications of Theory Y will have to be tested initially in more limited ways and under more favorable circumstances. However, a number of applications of Theory Y *in managing managers and professional people* are possible today. Within the managerial hierarchy, the assumptions can be tested and refined, techniques can be invented and skill acquired in their use. As knowledge accumulates, some of the problems of application at the worker level in large organizations may appear less baffling than they do at present.

Perfect integration of organizational requirements and individual goals and needs is, of course, not a realistic objective. In adopting this principle, we seek that degree of integration in which the individual can achieve his goals *best* by directing his efforts toward the success of the organization. "Best" means that this alternative will be more attractive than the many others available to him: indifference, irresponsibility, minimal compliance, hostility, sabotage. It means that he will continuously be encouraged to develop and utilize voluntarily his capacities, his knowledge, his skill, his ingenuity in ways which contribute to the success of the enterprise.[1]

Acceptance of Theory Y does not imply abdication or "soft" management, or "permissiveness." As was indicated above, such notions stem from the acceptance of authority as the *single* means of managerial control, and from attempts to minimize its negative consequences. Theory Y assumes that people will exercise self-direction and self-control in the achievement of organizational objectives *to the degree that they are committed to those objectives*. If that commitment is small, only a slight

---

[1] A recent, highly significant study of the sources of job satisfaction and dissatisfaction among managerial and professional people suggests that these opportunities for "self-actualization" are the essential requirements of both job satisfaction and high performance. The researchers find that "the wants of employees divide into two groups. One group revolves around the need to develop in one's occupation as a source of personal growth. The second group operates as an essential base to the first and is associated with fair treatment in compensation, supervision, working conditions, and administrative practices. *The fulfillment of the needs of the second group does not motivate the individual to high levels of job satisfaction and ... to extra performance on the job.* All we can expect from satisfying (this second group of needs) is the prevention of dissatisfaction and poor job performance." Frederick Herzberg, Bernard Mausner, and Barbara Bloch Snyderman, *The Motivation to Work.* New York: John Wiley & Sons, Inc., 2959, pp. 114-115. (Italics mine.)

degree of self-direction and self-control will be likely, and a substantial amount of external influence will be necessary. If it is large, many conventional external controls will be relatively superfluous, and to some extent self-defeating. Managerial policies and practices materially affect this degree of commitment.

Authority is an inappropriate means for obtaining commitment to objectives. Other forms of influence—help in achieving integration, for example—are required for this purpose. Theory Y points to the possibility of lessening the emphasis on external forms of control to the degree that commitment to organizational objectives can be achieved. Its underlying assumptions emphasize the capacity of human beings for self-control, and the consequent possibility of greater managerial reliance on the other means of influence. Nevertheless, it is clear that authority is an appropriate means for control under certain circumstances —particularly where genuine commitment to objectives cannot be achieved. The assumptions of Theory Y do not deny the appropriateness of authority, but they do deny that it is appropriate for all persons and under all circumstances.

Many statements have been made to the effect that we have acquired today the know-how to cope with virtually any technological problems which may arise, and that the major industrial advances of the next half century will occur on the human side of enterprise. Such advances, however, are improbable so long as management continues to organize and direct and control its human resources on the basis of assumptions— tacit or explicit—like those of Theory X. Genuine innovation, in contrast to a refurbishing and patching of present managerial strategies, requires first the acceptance of less limiting assumptions about the nature of the human resources we seek to control, and second the readiness to adapt selectively to the implications contained in those new assumptions. Theory Y is an invitation to innovation.

REFERENCES

Brown, J. A. C., *The Social Psychology of Industry*. Baltimore: Penguin Books, Inc., 1954.

Cordiner, Ralph J., *New Frontiers for Professional Managers*. New York: McGraw-Hill Book Company, Inc., 1956

Dubin, Robert, *The World of Work: Industrial Society and Human Relations.* Englewood Cliffs, N. J.: Prentice-Hall, Inc., 1958

Friedmann, Georges, *Industrial Society: The Emergence of the Human Problems of Automation.* Glencoe, Ill.: Free Press, 1955.

Herzberg, Frederick, Bernard Mausner, and Barbara Bloch Snyderman, *The Motivation to Work.* New York: John Wiley & Sons, Ind., 1959.

Krech, David, and Richard S. Crutchfield, *Theory and Problems of Social Psychology.* New York: McGraw-Hill Book Company, Inc., 1948

Leavitt, Harold J., *Managerial Psychology.* Chicago: University of Chicago Press, 1958.

McMurry, Robert N., "The Case for Benevolent Autocracy," *Harvard Business Review,* vol. 36, no. 1 (January-February), 1958.

Rice, A. K., Productivity and Social Organizations: *The Ahmedabad Experiment,* London: Tavistock Publications, Ltd., 1958.

Stagner, Ross, *The Psychology of Industrial Conflict.* New York: John Wiley & Sons, Inc., 1956.

THE ORGANIZATIONAL LEADER'S VIEW OF REALITY*

by Douglas McGregor

Introduction

The manager's view of reality is of course far wider and more complex than the following discussion will suggest. It includes his view of the physical world and, at a deeper level, his beliefs, however implicit, concerning "the meaning of it all." The function of cosmology[1] is to bring some semblance of order to experiences which otherwise would be so confusing that there would be no basis for action. It is difficult to imagine the anxiety that would result if man had no conception of cause and effect, no way of ordering his perception of reality and his experience with it. Thus, a cosmology is importantly associated with the individual's basic security, his confidence that he can cope successfully with physical and social reality.

The individual never experiences a complete lack of order in reality (except perhaps in early childhood), because he is endowed with a nervous system that enables him to perceive and remember selectively, to generalize, to relate, to discriminate, and to organize with respect to situations and events. Inevitably, he develops strong needs to find subjective order in what objectively is massive complexity. In fact, his needs frequently lead him to impose order on reality even when it is not objectively there. His possession of these characteristics, plus the fact that he lives in a culture in which there are already existing ordered views of reality, provides him with the basis for developing a cosmology.

In some sense every individual's cosmology is unique. In other respects all individuals share common beliefs about reality. However, no cosmology *is* reality; it is a human perception of reality. It is like a map of a territory that has been only partly explored and perhaps never will be completely known. The traveler therefore must rely to some extent on his own wits, using his map but remembering always that it is an imperfect representation of reality.

I try in this chapter to indicate a few ways in which the growth of behavioral science knowledge has changed the map upon which the managerial traveler in our society has tended to rely. But my analogy appears to break down, because some of this knowledge contradicts the evidence provided by the manager's own experience. He finds that the map does not correspond to his direct observation of the territory through which he is traveling. This is not, however, an unusual circumstance, nor is the tendency to reject the map that contradicts experience.

All of us have come to terms in some fashion with findings in *physical* science that contradict our direct experience. Such

---

[1] *"Cosmology" is defined as the theory of the universe as a whole and the laws governing it. (Eds.)*

knowledge asserts that the sun and the planets do not rise and set as they appear to do, that ordinary physical objects are in fact not solid as they seem to be, that invisible and unexperienced biological organisms affect our health and well-being, that what appear to be simple cause-effect relationships are in fact extremely complex.

Similarly, behavioral science knowledge involves assertions about the nature of man and of cause and effect in human behavior that challenge direct experience. Some of these findings are backed by sufficient research to give one considerable confidence that they are true. Some are still subject to controversy; like all scientific knowledge, they represent partial truth, and there may be material changes as new knowledge accumulates. Let us now consider some of this knowledge and determine its effect on the manager's view of cosmology.

Applying Behavioral Science Knowledge to Management

Useful scientific knowledge consists in (1) identification of the factors, characteristics, or variables that are sufficient and necessary causes of a given set of phenomena; and (2) statements about the relationships among these factors that are associated with changes in the phenomena. Thus the performance P of an individual at work in an industrial organization is a function of certain characteristics of the individual I, including his knowledge, skills, motivation, attitudes, and certain aspects of the environmental situation C, including the nature of his job, the rewards associated with his performance, and the leadership provided him.

$$P = f(I_{a,b,c,d\ldots} E_{m,n,o,p\ldots})$$

The relationships among these variables are many and complex. Existing behavioral science knowledge does not permit precise quantitative statements of most of them, but much that is useful can be said about their form and nature.

Perhaps the most general statement of the potential contribution that behavioral science can make to management would be this: Our present knowledge indicates that there are a number of important characteristics of individuals *and* of the work environment which conventional management practice does not take into account. The variables that most managers do recognize are necessary, but they are not sufficient to explain organized human effort. Behavioral science affords the possibility of improving organized human effort by identifying additional variables and their interrelationships so that, once recognized, they may be taken into account in managerial practice.

It is obvious, and demonstrably true scientifically, that man's behavior is influenced by certain characteristics of his environment. When we speak of motivating people, we are referring to the possibility of creating relationships between characteristics of man and characteristics of his environment that will result in certain desired behavior. "Reward" and "punishment" are the terms in common use to describe generally the environmental characteristics that are controlled to influence behavior.

It is important to recognize, however, that what is involved is always a *relationship* between E variables and I variables. Giving or withholding a particular sum of money or a particular kind of food will affect a particular individual's behavior in certain ways, *depending on his characteristics*. The offer of beef to a Hindu and a Christian will affect their behavior quite differently. A glass of water may have a powerful influence on a man dying of thirst and none on a man who already has access to water. A ten-dollar monthly raise in pay will affect a clerk and a top executive differently.

The relationships are indeed complex. They involve the individual's capabilities, his goals, his needs, his expectations, his attitudes, his perceptions concerning the scarcity of the reward that is being given or withheld. They involve relationships not only of reward or punishment to the individual, but of other characteristics of the environment. The threat of discharge will affect the behavior of an accounting clerk and a nuclear physicist differently in United States industry under present economic conditions. Knowledge about cause and effect in human behavior rests on knowledge of the relevant characteristics of I and E (which ones are "necessary" and which are "sufficient" to account for the behavior) and on knowledge about the relationships that hold between these characteristics.

There is substantial amount of unified knowledge about some of these relationships today; some are less well known and often disputed; and virtually nothing is known about others. A detailed analysis of the current state of knowledge would have little value for the manager. I propose, therefore, to present only certain general findings that seem to me to be fairly well established and, in addition, to be particularly relevant to the concerns of industrial managers. Even so, I shall ignore many qualifications and complications.

Rewards and Punishments as Incentives

One important body of knowledge has to do with two quite different kinds of motivational relationships. The first, and by far the most recognized and utilized today, involves what are called *extrinsic* rewards and punishments—they exist as characteristics of the environment, and their relationship to behavior is relatively direct. Money is the most obvious of them, but fringe benefits, promotion, praise, recognition, criticism, and social acceptance and rejection are other examples.

Intrinsic rewards, on the other hand, are inherent in the activity itself: The reward is the achievement of the goal. Intrinsic rewards cannot be *directly* controlled externally, although characteristics of the environment can enhance or limit the individual's opportunities to obtain them. Thus, achievements of knowledge or skill, of autonomy, of self-respect, of solutions to problems, are examples. So are some of the rewards associated with genuine altruism: giving love and help to others.

Management has rather fully exploited the possibilities of influencing behavior by controlling extrinsic rewards and punishments (although there are some important exceptions that will be considered later). In general, however, far less attention has been paid to intrinsic rewards. There are, I believe, two major reasons. The first is the difficulty in establishing a direct link between these rewards and performance. One can give money as a promotion for superior performance. The causal linkage is obvious to the recipient, as is the source of the reward. But one cannot give the sense of accomplishment that accompanies the individual's or group's recognition of having found a solution to a difficult and important problem. (This is quite different from the *extrinsic* reward of praise for the achievement.) In short, management cannot so easily or directly control intrinsic rewards. The individual *can* be prevented from obtaining such rewards—for example, by close supervision that gives him no opportunity to solve problems on his own. It is interesting and significant, however, that under such circumstances people will often obtain this reward by ingenious solutions that involve a kind of sabotage of management's control systems. "Beating the system" is a widely played game in which intrinsic rewards are highly motivational.

The second reason for management's failure to exploit the possibilities of intrinsic rewards is closely associated with beliefs about the nature of man that have been prominent in Western culture for at least two centuries. We need not become involved in the philosophical debate concerning the relationship between mind and body except to recognize that a central issue has been whether man's behavior can be explained in terms of purely mechanical analogies or whether it is necessary to assume the existence of "forces" that may be independent of physical law. However managers have resolved this issue personally, managerial practice appears to reflect at least a tacit belief that motivating people *to work* is a "mechanical" problem.

There are certain similarities between this view of man at work and Newton's laws of motion. To a considerable degree, man has been perceived to be like a physical body at rest. The application of external force is required to set him in motion—to motivate him to work. Consequently, extrinsic rewards and punishments are the obvious and appropriate forces to be utilized in controlling organized human effort.

Probably few managers today would accept these assertions as true of their own managerial philosophy. Most would insist that they recognize man to be to some degree self-activated. They would point particularly to that small proportion of the population that includes the "natural leaders." These men are ambitious by nature; they possess initiative and a desire to assume responsibility; they do not require the application of external force to set them in motion, although of course they are responsive to extrinsic rewards.

In addition, it would be argued that even the average man is self-activated in certain ways. He expends energy in play, in pursuing hobbies, and in other pleasure-seeking activities. Some individuals expend considerable energy, without obvious external cause, in destructive activities that undermine managerial objectives. They are self-motivated, but negatively.

The real point, it would then be argued, is not that man is set in motion only by external forces, but that the internal forces that activate him are—except for "the few"—antithetical to the requirements of organized human effort. He can be directed into productive effort at work only by means of extrinsic rewards and by punishments that counteract his "negative" motivation.

Whichever view one takes, then, the outcome in terms of managerial strategy is identical: Extrinsic rewards and punishments are the appropriate methods for controlling the behavior of the great majority of human beings.

This is an important issue. If human nature is essentially as thus described, intrinsic rewards and punishments have little or no value for the manager. In fact, a major part of the managerial task is to counteract natural human tendencies that are opposed to the goals of organization.

A view that is often expressed by managers today says that most people want maximum rewards for minimum effort. They want security—guarantees of employment and protection against most of the hazards of life. They tend to be indifferent or even negative toward reasonable standards of performance. As managers who hold this view see the situation, these characteristics of human nature are being steadily reinforced by government, labor unions, and some managements that have the unfortunate tendency to be too soft.

If, on the other hand, the self-activated characteristics of man are not *by their nature* antithetical to the requirements of organized human effort, the possibility exists that they could become assets to management rather than liabilities. If some substantial majority of human beings are not prevented *by nature* from being like the few (at least in a motivational sense), intrinsic rewards and punishments could be significant tools of management.

It is this view of human nature that is supported by much current knowledge and enlightened practice. The mechanical view is not wrong; it is insufficient to account for a considerable amount of man's behavior at work. A number of research studies have provided evidence of many ways in which intrinsic rewards can yield higher performance and reduce opposition to organization goals, and of many ways in which intrinsic punishment (often unwittingly imposed by management) can have the opposite consequences.

We shall examine some of these findings and their implications for managerial practice in later chapters. One example will serve as an illustration for the moment.

A series of studies in IBM revealed that the introduction of work standards in certain departments by a strategy utilizing extrinsic rewards and punishments brought about increased performance and also lowered morale. In certain other departments, managers opposed to this strategy brought about equivalent improvement *without* negative influences on morale. The essential difference in the latter case lay in the utilization of intrinsic rewards associated with the desire of workers to control their own fate, i.e., to have a greater degree of autonomy than was possible with the *imposition* of standards that was involved in the former case.[2]

These studies did not investigate the negative side effects, other than morale, that have been found typically to be associated with the conventional strategies of introducing work standards. In terms of cost and efficiency, these additional side effects (various methods invented by workers for beating the system) have been frequently demonstrated to be substantial.

A Theory of Motivation

Strictly speaking, the answer to the question managers so often ask of behavioral scientists—How do you motivate people?—is: You don't. Man is by nature motivated. He is an *organic* system, not a mechanical one. Inputs of energy (sunlight, food, water, etc.) are transformed by him into outputs of behavior (including intellectual activities and emotional responses, as well as observable actions). His behavior is influenced by relationships between his characteristics as an organic system I and the environment E. [Performance $P = f$(individual . . . environment)] Creating these relationships is a matter of *releasing* his energy in certain ways rather than others. We do not motivate him, because he *is* motivated. When he is not, he is dead. This is the sense in which the behavioral scientist distinguishes between an organic and a purely mechanical theory of human nature.

In an earlier volume,[3] I attempted to summarize a view of the motivational nature of man associated prominently with the name of Abraham Maslow.[4] This theory has gained considerable support from other behavioral scientists. Its central thesis

[2] D. Sirota, "A Study of Work Measurement," *Sixteenth Annual Proceedings of the Industrial Relations Research Association,* 1964; D. Sirota and S. M. Klein, "Employees' Attitudes toward Aspects of Work Measurement," *Personnel Research Studies* (IBM), 1961.

[3] D. McGregor, *The Human Side of Enterprise.* New York: McGraw-Hill Book Company, 1960.

[4] A. H. Maslow, *Motivation and Personality.* New York: Harper & Row, Publishers, Incorporated, 1954.

is that human needs are organized in a hierarchy, with physical needs for survival at the base. At progressively higher levels are needs for security, social interaction, and ego satisfaction. Generally speaking, when lower-level needs are reasonably well satisfied, successively higher levels of needs become relatively more important as motivators of behavior.

The relationships are by no means as simple as this brief statement implies. For example, "reasonable satisfaction" is culturally defined. A subsistence level of satisfaction of physical needs in our society today is far higher than that, say, in the villages of India. Moreover, man's higher-level needs are not completely absent, even at bare subsistence levels. He seeks ways of achieving his social and ego needs, even when he is relatively deprived with respect to his lower needs. Even in circumstances of severe deprivation, many may rebel against social and political restrictions in the interests of their higher needs. However, less energy is available if most of it must be used for sheer survival. In general, the relative strength of human needs is consistent with the hierarchy described above.

Another qualification is that severe deprivation of lower-level needs in early life may warp the individual's adjustment in a variety of ways and accentuate their importance for him permanently (except as psychotherapy may later modify his adjustment). Thus we find people with fixations on money, for example, or security, or power.

Man's goals associated with his physical, security, and social needs are achieved largely by means of extrinsic rewards that are controlled by others. It is because of this that mutual trust is such a basic requirement of effective organizational relationships. In its absence there is no assurance to employees of equity in the administration of wages and salaries, promotion, or discipline. In its absence also, management must establish tight controls and exercise close surveillance over employees.

Some of the goals associated with ego needs are achieved by means of extrinsic rewards—for example, recognition and status. Others, as noted earlier, are achieved solely by intrinsic rewards. The difficulty with intrinsic rewards, from management's point of view, is in utilizing them for purposes of control. I have argued above that part of the problem lies in the mistaken assumption that these needs are by their nature antithetical to the purposes of the industrial organization—that they are expressed in pleasure-seeking activities and not through work. Let us examine this assumption further.

If the expenditure of energy is work, it is clear that human beings often work hard at their hobbies and in other pleasureful activities. They work hard in acquiring skills or knowledge *that they wish to acquire*. They work hard in the service of causes to which they are committed—in civic or political or religious or social or humanitarian organizations. They expend energy in organized artistic activities—music or theater or graphic arts. It is often argued that most people are by nature dependent —that they prefer not to accept responsibility but to be led. If we observe their behavior on the job, the generalization appears to hold rather widely. Yet it is surprising how many of the same people not only accept but seek responsibility in a variety of organized activities away from the job.

Intrinsic rewards are significant in all these activities, although extrinsic rewards of status, recognition, and social acceptance are involved as well. The basic point is that intrinsic rewards are not associated exclusively with human activities of the kind that are defined as recreational. Nor are such activities carried on exclusively outside of organizational settings. It is not human nature that excludes the pursuit of goals yielding intrinsic rewards from the job environment. It is not human nature that defines pleasure-seeking activities as nonproductive. Human needs can be satisfied in a great variety of environments. With the exception of a very few (such as sleep and sex), they can be satisfied through activities that management would define as productive, as well as through activities that management would define otherwise.

It is my belief that a realistic perception of man in these respects has been obscured in our culture for a very long time by the moral conviction that pleasure is sinful and must therefore be disassociated from productive work. To earn his daily bread by the sweat of his brow is the punishment meted out to man ever since Adam and Eve were driven from the Garden; it is through painful and unpleasant effort that man atones for his sins and develops strength of character; what is good cannot be obtained through pleasureful activity. Certainly this is not the full explanation, but the influence of this social norm in our society is strong and pervasive.

The motivational theory under discussion asserts that man —if he is freed to some extent from using most of his energy to obtain the necessities of life and a degree of security from the major vicissitudes—will by nature begin to pursue goals associated with his higher-level needs. These include needs for a degree of control over his own fate, for self-respect, for using and increasing his talents, for responsibility, for achievement both in the sense of status and recognition and in the sense of personal development and effective problem solving. Thus freed he will also seek in many ways to satisfy more fully his physical needs for recreation, relaxation, and play. Management has been well aware of the latter tendency; it has not often recognized the former, or at least it has not taken into account its implications for managerial strategy.

Implications of the Theory for Management

A statement of strategy that has long seemed to me to be consistent with the goals of economic enterprise on the one hand, and with behavioral science knowledge of the motivational nature of man on the other, is this: Management must seek to create conditions (an organizational environment) such that members of the organization at all levels can best achieve their own goals by directing their efforts toward the goals of the organization. With respect to lower-level needs, this places before management the task of providing extrinsic rewards, *on an equitable basis,* for all kinds of contributions to the success of the enterprise. Since management controls these rewards, and can therefore both give and withhold them, this task also involves the equitable administration of extrinsic punishments for negative contributions. Note that this statement is careful not to relate these rewards and punishments to compliance or non-compliance with *management's wishes.* It cannot be assumed—in fact, it is often untrue—that a given manager's wishes are the expression of the goals of the enterprise (even sometimes when he is a top-level executive).

With respect to higher-level ego needs (and some middle-level social needs) management's task is to provide opportunities for members of the organization to obtain intrinsic rewards from contributions to the success of the enterprise. Since management does not directly control such rewards, the problem of equity in their administration does not arise. The task is to provide an appropriate environment—one that will permit and encourage employees to seek intrinsic rewards *at work.* Its performance will involve managers at every level in an examination of the way work is organized; the nature and administration of managerial controls; the way responsibilities are assigned and supervised; the way goals are set, policies established, planning done—in short, almost every aspect of managerial practice. Often the provision of opportunities for intrinsic rewards becomes a matter of removing restraints. Progress is rarely fast because people who have become accustomed to control through extrinsic rewards exclusively must learn new attitudes and habits before they can feel secure in accepting opportunities for intrinsic rewards at work. If there is not a fair degree of mutual trust, and some positive support, the whole idea may appear highly risky to them.

It will not be fruitful for management to undertake this task unless there is genuine open-mindedness (if not acceptance) with respect to the motivational character of human nature outlined in the preceding pages.[5]

One of the generalizations which emerges from these considerations about motivation and human nature is this: When a manager asserts, on the basis of his experience and observation, that most people are by nature either indifferent or antagonistic toward the goals of the industrial enterprise, there is more than a small possibility that he may be confusing cause and effect. The indifference and hostility are often observable, but they may be the *result* of a managerial strategy that has, over a long period, provided adequate extrinsic rewards for lower-level needs but has ignored or even prevented the achievement of intrinsic rewards associated with higher-level needs. The former needs, being reasonably well satisfied, have become less motivational; the latter, being frustrated, are finding expression outside the organization (and perhaps also in the exercise of ingenuity to beat the system inside the organization).

Another generalization emerging from an organic conception of human nature is that all human relationships are *transactional*. Since the normal individual is not passive toward his environment, but is actively coping with it, *influence in any form is a two-way process.*

Raymond Bauer, in a penetrating analysis of research on social communication, indicates how behavioral scientists

---

[5] *In one area of industrial organizations—namely, the scientific research laboratory involved primarily in basic research—management has gone a considerable way toward accomplishing this task. The reasons for doing so have been largely connected with the problem of obtaining and keeping competent scientists, rather than with the acceptance of new ideas about human nature. (In fact, I have heard many managers assert vehemently that scientists are not at all representative of Homo sapiens!) I doubt that these results would have been achieved except for the external pressures that have almost literally forced changes in policy and practice on some of these managements. Those pressures are not evident to anything like the same degree in the rest of the industrial organization today. (Eds.)*

have gradually come to recognize that even communication by means of mass media ("obviously" a one-way form of influence) is transactional in significant ways. The reciprocal influence in social communication is not necessarily balanced—there may be inequities either way. The essential point is that it is never fully one way.[6]

The reactions of the influenced may not be directly or immediately observable to the influencer, but this does not mean they are absent.

The manager whose conception of cause and effect in human behavior is mechanical must rely on the "orneriness" of human nature for an explanation of the many forms of indifference or resistance to managerial influence. The only way he can conceive of to counteract them is to increase the threat of extrinsic punishment (which often aggravates the symptoms he is trying to eliminate).

The manager whose conception of cause and effect is organic will recognize the transactional character of influence. When he encounters indifference or resistance, he will attribute the reaction not to human nature, but to aspects of the relationship between E variables and I variables that can be analyzed and probably corrected by *mutual* interaction.

The values in *participation* as a tactic of management do not lie merely, or even primarily, in the fact that people like to be consulted about decisions affecting them. The significant point is that participation, when it is sincere and genuine, is an open recognition of the interactional character of influence. When resistance to or sabotage of managerial decisions is anticipated, participation provides a natural method for minimizing or eliminating either in advance.

Thus a manager's view of human nature powerfully influences his selection of a strategy. (See Chapter 5 for a discussion of managerial strategies.) His strategy, in turn, powerfully influences the behavior of his subordinates. Naturally, he takes the evidence provided by their behavior as proof of his views of human nature. Such circular reactions can occur with incorrect or inadequate beliefs about human nature as well as with adequate ones. Once they are established, contrary evidence is often rejected on the ground that it is inconsistent with directly observable reality.

[6] R. Bauer, "The Obstinate Audience: The Influence Process from the Point of View of Social Communications," *American Psychologist*, vol. 19, no. 5, pp. 319-328, May, 1964.

Such situations are by no means limited to management or to the behavioral sciences. They have been repeated countless times throughout history in the physical sciences, as man has rejected evidence contradicting his direct experience of reality. It is often decades, and sometimes centuries, before these issues are finally resolved.

Perceived Versus Objective Reality

Another important property of human nature has been elaborated as a result of behavioral science research. It is that human behavior is seldom a *direct* response to objective reality, but is rather a response to the individual's perception of that reality. A simple reflex, such as the removal of the finger from a hot stove, appears to be a direct response to reality. But even it is mediated by the nervous system. Impulses must flow in through sensory nerves and back out through nerves controlling muscular action before the response can occur. Moreover, as a result of learning, the individual may on occasion refrain from touching a stove in the belief that it is hot when in fact it is not. He responds to *his perception* of reality.

Human response to more complex aspects of reality involves higher levels of the nervous system that have certain important characteristics. Among the most important of these are the processes of selective perception and memory by which the individual organizes his perception of reality.

We recognize these processes readily enough in some circumstances. A common expression is: "That's not the way I see it." However, we tend to think of this phenomenon as being restricted to ambiguous situations such as those associated with politics or broad social issues. It is not easy to accept the fact that even our perceptions of relatively simple aspects of physical reality are mediated by the selectivity of our perception, by our capacity to see what we expect to see, by the theory we have developed about the nature of the world (our cosmology), and by our needs and wishes or our fears and anxieties. It is to a large extent our perception of reality, not reality itself, that influences and determines our behavior.

Consider the behavior of man as it was influenced until the end of the fifteenth century by his perception of a flat rather than a spherical earth. Consider the differences in behavior between a doctor and a layman. If the layman undertakes to treat himself, his perception of the reality of his own disease will in many instances lead him to adopt a method of treatment quite different from what the doctor would prescribe on the basis of his own more professional perception. Consider the question of equity with respect to the administration of salaries or promotions and the quite different perceptions of management and of workers concerning reality. The effort, time, and money devoted to the development of an appropriate corporate image by some companies today are at least a tacit admission that man responds not to reality directly but to his perception of it.

Rational Versus Emotional Man

Another important aspect of the nature of human nature from the managerial point of view has to do with the emotional characteristics of behavior and their control. The thoughtful manager today is relatively well informed about at least some of these characteristics of human nature. He accepts the fact that some are unconscious and thus uncontrollable by the individual. He is aware of the general findings in psychosomatic medicine and clinical psychology.

Many managers act, however, as though they believe that man is divisible into two *separate* individuals: (1) a rational person who can operate logically, deal with facts, and reach purely objective conclusions and (2) an emotional person who is blindly irrational, ignores or misinterprets facts, and operates in a highly biased fashion. Managers. of course, desire to deal with the former "person" and to exclude the influence of the latter. The ability to make the separation, it is assumed, rests in part on the individual's education and intellectual skills, but primarily on the exercise of will power and the conscious intention to be rational. This ability is believed to be particularly characteristic of the few.

Thus, the tacit belief, reflected in much managerial behavior, is that at least some men can become, if they choose, rational, logical decision-making machines with respect to business problems. Verbal persuasion is usually applied to make man over into this kind of machine: "Let's keep personalities out of this"; "Let's deal with the facts"; "Consider the problem coldly and objectively." If man can only be persuaded to make the attempt, he can largely eliminate from his thinking or behavior the influences of his needs, fears, wishes, anxieties, hostilities, and guilts.

This conception of the nature of man is sharply challenged

by the evidence from the psychological clinic and by a considerable body of experiemental research. Except possibly for the most trivial acts, man's behavior—whether he is thinking, analyzing, reasoning, or interacting with others—is *always* influenced significantly by emotional factors. He is aware of some of these but not of many others. Generally speaking, the more important the problem or issue under consideration is to him, the greater the influence of emotional factors on his responses. Others cannot eliminate these influences by giving orders or making requests, nor can he eliminate them in himself by the conscious, willful effort to do so. *The emotional and the rational aspects of man are inextricably interwoven; it is an illusion to believe they can be separated.*

A massive body of physiological and psychological evidence supports this generalization. For example, there are specific, differential patterns of response of the autonomic nervous system and the glandular system (which are only to a slight degree under conscious control) associated with different kinds of activity. These physiological subsystems are known to be closely tied to emotional reactions.

> The rate of heartbeat, the blood pressure, the electrical conductivity of the skin vary measurably and systematically depending on the behavior in which the organism is involved.
>
> The relationships are exceedingly complex, but there is tentative evidence that heart rate *accelerates* somewhat as an individual prepares to undertake a problem-solving task in which he will use his intellectual abilities and knowledge. It accelerates still more as he engages in the task. On the other hand, the heart rate decelerates when he prepares for and later engages in observing, in taking in information from his environment. Moreover, there are significant physiological differences, for example, between an activity associated with "anger toward peers" and one associated with "anger at mother." The subjects are unaware of these differences.

It is well known today that activities in the central nervous and glandular sysyems can modify the receptivity of sense organs. The accelerated heartbeat rate, as man engages in mental activities of certain kinds, appears to be part of a physiological pattern that partially shuts out certain kinds of stimulation from the environment, while deceleration of the heartbeat is connected with a lowering of the barriers to inputs. Beyond this, to find differential changes associated with reactions to "peers" as opposed to reactions to "mother" is indeed significant.[7] The important implication for our purposes, from this rapidly growing body of research knowledge, is that emotional responses, many of which are completely unconscious, are associated with virtually all human behavior. It is clear that attempts to eliminate them by verbal persuasion are futile.

A careful study of performance reviews in a division of a large manufacturing company led to a conclusion consistent with these generalizations. It is virtually impossible within the content of the conventional appraisal interview for a superior to communicate a negative evaluation of a subordinate's performance to him without producing defensive reactions. The more severe the criticism (as perceived by the subordinate), the more the defensiveness. Thus, the subordinate does not react rationally to the facts. He fails to hear them, or he misinterprets them, or he rejects them as untrue. Much as he may wish to do so, he cannot in these circumstances turn himself into a rational machine. In consequence, changes in behavior attributable to requests by superiors in the context of the appraisal interview turned out in this study to be few indeed.[8]

Human beings in relationships that involve differences in power and status are particularly vulnerable to the effects of emotional forces (note the example above concerning peers versus mothers). The highly sensitive nature of these relationships in childhood and adolescence creates lasting tendencies to react emotionally as well as rationally to them. There are, for example, always subtle and sometimes obvious changes in a subordinate's behavior when he deals directly with those above him in the managerial hierarchy.

It is true that the individual may gain some control over emotional factors influencing his own behavior if he can accept his feelings as facts. If he can come to recognize them, to understand something of the circumstances that arouse them, to accept them as inevitable and integral aspects of his behavior, he

[7] H. F. Harlow, "The Affectional System in Monkeys," *The American Psychologist,* January, 1962.

[8] E. Kay, H. H. Meyer, and J. R. P. French, Jr., "Effects of Threat in a Performance Appraisal Interview," *Journal of Applied Psychology,* vol. 49, no. 5, pp. 311-317, 1965. H. H. Meyer, E. Kay, and J. R. P. French, Jr., "Split Roles in Performance Appraisal," *Harvard Business Review,* January-February, 1965, pp. 123-129.

can control to some extent their effects.

The process of gaining control over undesired emotional reactions in this fashion is greatly aided if it is one of social interaction. An obvious reason is that, under proper circumstances, the interaction can aid in the recognition of the existence of unconscious emotional reactions and in the discovery of the conditions that arouse them. This is well recognized in everyday life. We seek help along these lines from many sources —from friends, relatives, consultants, colleagues, ministers, psychiatrists. There are tremendously valuable possibilities of achieving more rational business decisions if we can accept certain wider implications of the relationship between social interaction and control of emotional influences on behavior.

A top executive calls a meeting of his associates to discuss an important policy decision. Most—perhaps all—of the participants will be affected by the outcome. It is inevitable, therefore, that emotional influences will be operative. It is clear that ignoring them, or trying to banish them by verbal magic, will not eliminate them. Why not, then, attempt to neutralize them by openly accepting their presence and utilizing the process of social interaction for their control? *We are considerably more capable of detecting the presence of emotional influences in the behavior of others than we are in ourselves.* It is not necessary to engage in psychotherapy or to probe into the causes of such emotional influences in order to compensate reasonably well for them, provided there is recognition of what they are. A group of individuals can help one another to recognize and accept them as facts and in so doing can remove or reduce the very barriers which stand in the way of rational, objective decisions.

We say that an important reason for group consideration of important decisions is to get the benefit of different points of view. Yet by denying or suppressing the emotional factors *which are among the major causes of different points of view,* we defeat our stated purpose.

It is well recognized in everyday life that the effectiveness of social interaction in improving control over emotional influences depends profoundly on the nature of the relationship between the parties involved. It would be critical, therefore, to the success of a strategy such as I am suggesting that the relationships between the members of the group be of a certain kind. Moreover, there are obviously skills involved in successful interaction of this kind. There is good evidence that these skills can be acquired by most normal people. We shall examine such considerations in some detail in Chapters 10 and 11.

It is perhaps not too difficult for the manager to give lip service to these findings about the emotional nature of man. Many do. To include them genuinely in his view of reality so that they become part of the basis for his actions is another matter. The manager is also an example of rational-emotional human nature. His own feelings—partly conscious and partly unconscious —exert important influence on his ability to accept fully that man is not separable into a rational being and an emotional one. To accept the implications of the fact would, for example, alter considerably his view of what is predictable and controllable in the organizational reality that surrounds him.

An important aspect of the lives of forty-five to fifty Sloan Fellows during the year they spend at M.I.T. in the Executive Development Program is the organization of their own social activities. Since their families move with them to the Boston area for the year, and since they are quite different as a group from the other students at M.I.T., they tend to do many things together.

The management of their extracurricular activities is entirely up to the group. Experience indicates that if they leave these matters to chance, they are likely to lose kinds of control that most of them consider important. They become "managed" by implicit norms and standards that develop in any organization unless explicit attention is given to them.

These matters received rather full discussion in the initial phases of the program for a recent group of Sloan Fellows. The discussion took place in subgroups of a dozen men each. Afterward, in a general session, the suggestion was made and adopted that each subgroup select two representatives to meet together to explore these issues further, preparatory to dealing with them formally. The subgroups then met to select their representatives.

In one group, which I observed, there were clearly different feelings about the issues involved and about the task of choosing representatives. These, however, were ignored, and the suggestion of one member that they select their representative by secret ballot was immediately accepted. Then the suggestion was made that people might feel quite different about the importance of this problem, that some would welcome the opportunity to serve as representatives whereas others would resent being chosen. The group then encouraged individual members to express their feelings. Because the power relationships were negligible (the group consisted of peers), several members did so. It became apparent that, out of twelve, six felt that the issues were trivial, that they had more important things to do and would therefore much prefer not to be chosen. Three others were relatively neutral and would serve willingly if asked. Three, for various reasons, expressed interest in the issues and a genuine desire to have the opportunity to join the "task force."

With this knowledge the group then proceeded to the secret ballot. Two of the three who had expressed a desire to serve were elected.

This was not a critical managerial decision obviously. The consideration of emotional factors, however, influenced the result materially. What impressed me was that if the issue had been genuinely important, it is more likely that feelings would have been denied, ignored, or suppressed in making of the decision. In this particular case, the implementation of the decision (the work of the task force) might not have been materially affected by the presence of representatives who disliked the task. If the issue had been important, it is not hard to imagine that the implementation desired would have been far less than optimal.

Some of my academic colleagues are fond of saying that emotion is a dirty word in management's lexicon. This is a pointed and largely accurate description. A less colorful but equally correct statement is that management appears to want to eliminate the effects of emotion on behavior in the organizational setting. To the extent that this objective were to be achieved, the organization would reduce its ability to survive! The essential difficulty is that the typical managerial view of emotion is highly restricted. It ignores the fact that human loyalty, enthusiasm, drive, commitment, acceptance of responsibility, and self-confidence are all emotional variables. So are all the "values we hold dear." Motivation is an *emotional* force. Moreover, the evidence grows that intellectual creativity (as well as artistic creativity) is a process involving emotional factors. Clearly, management does not desire to eliminate these characteristics of human nature from its own or its employees' behavior. In fact, if a human being existed who was completely unemotional, objective, and logical, he would by definition have no *interest* in the success of any organization. He would not be motivated.

The real desire of the manager is that human beings (particularly those with whom he must interact) should express certain emotions and suppress others. He would like to eliminate such emotional characteristics as antagonism, hostility, resistance, defiance, uncooperative attitudes, and unrealistic points of view. He would like to eliminate emotional forces that are associated in his mind with bad, selfish, immature, and unreasonable behavior. (In fact, many of these are at least partly unconscious and therefore are precisely those which cannot be eliminated by conscious intent.)

A cultural factor is also involved in these implicit desires. The model of the successful manager in our culture is a masculine one. The good manager is aggressive, competitive, firm, just. He is not feminine: he is not soft or yielding or dependent or intuitive in the womanly sense. The very expression of emotion is widely viewed as a feminine weakness that would interfere with effective business processes. Yet the fact is that all these emotions are part of the human nature of men and women alike. Cultural forces have shaped not their existence but their acceptability; they are repressed, *but this does not render them inactive.* They continue to influence attitudes, opinions, and decisions.

It can be stated with some assurance that emotions will influence behavior, including thinking, reasoning, and decision making, whenever they are aroused. Second, they will be aroused to the degree that the issue or problem is important. Third, importance is a function of the (conscious or unconscious) meaning of the issue or the problem or the situation *to the individual.* One of the potential values of the outside consultant in certain situations is that he is more likely to be neutral so far as his emotional involvement in the issues is concerned. However, this is by no means always true. Often the issues, and his role in the resolution of them, are genuinely important to the consultant although for reasons different from those affecting the client.

It is possible for objective reality to be so coercive that the effects of emotional factors upon behavior become negligible, at least for the moment. Thus the "facts" can sometimes determine a decision completely, although the subsequent implementation of the decision may be substantially affected positively or negatively by emotional influences. It is rare, however, for a managerial decision of more than trivial significance to be completely determined by the facts. Even when the facts appear to be coercive, there is usually room for doubt concerning their interpretation or their veracity. Scientific findings are the subject of frequent and sometimes bitter dispute on this score, despite the elaborate safeguards characteristic of scientific methods.

Complete objectivity is a rare phenomenon unless the issues are of little consequence to the individual. This is not to deny the possibility of some gain in striving for it. The general implication from behavioral science knowledge is that man is *by nature* an inseparable mixture of rational and emotional components. He cannot turn himself into a rational "machine" by any known means, nor can he eliminate the effects of emotion on intellectual activity in others by persuasion or by command. He can, however, under certain conditions, utilize the help of others to reduce or compensate for the effects of emotion on their own behavior.

Social Man

It is hardly necessary to call attention to the degree to which our society stresses the values of individualism. We have done so for three and a half centuries. Negative attitudes toward conformity, dislike of being "other-directed," carefully contrived legal protection of individual rights, certain attitudes toward government—all reflect these values. The manager, as a member of our society, tends to share them. Thus he stresses the desirability of dealing with individuals as he carries out his managerial responsibilities, for he thinks of the individual as the primary (and only) unit of organized human effort, and of competition between individuals as a major source of motivation.

Of course, complete individual freedom in organizational life is impossible. A degree of control and standardization of individual behavior is obviously necessary. Nevertheless, the manager tends to respond negatively to what he is likely to perceive as "collectivization," whether in the form of face-to-face work groups or in the form of a union. Oddly, he doesn't frown on teamwork, perhaps because he doesn't perceive the team as a collective. I suspect that usually teamwork merely means

cooperation between people without reference to an entity
called a "team." (Of course, this view of reality has its emotional aspects, whether or not they are recognized. The manager's power may be appreciably affected, depending on
whether he deals with individuals or with groups.)

In many cases, the manager's cosmology includes the view
that a group is an inefficient means for getting work done, particularly when it comes to activities like planning, decision
making, innovating, and problem solving. It is in the nature of
human nature, as he views it, that intellectual activities in particular are properly individual activities and are therefore im-
paired by being carried on in a group. There is much in experience and everyday observation to support this belief. By and
large, groups, committees, and task forces *are* grossly inefficient in these respects. Again, however, the question arises
whether these are *inherent* characteristics of group activity—unchangeable human nature—or whether they are the *result* of the
way groups are managed.

In the last few years, there has been some change in this
aspect of managerial cosmology. Formal educative processes
designed to improve understanding and skill with respect to
group activity have had an impact. The controversy concerning
the individual versus the group is by no means settled, but the
complexity of reality in a modern industrial organization is
gradually producing a reluctant acceptance of the view that
groups are appropriate for some kinds of managerial activity.
Nevertheless, most managers perceive human nature fundamentally in terms of individual nature. Individual man is the
unit of society and of all its organizations.

But man is a social organism, too, and recent studies indicate a close evolutionary relationship between man's emotional
and social nature. Knowledge in this field has increased dramat-
ically in recent years, partly as a result of the development of
techniques in physiology that permit observation of relationships between behavior and the precise stimulation of certain
areas of the brain in living animals (and to a limited extent in
man). Also, surgical removal of portions of the brain result in behavior changes, which have been extensively studied.

One region of the mammalian brain is associated with patterns of behavior related to functions like eating and swal-
lowing and to fighting, searching, and self-defense—activities concerned with self-preservation. A related region is

associated with grooming reactions and preliminary sexual responses—activities concerned with sustaining the species rather than the self. The latter portion of the nervous system is not found below the level of mammals and is most highly developed in man.[9]

A variety of other findings, coupled with the results of anthropological research, point quite definitely to the conclusion that evolution has been a process not only of competition but of cooperation and mutual support. As one ascends the evolutionary ladder, altruism, idealism, generosity, admiration, and behavior stemming from emotions such as these (which affect survival of the *species*) are gradually added to the more primitive emotions of hostility and acquisitiveness (which affect survival of the *individual*). As one researcher phrased it, "In the complex organization of the old and new structures [of the brain] we presumably have a neural ladder . . . for ascending from the most primitive sexual feeling to the highest level of altruistic sentiments."[10]

Many developments have led to modifications and refinements in evolutionary theory. Although adaptation as a result of natural selection is still a cornerstone of the theory, it is recognized today that natural selection favors the reproductive success of a *population* and that alone. Survival of the individual is irrelevant. A set of conclusions concerning results of a synthesis of findings from several behavioral science disciplines includes the following:

Individuals seek and find gratifying those situations that have been highly advantageous in survival of the species. That is, tasks that must be done (for species survival) tend to be quite pleasurable; they are easy to learn and hard to extinguish. Their blockage or deprivation leads to tension, anger, substitutive activity and (if prolonged) depression. Such blockage is often accompanied by emergency-type physiological responses that support actions necessary to correct the situation. In the post-infancy human, a remarkable variety of coping behavior may be mobilized by such blockage or deprivation, determined in substantial part by cultural patterning.[11]

[9] P. H. Knapp (ed.), *The Expression of the Emotions in Man*. New York: International Universities Press, Inc., 1963.
[10] P. D. Maclean, "Phylogenesis," in *ibid.*, p. 32.
[11] D. A. Hamburg, "Emotions in the Perspective of Human Evolution," in *ibid.*, p. 312.

Man is by nature committed to social existence, and is inevitably, therefore, involved in the dilemma between serving his own interests and recognizing those of the group to which he belongs. Insofar as this dilemma can be resolved, it is resolved by the fact that man's self-interest can best be served through his commitment to his fellows. . . . Need for positive effect means that each person craves response from his human environment. It may be viewed as a hunger, not unlike that for food, but more generalized. Under varying conditions it may be expressed as a desire for contact, for recognition and acceptance, for approval, for esteem, or for mastery. . . . As we examine human behavior, we find that persons not only universally live in social systems, which is to say they are drawn together, but also universally act in such ways as to obtain the approval of their fellow men.[12]

Finally:

The available evidence strongly indicates that, throughout the long course of his evolution, man has been a group-living form. Moreover it is very likely that *the human group,* throughout the history of the species, *has been a powerful problem-solving tool, coping with all sorts of harsh and taxing environmental contingencies.* It has been an adaptive mechanism *par excellence.*[13] (Italics mine.)

One would expect to find evidence supporting these conclusions in the context of organized human effort in industry, and this is what we do find. The classic studies by the Harvard researchers at the Hawthorne works of the Western Electric Company in the late 1920s are a major case in point.[14] The studies of William Foote Whyte on incentive systems,[15] the evidence accumulated by the Institute for Social Research at the University of Michigan,[16] the work of Kurt Lewin and his successors,[17] and many other studies have served to extend and refine knowledge about group behavior.

[12] *Ibid.,* p. 308.
[13] *Ibid.,* p. 309.
[14] F. J. Roethlisberger and W. J. Dickson, *Management and the Worker.* Cambridge, Mass.: Harvard University Press, 1939.
[15] W. F. Whyte et al., *Money and Motivation.* New York: Harper & Row, Publishers, Incorporated, 1955.
[16] R. Likert, *New Patterns in Management.* New York: McGraw-Hill Book Company, 1961; and R. Kahn et al., *Organizational Stress.* New York: John Wiley & Sons, Inc., 1964.
[17] R. Lippitt et al., *The Dynamics of Planned Change.* New York: Harcourt, Brace & World, Inc., 1958

Both extrinsic and intrinsic rewards and punishments are associated with man's social needs. He needs not only to receive acceptance, support, and recognition in group settings, but also to give these rewards to fellow members. In giving, the rewards are inherent in the action; they are intrinsic. Their evolutionary base is suggested above.

Under appropriate conditions, the group can also be a setting within which the individual satisfies many of his most important ego needs, including those for learning, autonomy (despite a common belief to the contrary), leadership, and self-fulfillment.

A view of reality that ignores or denies these possibilities for goal achievement, or that sees them as inherently incompatible with organizational objectives and requirements, is greatly limited with respect to the managerial task of motivating people to work. Moreover, the theory cited above would suggest that when these social needs are thwarted, individuals will retaliate with aggressive behavior (such as beating the system) and with strong attempts to recreate situations in which needs are met. Evidence and experience in the industrial sphere support this idea: The formation of informal face-to-face work groups, and their powerful influence, is not accidental when management coercively adopts a strategy of dealing exclusively with individuals.

It is important to recognize that the growth of behavioral science knowledge about groups has not resulted in the conclusion that it is necessary to *choose* between the individual and the group. Just as in the physical sciences, understanding of the phenomena at different levels is necessary for prediction and control. The physical particle exhibits properties that are replicated in the atom, in the molecule, and even in a planetary system. However, there are also properties that are unique to each level, and our ability to control natural phenomena is increased by knowledge of the properties of physical systems at different levels.

The same is true of human behavior. We study characteristics of cells, of organs, of the nervous system as a whole, of the human being as an organism, of groups, and of larger aggregations of human beings. Certain characteristics are common to all these "systems"; others are unique to each level. Water, for example, is composed of atoms of hydrogen and oxygen. Knowledge about these at the level of the atom would not give us knowledge of the properties of water, nor of the fact that water at temperatures below 32 degrees Fahrenheit becomes solid and floats.

Management's insistence that the individual is the unit of organization is as limiting as an engineer's insistence that the atom is the unit of physical systems. The limitations of a physical technology based on knowledge at one level alone would be great indeed. A molecule is an assembly of atoms, to be sure, but certain *relationships* among the atoms result in molecules with given properties, whereas other relationships result in molecules with entirely different properties. These properties of molecules cannot be predicted solely on the basis of knowledge of the properties of atoms.

Considerations of a similar nature lead the behavioral scientist to question many managerial assertions about the inherent characteristics of human groups. These assertions are based almost entirely on attempts to deal with groups in terms of knowledge of individuals. The accumulated behavioral science knowledge about *group* behavior tends to contradict the idea that the properties of groups are inherently or inevitably those which we typically observe when we deal with groups as mere collections of individuals. It is also demonstrably possible to create relationships between individuals comprising a face-to-face group such that the group exhibits properties almost diametrically opposed to those observed in the typical committee or staff group or task force in everyday organizational life.

Such groups *do* make decisions that are effectively implemented without the necessity for external pressure or surveillance. They are creative and innovative; they operate efficiently; they are not crippled by disagreements or hampered by dominant personalities. Pressures for conformity are minimal, and the knowledge and skills of each member are effectively utilized. The outputs of the group are not mediocre least-common-denominator compromises, but can often yield decisions and problem solutions at a general level of performance superior to the sum of the outputs of the individual members operating separately. Finally, the members perceive the group to be a setting within which there are attractive opportunities to achieve many of their individual goals and to gain intrinsic rewards while *at the same time* contributing to the goals of the organization.

The characteristics of such effective groups will be considered in later chapters, as well as some practical considerations with respect to their development. For the moment, the essential point is that a managerial cosmology limited to "man the individual" excludes important possibilities of improved organizational effectiveness.

Summary

The manager's view of reality exerts profound effects upon his every managerial act. His acts in turn affect the achievement of both his own goals and those of the organization of which he is a member. I have suggested so far a few important ways in which some common managerial perceptions of reality differ from present-day behavioral science knowledge about that reality. These have had to do with the nature of man: how he is motivated, the role of emotion in his behavior, and the significance of his social nature.

It will be fruitful now to consider other aspects of the manager's reality—his view of the industrial organization and his understanding of his own behavior, his identity, and his role. Then we will be in a position to examine, practically, some of the ways in which management styles and strategies might be altered if a view of reality consistent with these behavioral science findings were to be adopted, and what consequences this might have for the achievement of the manager's and the organization's goals.

POST-BUREAUCRATIC LEADERSHIP*

by Warren G. Bennis

In an early issue of this magazine (*Trans-action*, June-July 1965), I forecast that in the next 25 to 50 years we would participate in the end of bureaucracy as we know it and in the rise of new social systems better suited to the 20th century demands of industrialization. The prediction was based on the evolutionary principle that every age develops an organizational form appropriate to its genus, and that the prevailing form today—the pyramidal, centralized, functionally specialized, impersonal mechanism known as bureaucracy—was out of joint with contemporary realities.

The breakdown of a venerable form of organization so appropriate to 19th century conditions is caused, I argued, by a number of factors, but chiefly the following four: (1) rapid and unexpected change; (2) growth in size beyond what is necessary for the work being done (for example, inflation caused by bureaucratic overhead and tight controls, impersonality caused by sprawls, outmoded rules, and organizational rigidities); (3) complexity of modern technology, in which integration between activities and persons of very diverse, highly specialized competence is required; (4) a change in managerial values toward more humanistic democratic practices.

Organizations of the future, I predicted, will have some unique characteristics. They will be adaptive, rapidly changing temporary systems, organized around problems-to-be-solved by groups of relative strangers with diverse professional skills. The groups will be arranged on organic rather than mechanical models; they will evolve in response to problems rather than to programmed expectations. People will be evaluated, not in a rigid vertical hierarchy according to rank and status, but flexibly, according to competence. Organizational charts will consist of project groups rather than stratified functional groups, as is now the case. Adaptive, problem-solving, temporary systems of diverse specialists, linked together by coordinating executives in an organic flux—this is the organizational form that will gradually replace bureaucracy.

Ironically, the bold future I had predicted is now routine and can be observed wherever the most interesting and advanced practices exist. Most of these trends are visible and have been surfacing for years in the aerospace, construction, drug, and consulting industries as well as professional and research and development organizations, which only shows that the distant future now has a way of arriving before the forecast is fully comprehended.

A question left unanswered, however, has to do with leadership. How would these new organizations be managed? Are there any transferable lessons from present managerial practices? Do the behavioral sciences provide any suggestions? How can these complex, ever-changing, free-form, kaleidoscopic patterns be coordinated? Of course there can be no definitive answers, but unless we can understand the leadership requirements for organizations of the future, we shall inevitably back blindly into it rather than cope with it effectively. Accepted theory and conventional wisdom concerning leadership have a lot in common. Both seem to be saying that the success of a leader depends on the leader, the led, and the unique situation. This formulation—abstract and majestically useless—is the best that can be gleaned from over 100 years of research on "leadership."

On the other hand, any formulations may be inadequate and pallid compared to the myths and primitive psychological responses that surround such complexities as leadership and power. Our preoccupation with the mystiques of the Kennedys is sufficient reminder of that.

Thus, leadership theory coexists with a powerful and parallel archetypal reality. But in what follows, we shall see that it is the latter myth that is threatened—the aggressive, inner-directed 19th century autocrat. For the moment, though, I want to quickly review some of the key situational features likely to confront the leader of the future.

The overarching feature is change itself, its accelerating rate and its power to transform. The phrase "the only constant is change" has reached the point of a cliche, which at once anesthetizes us to its pain and stimulates grotesque fantasies about a Brave New World with no place in the sun for us. Change is the "godhead" term for our age as it has not been for any other. One has only to recall that the British Parliament was debating in the last part of the 19th century whether to close up the Royal Patent Office, as it was felt that all significant inventions had already been discovered.

Situational Features

But what are the most salient changes affecting human organization, the ones with most relevance to their governance? Foremost is the changing nature of our institutions. In 1947, employment stood at approximately 58 million and now is at about 72 million. According to V. K. Fuchs, "Virtually all of this increase occurred in industries that provide services, for example, banks, hospitals, retail stores, and schools." This nation has become the only country to employ more people in services than in production of tangible goods. The growth industries today, if we can call them that, are education, health, welfare, and other

professional institutions. The problem facing organizations is
no longer manufacturing—it is the management of large-scale
sociotechnical systems and the strategic deployment of high-
grade professional talent.

There are other important correlates and consequences of
change. For example, the working population will be younger,
smarter, and more mobile. Half of our country's population is
under 25, and one out of every three persons is 15 years of age
or younger. More people are going to college; over half go to
college in certain urban areas. The United States Postal Department reports that one out of every five families changes its address every year.

Most of these changes compel us to look beyond bureaucracy for newer models of organizations that have the capability to cope with contemporary conditions. The general direction
of these changes—toward more service and professional organizations, toward more educated, younger, and mobile employees, toward more diverse, complex, science-based systems, toward a more turbulent and uncertain environment—forces us to
consider new styles of leadership. Leading the enterprise of the
future becomes a significant social process, requiring as much,
if not more managerial than substantive competence. Robert
McNamara is a case in point. Before he came to Washington, he
was considered for three Cabinet positions: Defense, State, and
Treasury. His "only" recommendation was that he was a superior administrator. Chris Argyris has concluded that success or
failure in the United States Department of State depends as
much or more on one's interpersonal and managerial comp-
tence as one's substantive knowledge of "diplomacy." It can
also be said that leadership of modern organizations depends
on new forms of knowledge and skills not necessarily related to
the primary task of the organization. In short, the pivotal function in the leader's role has changed away from a sole concern
with the substantive to an emphasis on the interpersonal and
organizational processes.

MAIN TASKS OF LEADERSHIP

One convenient focus for a discussion of leadership is to
review the main problems confronting modern organizations,
and to understand the kinds of tasks and strategies linked to
the solution of these problems.

Contributions and Inducements

A simple way to understand this problem is to compute the ratio between what an individual gives and what he gets in his day-to-day transactions. In other words, are the contributions to the organization about equivalent to the inducements received? Where there is a high ratio between inducements and contributions, either the organization or the employee gets restless and searches for different environments, or different people. There is nothing startling or new about this formulation. Nevertheless, organizations frequently do not know what is truly rewarding, especially for the professionals and highly trained workers who will dominate the organizations of the future. With this class of employee, conventional policies and practices regarding incentives, never particularly sensitive, tend to be inapplicable.

Most organizations regard economic rewards as the primary incentive to peak performance. These are not unimportant to the professional, but if economic rewards are equitable, other incentives become far more potent. Avarice, to paraphrase Hume, is not the spirit of industry, particularly of professionals. Professionals tend to seek such rewards as full utilization of their talent and training; professional status (not necessarily within the organization, but externally with respect to their profession); and opportunities for development and further learning. The main difference between the professional and the more conventional, hourly employee is that the former will not yield "career authority to the organization."

The most important incentive, then, is to "make it" professionally, to be respected by professional colleagues. Loyalty to an organization may increase if it encourages professional growth. (I was told recently that a firm decided to build all future plants in university towns in order to attract and hold on to college-trained specialists.) The "good place to work" re sembles a super-graduate school, alive with dialogue and senior colleagues, where the employee will not only work to satisfy organizational demands, but, perhaps primarily, those of his profession.

The other incentive is self-realization, personal growth that may not be task-related. I'm well aware that the remark questions four centuries of an encrusted Protestant ethic, reinforced by the indispensability of work for the preservation and justification of existence. But work, as we all must experience it, serves at least two psychic functions: first, that of binding man more closely to reality; and secondly, in Freud's terms, "of displacing a large amount of libidinal components, whether narcissistic, aggressive, or even erotic, onto professional work and onto human relations connected with it..."

It is not at all clear as to how, or even if, these latter needs can be deliberately controlled by the leadership. Company-sponsored courses, sensitivity training sessions, and other so-called adult education courses may, in fact, reflect these needs. Certainly attitudes toward "continuing education" are changing. The idea that education has a terminal point and that college students come in only 4 sizes—18, 19, 20, and 21—is old-fashioned. A "dropout" should be redefined to mean anyone who hasn't returned to school.

Whichever way the problem of professional and personal growth is resolved, it is clear that many of the older forms of incentives, based on the more elementary needs (safety-economic-physiological) will have to be reconstituted. Even more profound will be the blurring of the boundaries between work and play, between the necessity to belong and the necessity to achieve, which 19th century mores have unsuccessfully attempted to compartmentalize.

The Problem of Distributing Power

There are many issues involved in the distribution of power: psychological, practical, and moral. I will consider only the practical side, with obvious implications for the other two. To begin with, it is quaint to think that one man, no matter how omniscient and omnipotent, can comprehend, let alone control, the diversity and complexity of the modern organization. Followers and leaders who think this is possible get trapped in a child's fantasy of absolute power and absolute dependence.

Today it is hard to realize that during the Civil War, "government" (Lincoln's executive staff) had fewer than 50 civilian subordinates, and not many executives at that, chiefly telegraph clerks and secretaries. Even so recent an administration as Franklin Roosevelt's had a cozy, "family" tone about it. According to his doctor, for example, Roosevelt "loved to know everything that was going on and delighted to have a finger in every pie."

"Having a finger in every pie" may well be an occupational disease of presidents, but it is fast becoming outmoded. Today's administration must reflect the necessities imposed by size and complexity. In fact, there has been a general tendency to move tacitly away from a "presidential" form of power to a "cabinet" or team concept, with some exceptions (like Union Carbide) where "team management" has been conceptualized and made explicit. There is still a long-standing pseudomasculine tendency to disparage such plural executive arrangements, but they are on the increase.

This system of an "executive constellation" by no means implies an abdication of responsibility by the chief executive. It should reflect a coordinated effort based on the distinct competencies of the individual. It is a way of multiplying executive power through a realistic allocation of effort. Of course, this means also that top executive personnel are chosen not only on the basis of their unique talents but on how these skills and competencies fit and work together.

Despite all the problems inherent in the executive constellation concept—how to build an effective team, compatibility, etc.—it is hard to see other valid ways to handle the sheer size and overload of the leader's role.

The Control of Conflict

Related to the problem of developing an effective executive constellation is another key task of the leader—building a climate in which collaboration, not conflict, will flourish. An effective, collaborative climate is easier to experience and harder to achieve than a formal description of it, but most students of group behavior would agree that it should include the following ingredients: flexible and adaptive structure, utilization of individual talents, clear and agreed-upon goals, standards of openness, trust, and cooperation, inter-dependence, high intrinsic rewards, and transactional controls—which means a lot of individual autonomy, and a lot of participation in making key decisions.

Developing this group "synergy" is difficult, and most organizations take the easy way out—a "zero-synergy" strategy. This means that the organization operates under the illusion that they can hire the best individuals in the world, and then adopt a Voltairean stance of allowing each to "Cultivate his own garden." This strategy of isolation can best be observed in universities, where it operates with great sophistication. The Berkeley riots were symptomatic of at least four self-contained, uncommunicating social systems (students, faculty, administration, regents) without the trust, empathy, and interaction—to say nothing of the tradition—to develop meaningful collaboration. To make matters worse, academics by nature, reinforced by tradition, see themselves as "loners." They want to be independent together, so to speak. Academic narcissism goes a long way on the lecture platform, but may be positively dysfunctional for developing a community.

Another equally pernicious strategy with the same effects, but different style (and more typical of American business institutions), is a pseudodemocratic "groupiness" characterized by false harmony and avoidance of conflict.

Synergy is hard to develop. Lack of experience and strong cultural biases against group efforts worsen the problem. Groups, like other highly complicated organisms, need time to develop. They need a gestation period to develop interaction, trust, communication, and commitment. No one should expect an easy maturity in groups any more than in young children.

Expensive and time-consuming as it is, building synergetic and collaborative cultures will become essential. Modern problems are too complex and diversified for one man or one discipline. They require a blending of skills and perspectives, and only effective problem-solving units will be able to master them.

Responding to a Turbulent, Uncertain Environment

In the early days of the last war when armaments of all kinds were in short supply, the British, I am told, made use of a venerable field piece that had come down to them from previous generations. The honorable past of this light artillery stretched back, in fact, to the Boer War. In the days of uncertainty after the fall of France, these guys, hitched to trucks, served as useful mobile units in the coast defense. But it was felt that the rapidity of fire could be increased. A time-motion expert was, therefore, called in to suggest ways to simplify the firing procedures. He watched one of the gun crews of five men at practice in the field for some time. Puzzled by certain aspects of the procedures, he took some slow-motion pictures of the soldiers performing the loading, aiming and firing routines.

When he ran those pictures over once or twice, he noticed something that appeared odd to him. A moment before the firing, two members of the guy crew ceased all activity and came to attention for a three second interval extending throughout the discharge of the gun. He summoned an old colonel of artillery, showed him the pictures, and pointed out this strange behavior. What, he asked colonel, did it mean? The colonel, too, was puzzled. He asked to see the pictures again. "Ah," he said when the performance was over, "I have it. They are holding the horses." (Elting Morison, *Man, Machines and Modern Times,* 1966)

This fable demonstrates nicely the pain with which man accommodates to change. And yet, characteristically and ironically, he continues to seek out new inventions which disorder his serenity and undermine his competence.

One striking index of the rapidity of change—for me, the single, most dramatic index—is the shrinking interval between the time of a discovery and its commercial application. Before World War I, the lag between invention and utilization was 33 years, between World War I and World War II, it was 17 years. After World War II, the interval decreased to about nine years, and if the future can be extrapolated on the basis of the past, by 1970 it will be around five to six years. The transistor was discovered in 1948, and by 1960, 95 percent of all the important equipment and over 50 percent of all electronic equipment utilized them in place of conventional vacuum tubes. The first industrial application of computers was as recent as 1956.

Modern organizations, even more than individuals, are acutely vulnerable to the problem of responding flexibly and appropriately to new information. Symptoms of maladaptive responses, at the extremes, are a guarded, frozen, rigidity that denies the presence or avoids the recognition of changes that will result most typically in organizational paralysis; or, at the opposite extreme, an overly receptive, susceptible gullibility to change resulting in a spastic, unreliable faddism. It is obvious that there are times when openness to change is appropriate and other times when it may be disastrous. Organizations, in fact, should reward people who act as counterchange agents to create forces against the seduction of novelty for its own sake.

How can the leadership of these new style organizations create an atmosphere of continuity and stability amidst an environment of change? Whitehead put the problem well:

The art of society consists first in the maintenance of the symbolic code, and secondly, in the fearlessness of revision . . . Those societies which cannot combine reverence to their symbols with freedom of revision must ultimately decay . . .

There is no easy solution to the tension between stability

and change. We are not yet an emotionally adaptive society, though we are as close to having to become one as any society in history. Elting Morison suggests in his brilliant essay on change that "we may find at least part of our salvation in identifying ourselves with the adaptive process and thus share some of the joy, exuberance, satisfaction, and security . . . to meet . . . changing times."

The remarkable aspect of our generation is its commitment to change in thought and action. Executive leadership must take some responsibility in creating a climate that provides the security to identify with the adaptive process without fear of losing status. Creating an environment that would increase a tolerance for ambiguity and where one can make a virtue out of contingency, rather than one that induces hesitancy and its reckless counterpart, expedience, is one of the most challenging tasks for the new leadership.

Clarity, Commitment, and Consensus

Organizations, like individuals, suffer from "identity crises." They are not only afflictions that attack during adolescence, but chronic states pervading every phase of organizational development. The new organizations we speak of, with their bands of professional problem-solvers, coping within a turbulent environment, are particularly allergic to problems of identity. Professional and regional orientations lead frequently to fragmentation, intergroup conflicts, and power plays and rigid compartmentalization, devoid of any unifying sense of purpose or mission.

Universities Surpass Business in Subterfuge

The university is a wondrous place for advanced battle techniques, far surpassing their business counterparts in subterfuge and sabotage. Quite often a university becomes a loose collection of competing departments, schools, institutes, committees, centers, programs, largely noncommunicating because of the multiplicity of specialist jargons and interests, and held together, as Robert Hutchins once said, chiefly by a central heating system, or as Clark Kerr amended, by questions of what to do about the parking problem.

The modern organizations we speak of are composed of men who love independence as fiercely as the ancient Greeks; but it is also obvious that they resist what every Athenian, as a matter of course, gave time and effort for: "building and lifting up the common life."

Thucydides has Pericles saying:

We are a free democracy . . . . We do not allow absorption in our own affairs to interfere with participation in the city's. We regard men who hold aloof from public affairs as useless; nevertheless we yield to none in independence of spirit and complete self-reliance.

A modern version of the same problem (which the Greeks couldn't solve either, despite the lofty prose) has been stated by the president of a large university:

The problem with this institution is that too few people understand or care about the overall goals. Typically they see the world through their own myopic departmental glasses; i.e., too constricted and biased. What we need more of are professional staff who can wear not only their own school or departmental "hat" but the overall university hat.

Specialism, by definition, implies a peculiar slant, a skewed vision of reality. McLuhan tells a good joke on this subject. A tailor went to Rome and managed to get an audience with his Holiness. Upon his return, a friend asked him, "What did the Pope look like?" The tailor answered, "a 41 regular."

Having heard variations of this theme over the years, a number of faculty and administrators, who thought they could "wear the overall university hat" formed what later came to be known as "the HATS group." They came from a variety of departments and hierarchical levels and represented a rough microcosm of the entire community. The HATS group has continued to meet over the past several years and has played an important role in influencing university policy.

There are a number of functions that leadership can perform in addition to developing HATS groups. First, it can identify and support those persons who are "linking pins," individuals with a psychological and intellectual affinity for a number of languages and cultures. Secondly, it can work at the places where the different disciplines and organizations come together (for example, setting up new interdisciplinary programs), in order to create more intergroup give and take.

The third important function for leadership is developing and shaping identity. Organizations, not only the academic disciplines, require philosophers, individuals who can provide articulation between seemingly inimical interests, and who can break down the pseudospecies, transcend vested interests, regional ties, and professional biases. This is precisely what Mary Parker Follett had in mind when she discussed leadership in terms of an ability to bring about a "creative synthesis" between differing codes of conduct.

Chester Barnard in his classic *Functions of the Executive* (1938) recognized this, as well as the personal energy and cost of political process. He wrote, "it seems to me that the struggle to maintain cooperation among men should as surely destroy some men morally as battle destroys some physically."

The Problem of Growth and Decay

For the leader, the organization has to take a conscious responsibility for its own evolution; without a planned methodology and explicit direction, the enterprise will not realize its full potential. For the leader, this is the issue of revitalization and it confronts him with the ultimate challenge: growth or decay.

The challenge for the leader is to develop a climate of inquiry and enough psychological and employment security for continual reassessment and renewal. This task is connected with the leader's ability to collect valid data, feed it back to the appropriate individuals, and develop action planning on the basis of the data. This three-step "action-research" model sounds deceptively simple. In fact, it is difficult. Quite often, the important data cannot be collected by the leader for many obvious reasons. Even when the data are known, there are many organizational short circuits and "dithering devices" that distort and prevent the data from getting to the right places at the right time. And even when data-gathering and feedback are satisfactorily completed, organizational inhibitions may not lead to implementation.

In response to the need for systematic data collection, many organizations are setting up "Institutional Research" centers that act as basic fact-gathering agencies. In some cases, they become an arm of policy-making. Mostly, they see as their prime responsibility the collection and analysis of data that bear on the effectiveness with which the organization achieves its goals.

Fact-gathering, by itself, is rarely sufficient to change attitudes and beliefs and to overcome natural inertia and unnatural resistance to change. Individuals have an awesome capacity to "selectively inattend" to facts that may in the eyes threaten their self-esteem. Facts and reason may be the least potent forms of influence that man possesses.

Some progressive organizations are setting up organizational development departments that attempt to reduce the "implementation gap" between information and new ideas and action. These OD departments become the center for the entire strategic side of the organization, including not only long-run planning, but plans for gaining participation and commitment to the plans. This last step is the most crucial for the guarantee of successful implementation.

NEW CONCEPTS FOR LEADERSHIP

In addition to substantive competence and comprehension of both social and technical systems, the new leader will have to possess interpersonal skills, not the least of which is the ability to defer his own immediate desires and gratifications in order to cultivate the talents of others. Let us examine some of the ways leadership can successfully cope with the new organizational patterns.

Understanding the "social territory"

"You gotta know the territory," sang "Professor" Harold Hill to his fellow salesmen in *The Music Man*. The "social territory" encompasses the complex and dynamic interaction of individuals, roles, groups, organizational and cultural systems. Organizations are, of course, legal, political, technical, and economic systems. For our purposes, we will focus on the social system.

Analytic tools, drawn primarily from social psychology and sociology, are available to aid in the understanding of the social territory. But we need more than such tools to augment and implement these understandings. Leadership is as much craft as science. The main instrument or "tool" for the leader-as-a-craftsman is himself and how creatively he can use his own personality. This is particularly important for leaders to understand, for, like physicians, they are just as capable of spreading as of curing disease. And again, like the physician, it is important that the leader heed the injunction "heal thyself" so that he does not create pernicious effects unwittingly. Unless the leader understands his actions and effects on others, he may be a "carrier" rather than a solver of problems. Understanding the social territory and how one influences it is related to the "action-research" model of leadership mentioned earlier: (1) collect data, (2) feed it back to appropriate sources, and (3) action-planning. The "hangup" in most organizations is that people tend to distort and suppress data for fear of real or fancied retaliation. (Samuel Goldwyn, a notorious martinet, called his top staff together after a particularly bad box-office flop and said: "Look, you guys, I want you to tell me exactly what's wrong with this operation and my leadership—even if it means losing your job."!)

The Concept of 'System-Intervention"

Another aspect of the social territory that has key significance for leadership is the idea of system. At least two decades of research have been making this point unsuccessfully. Research has shown that productivity can be modified by what the group thinks important, that training effects fade out and deteriorate if they do not fit the goals of the social system, that cohesiveness is a powerful motivator, that conflict between units is a major problem in organizations, that individuals take many of their cues and derive a good deal of their satisfaction from their primary work group, that identification with the small work group turns out to be the only stable predictor of productivity, and so on.

The fact that this evidence is so often cited and rarely acted upon leads one to infer that there is some sort of involuntary reflex that makes us locate problems in faulty individuals rather than in malfunctioning social systems. What this irrational reflex is based upon is not altogether clear. But individuals, living amidst complex and subtle organizational conditions, do tend to oversimplify and distort complex realities so that people rather than conditions embody the problem. This tendency toward personalization can be observed in many situations. In international affairs, we blame our troubles with France on de Gaulle, or talk sometimes as though we believe that replacing Diem, or Khanh, or Ky will solve our problems with the Saigon government. Other illustrations can be seen when members of organizations take on familial nicknames, such as "Dad," "Big Brother," "Man," "Mother Hen," "Dutch Uncle," etc. We can see it in distorted polarizations such as the "good guy" leader who is too trusting, and his "hatchet man" assistant who is really to blame. These grotesques seem to bear such little resemblance to the actual people that one has to ask what psychological needs are being served by this complex labeling and stereotyping.

One answer was hinted at earlier in the Freud quote. He said that work provides an outlet for displacing emotional components onto professional work and the human relations associated with work. If there were no "Big Daddys" or "Queen Bees," we would have to invent them as therapeutic devices to allay anxieties about less romantic, more immediate mothers and fathers, brothers and sisters.

Another reason for this tendency toward personalization is related to the wounded narcissism leaders often suffer. Organizations are big, complex, wondrous—and hamstrung with inertia. Impotence and alienation imprison the best of men, the most glorious of intentions. There is a myth that the higher one goes up the ladder, the more freedom and potency one experiences. In fact, this is frequently not the case, as almost any chief executive will report: the higher he goes the more tethered and bound he may feel by expectations and commitments. In any case, as one gets entrapped by inertia and impotence, it is easier to blame heroes and villains than the system. For if the problems are embroidered into the fabric of the social system, complex as they are, the system can be changed. But if the problems are people, then the endemic lethargy can be explained away by the difficulty—the impossibility—of "changing human nature."

If management insists on personalizing problems that arise from systems, serious repercussions must result. In the new organizations—where roles will be constantly changing and ambiguous, where changes in one subsystem will clearly affect other subsystems, where diverse activities have to be coordinated and integrated, where individuals work simultaneously in many different jobs and groups—a system viewpoint must be developed. Just as psychotherapists find it difficult to treat a "problem child" without treating the entire family, it will be more difficult to influence individual behavior without working with his particular subsystem level if the intervention is to last and serve its purpose.

An Agricultural Model of Leadership

I have not found the right word or phrase that accurately portrays the concept of leadership I have in mind—which can be summarized as follows: an active method for producing conditions where people and ideas and resources can be seeded, cultivated, and integrated to optimum effectiveness and growth.

The phrase "other-directedness," unfortunately, has taken on the negative tone of "exclusively tuned into outside cues." For awhile I thought that "applied biology" might capture the idea, for it connotes an ecological point of view; a process of observation, careful intervention, and organic development. I have also noticed that many biologists and physicians (particularly those physicians who either have no practices or went into public health, psychiatry, or research) are excellent administrators. Socrates used a close and congenial metaphor to symbolize the role of the teacher, the "mid-wife," someone who helped others to give birth to creations. . . .

The most appropriate metaphor I have found to characterize adaptive leadership is an "agricultural" model. The leader's job, as I have stated, is to build a climate where growth and development are culturally induced. Roy Ash, an astute industrialist and chairman of Litton Industries, remarked recently, "If the larger corporations, classically viewed as efficient machines rather than hothouses for fomenting innovation, can become both of these at once, industrial competition will have to take on new dimensions." I think Ash captures exactly the shift in metaphor I am getting at, from a mechanical model to an organic one. Up until very recent times, the metaphor most commonly used to describe power and leadership in organizations derived from Helmholtz's laws of mechanics. Max Weber, who first conceptualized the model of bureaucracy, wrote, "Bureaucracy is like a modern judge who is a vending machine into which the pleadings are inserted along with the fee and which then disgorges the judgment with its reasons mechanically derived from the code."

The language of organizational dynamics in most contemporary writings reflects the machine metaphor: social engineering, equilibrium, friction, resistance, force-field, etc. The vocabulary for adaptive organizations requires an organic metaphor, a description of a process, not structural arrangements. This process must include such terms as open, dynamic systems, developmental, organic, adaptive, etc.

All of these strategic and practical considerations lead to a totally new concept of leadership. The pivotal aspect of this concept is that it relies less on the leader's substantive knowledge about a particular topic than it does on the understanding and possession of skills summarized under the agricultural model.

This new concept of leadership embraces four important

sets of competencies: (1) knowledge of large, complex human systems; (2) practical theories of intervening and guiding these systems, theories that encompass methods for seeding, nurturing, and integrating individuals and groups; (3) interpersonal competence, particularly the sensitivity to understand the effects of one's own behavior on others and how one's own personality shapes his particular leadership style and value system; and (4) a set of values and competencies which enables one to know when to confront and attack, if necessary, and when to support and provide the psychological safety so necessary for growth.

It is amusing and occasionally frustrating to note that the present view of leadership which I have referred to as an agricultural model, is often construed as "passive" or "weak" or "soft" or more popularly "permissive," and generally dismissed with the same uneasy, patronizing shrug one usually reserves for women who try, however clumsily, to play a man's game. The fact is that the role of leadership described here is clearly more demanding and formidable than any other historical precedent, from king to Pope.

It may be that the common tendency to give this new leadership role such passive and effeminate names betrays the anxiety that many must feel at the downfall of that distant, stern, strict Victorian father, whose surrogate has led us so often as teacher, military commander, and corporation president. Perhaps that is the only kind of authority we have experienced first hand, or know intimately, or consider legitimate. But if this new man of power—other-directed and interpersonally competent—takes over the dominant role, as he now seems to be doing, then not only will new myths and archetypes have to substitute for the old, family ones, but new ways—perhaps new legends—will have to be developed to dramatize the rise of new heroes. Let us hope that this new tradition of leadership is not only more potent, but in the long run more gratifying.

PEOPLE—THE WELLSPRINGS OF ORGANIZATIONAL ENERGY*

by Robert R. Blake and Jane Srygley Mouton

It is one thing to recognize that changes may be essential to the achievement of corporate success. It is quite a different thing to do something about it. The bridge that can carry an organization from recognition to action is *people*. Human energy is what powers every corporate achievement. Corporate excellence on paper is nothing more than a statement of good intentions until human energy is applied through the exercise of business skills and judgment. For one man to manage another man effectively, he must comprehend and utilize his understanding of at least four issues: how corporate culture influences the way men think and feel and their will to the behavior of others; and the dynamics of his own behavior. Without these kinds of behavior and the skills of using them in managerial situations, boundless energies otherwise available remain locked up or are at least only partially released. The full potential is unrealized. Striving for corporate excellence becomes driving for corporate excellence. Driving for corporate excellence, no matter how well intended, produces resistance to change in the form of antagonisms, feelings of being taken advantage of, exploited, or left out. Driving for change only ensures that this major barrier to corporate excellence, resistance, which seems always present in some degree, is not eliminated or overcome. Indeed, the barrier of resentments may be expanded.

Many companies have endeavored to improve themselves without taking advantage of knowledge of the dynamics of behavior. They have assumed that barriers to excellence are found on the business side of the business only. Usually, problems *are*

* Reprinted with permission from *Building a Dynamic Corporation Through Grid Organization Development* by Robert R. Blake & Jane Srygley Mouton, Addison-Wesley Publishing Company, 1969.

162

on the business side of the business. Problems of the corporation obviously do show up in operational difficulties, but reasons for the operational difficulties are most likely to be human in character and origin. Pressure for improving operational results without resolving the human problems causing operational limitations is but the treatment of symptons.

A foundation to operational excellence is in the comprehension and use of a model of what constitutes excellence in problem-solving behavior. When people have acquired skills of solving problems in their human interactions, these skills can be used to eliminate and confront operational barriers to excellence.

Properties in a model of excellence for human behavior can be specified just as in other parts of business life. In the following section, key properties in managerial behavior are specified. For each property, the Grid, briefly described below, is used to demonstrate options and alternatives available to the management in any company.

The Grid

The Grid clarifies and crystallizes many of the fundamentals of behavior dynamics in business. Here is the basis of it. Any man who is working for a firm has assigned responsibilities. This is true whether he works at a very low level or high up in the organization. Whenever he acts as a manager, there are two matters on his mind. One is production—the results of his efforts. How much he thinks about results can be described as his degree of concern for production. (See Figure 1) The horizontal axis of the Grid stands for concern for production. It is a nine-point continuum, where 9 shows high concern for production and 1, low concern. A manager is also thinking about those around him, either bosses, colleagues, or those whose work he directs. The vertical axis represents his concern for people. This too is on a nine-point continuum with 9 a high degree and 1 a low degree.

The Grid reflects these two concerns. It does so in a way that enable men to comprehend how the two concerns interact. At points of intersection are theories. They are theories that every manager uses when he thinks about how to get results through people, whether he realizes it or not. They also can be used to analyze the patterns of interactions among managers which comprise the corporate culture. Five of the many possible theories or styles stand out clearly. They appear in the four corners and in the center of the Grid.

As can be seen from the Grid diagram, in the lower right corner, 9,1 represents a great deal of concern for output but little for the people who are expected to produce. At the opposite corner of the Grid, the top left, is the 1,9 theory. It is the style that puts major emphasis on people and little on the results required for a healthy business. In the lower left Grid corner is 1,1. It may not seem that any manager could have almost no concern for either people or production, yet people managing in this manner have been found in many businesses, going

THE MANAGERIAL GRID

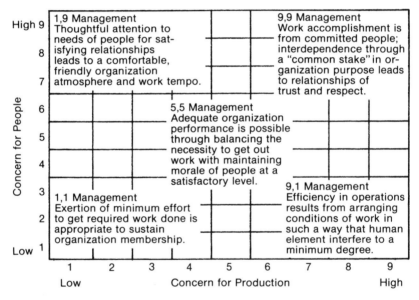

Fig. 1 The Grid®. (*Source:* R. R. Blake and J. S. Mouton, *The Managerial Grid.* Houston: Gulf Publishing Company, 1964, p. 10. Reproduced by permission.)

through the motions of being part of the firm but really not contributing to it. They are not doers but freeloaders. They have not quit their jobs, but they walked out mentally, perhaps many years ago.

In the center is the 5,5 style. The manager with this approach is seeking the middle of the road. His attitude is, "Get results but don't kill yourself. Do the job but find a comfortable tempo. Do not push too much or you will be seen as a *hard nose.* Do not let people off too easily or they will think you are *soft.* Be *fair but firm.*" The 5,5 manager is an "organization man." The upper right corner, the 9,9 position, denotes high concern for production united with high concern for people. A man who manages according to this theory stresses fact-finding as the key to solving problems. Whenever disagreements arise, he sees to it that facts are dug into. The problem is thrashed through to solution in an open and aboveboard way that can result in mutual understanding with full commitment to conclusions reached. A team of men working together in a 9,9 manner know that they have a common stake in the outcome of their endeavors. They therefore mesh effort in an interdependent way. The 9,9 theory is a synergistic theory.

The single most significant premise on which Grid Organization Development rests is that the 9,9 way of doing business is acknowledged universally by managers as the soundest way to manage to achieve excellence. This conclusion has been verified through empirical studies of a statistical character in North and South America, Asia, the Middle East, Europe, and Africa. The 9,9 theory defines a model that men, based on their own convictions, say they want not only for a model of their own conduct but also for a model of what they want their companies to become. Key properties of behavioral dynamics are outlined below to clarity 9,9. Characteristics of a 9,9 corporate culture are contrasted with corporate cultures that reflect other theories of management.

Personal Goals and Corporate Objectives

Every manager has at some time in his career set a personal goal of success. Inherent in the idea of personal success is the advancement of self-interest by accomplishments which will further one's personal situation. According to older theories of motivation, pursuit of self-interest was the all-consuming factor in the personal drive for success.

Self-interest is certainly at the very foundation of personal effort. This is as it should be. A free-enterprise system places the obligation on each individual to take responsibility for himself and his own welfare. It presumes that the motivation of men is dominated by self-interest. The reason that so much corporate emphasis is placed on reward for merit is to bring self-interest in line with corporate needs, for men can compete with one another under rules of reward for merit and find that self-interest and social justice are closely connected. This does not mean that managers are always capable of exercising valid judgments of merit, or that they always do so. It does mean that the desirability of doing so is widely acknowledged. It is not to say that politics, old-school ties, and being in the right place at the right time are uninfluential. It is to say that when these matters are thought about more deeply, their lack of objectivity is recognized.

But is all action motivated by self-interest, by "looking out for Number One?" Are the motivations of service, altruism, or making a worthwhile contribution no more than delusions? No. Once an individual identifies with a larger cause and takes it within himself, his actions often are better understood as being motivated by his contributing to the solution of larger and broader issues with a minimum of self-reference. It might be said that because he has taken a larger concern within himself, this is still self-interest. But whether it is or is not is irrelevant. What is important is that he is applying his energies in pursuit of other objectives which, at the least, are only indirectly selfish.

It is in the character of human behavior that people identify with and work toward the achievement of broader objectives in contrast with objectives narrowly defined as self-interests. Patriotism is one example. The professor who becomes so absorbed in his subject that he loses himself in it is another. How parents work toward the health, success, and security of their children is a third. A fourth is the manager who finds his job so absorbing that the day is gone before he knows it. These are examples of people who are not motivated by self-interest, at least in any narrow concept of what that means.

All this is fundamental to an understanding and appreciation of corporate excellence and how it happens that people are prepared to commit their full energies to achieving it.

In any well-managed company, those who manage it have taken upon themselves a personal responsibility for its success. Corporate success and personal contribution to it replaces or becomes identical with self-interest. The manager's motivation seems to be selfless much as a patriot's motivation is genuinely selfless, but self-interest and corporate interest have become so merged and blended that it is meaningless to view them as distinct. They are one and the same.

Achieving conditions of motivation throughout a company

is essential for the pursuit of excellence. Otherwise striving for excellence becomes driving for excellence, because corporate interests and self-interests have not been merged. When men master success by being effective in working with and through others in the achievement of the purposes of the firm, there is no contradiction between personal objectives and corporate objective (9,9). They are congruent.

Is the corporation, with profitability its ultimate objective, the kind of institution that people can be asked to identify their interests with in this manner? Or do its financial objectives disqualify it from meriting this kind of identification? This is a question that many managers have asked themselves. Young people of today seem to be more frequently answering it in the negative. Every person working for a corporation is confronted with answering this question for himself. It is unlikely that others can answer it for him, or that this book can do so. But some further questions can put another perspective on this matter. For example, what other institutions have furthered the well-being of societies as much as the corporation? What others are able to provide the kind of meaningful experiences a corporation provides to the individuals who work within them? What other institutions have been able to create as many opportunities for individual growth and development and success in return for meritorious effort and contribution? This is not to say that corporations have achieved a high degree of skill in the utilization of people. Nor is it to say that for many work is little more than repetitious and humdrum. These are signs of weaknesses in the conduct of the corporation rather than limitations of the concept of it. Organization development has a major objective of strengthening the capacities of corporations to utilize people to permit the sound merging of self-interests with corporate interest. Corporate excellence is approached when this merger has been achieved.

In much of corporate life today, personal success and corporate success are not integrated. Sometimes a man's efforts toward personal success are maintained continually at a high level. Yet he is ineffective in working with and through others, unable to arouse their commitment or to release their creativity. He attempts to achieve organization goals by driving others (9,1). The goal of success is not absent, but the likelihood of achieving it is lessened. The side effects of bottling up resentments rather than liberating the motivations of others reduce the problem-solving capacity of the firm.

Sometimes men find a replacement for goals of high success for themselves or the corporation. They substitute just going along to get along, with all that is implied for adjustment rather than problem solving, of accepting a half loaf rather than a whole (5,5). Usually the manager who acts in this manner accepts the *status quo* arrangements of cultural practices and seeks evolutionary change and improvement.

Sometimes the desire to be liked and accepted becomes the model of success (1,9) rather than the desire to be effective, to contribute, and to be respected. This results in appeasement, backing off from convictions to be accepted, and embracing the views of others. Then organization members can be warm, tranquil, friendly, and well related. Meanwhile the firm is becoming soft and flabby, sluggish, and unresponsive to its real problems and opportunities.

Occasionally men abandon objectives of personal success. They do not seek to contribute to the firm, nor do they try to maintain membership in a congenial network of social relationships. They desire to make only the minimum contribution that will permit them to stay in the company, to be paid, and to enjoy the advantages of welfare and retirement benefits (1,1).

Sometimes one of these postures becomes deeply entrenched in an organization. What has been used here to describe the character of a manager becomes the character of all management. This is why significant emphasis is placed upon the management of culture as the gateway to excellence. It is most unusual for a model of corporate excellence to find fulfillment in a company where the management style is 9,1, 5,5, 1,9, or 1,1. Trying to achieve corporate excellence without achieving managerial objectives which are built upon a 9,9 foundation of managerial excellence produces a fusion which unites the two. The result can be corporate achievement based upon the personal success and gratification of its managers.

THE FUNCTION OF LEADERSHIP IN ACADEMIC INSTITUTIONS

by T. R. McConnell

Speaking some years ago at an institute for new college presidents, I observed that as I had visited colleges and universities, I had been struck by the aimlessness, the drift, the opportunism, the disunity of some, and the purposefulness, the economy, the integrality of others—although the latter were much less numerous. There was enormous disparity among institutions, large and small, in the clarity and coherence of their purposes, and in the pertinence of activities to professed aims.

I noted that many institutions that called themselves liberal arts colleges had lost a distinctive character, and, in fact, had ceased to be liberal arts colleges by making all sorts of concessions to vocationalism. I had visited several self-styled liberal arts institutions in which the largest number of majors were in such fields as business administration, recreation, physical education, industrial arts, home economics, petroleum geology, medical technology, and education. McGrath, of course, has carefully documented this phenomenon.[1]

It could have been said also that a large number of state colleges, many of them newly designated as universities, were busy multiplying majors and specialties and organizing schools and colleges, apparently preferring to become pale reflections of major universities instead of serving a narrower range of purposes with some quality and distinction.

In my address, I went on to say that many universities were essentially collections of relatively autonomous professional schools and specialized departments; these loosely connected parts were *in* the university but not *of* the university, in spite of

[1] From *Educational Record*, Spring 1968. © Copyright 1968 by the American Council on Education. Reprinted with permission. Earl J. McGrath, *Are Liberal Arts Colleges Becoming Professional Schools?* (New York: Teachers College Press, Columbia University, 1958).

the fact that modern scholarship had become more dependent on related disciplines at the same time that it had become more specialized. I added that it would take vigorous and creative leadership to make a true university out of what was now a multiuniversity. Some years later, as you are well aware, President Clark Kerr documented the disunity of the university and popularized the term "multiversity." His widely quoted characterization will come to mind:

The multiversity is an inconsistent institution. It is not one community but several—the community of the undergraduate and the community of the graduate; the community of the humanist, the community of the social scientist, and the community of the scientist; the communities of the professional schools; the community of all the nonacademic personnel; the community of the administrators. . . . In the multiversity many parts can be added and subtracted with little effect on the whole or even little notice taken or any blood spilled.

He described the modern university as a mechanism held together by administrative rules and powered by money.[2] At the moment, in the University of California, we seem to have more administrative rules than money.

Kerr wrote as if he considered the progressive disintegration of the university to be inevitable. In writing on the problem of leadership in the university, Mooney expressed the same fatalism and deplored the consequences of disunity.

The net effect . . . (he said) is that no one has the power to take positive leadership in the development of the university as an integral enterprise—not the line administrator, his staff, the faculty councils, the departments, or the colleges. Such power as any individual or group possesses is functionally negative with respect to the whole, fully effective only in denial of what others may try, destructive of initiative and integration, self-propelling into further snarls and splits, productive of deeper paralysis.[3]

Mostly a mediator

Combine the progressive dissipation of authority, the seg-

[2] Clark Kerr, *The Uses of the University* (Cambridge: Harvard University Press, 1963), pp. 19, 20.

[3] Ross L. Mooney, "The Problem of Leadership in the University," *Harvard Educational Review*, Winter 1963 (33), pp. 42-57.

mental autonomy of numerous units of organization, the personal authority of the faculty professional, the empire building of the faculty enterpreneur, numerous and often conflicting external pressures on the university, and default of strong unifying leadership, and you get a multiversity. One of the effects of these phenomena is to curtail administrative initiative. The president's role, according to Kerr, is reduced to that of negotiating among competing and often conflicting forces.

The president in the multiversity is leader, educator, creator, initiator, wielder of power, pump; he is *also* office holder, caretaker, inheritor, consensus seeker, persuader, bottle-neck.

After listing the president's multiple roles, Kerr added, "But he is mostly a mediator."[4]

Kerr declared that the first job of the mediator. is to establish peace among the competing parties. The second is to promote progress. "Progress" may, however, be toward greater disunity, and the process may be irreversible.

But all hope for internal coherence may not be lost. Some college and university presidents may take a strong hand in determining the central directions of institutional development. The presidents who succeed in exercising such leadership will not confuse their incidental and their principal functions. The late Chancellor Samuel P. Capen of the University of Buffalo once said that a university president should be preoccupied with his institution's purposes and with the relevance of means to ends. He declared that a president qualified for his position buries himself—but not on routine, or in trivial detail, or in mediation between competing interests, or even in the serious emergencies which inevitably occur.

He buries himself in the grand plan of his institution's future . . . Except for the elaboration and the furtherance of the grand plan, there is no need of a president. Almost everything else he does could be done by some other officer, a good deal of it by a clerk; and just about as well, perhaps better.[5]

President Perkins of Cornell, after conceding that the faculty must always determine the shape of educational policy,

---

[4] Kerr, p. 36.
[5] Samuel P. Capen, *The Management of Universities* (Buffalo: Steward & Foster, 1953), pp. 69, 70.

went on to say:

But someone must be concerned with the institution as a whole, the activities it supports, the public face it presents, and the private concerns with which it is occupied. This job cannot be divided among disparate elements of the university. So it is the administrator—the president and others with management responsibility, cooperating with faculty and student leaders—who must be concerned both with the apparatus of the university and with the idea it represents. He must be able to involve himself directly in the central academic business of the university, to exert educational leadership, to be an agent for both stability and change.

Perkins then concluded:

While it is true that the president and dean must not be too vigorous in throwing their weight around, the role of university president as bashful educational leader is mostly non-sense and greatly overplayed.[6]

Perkins was not suggesting, of course, that a university president should try to ride roughshod over his faculty. He observed, in fact, that faculty arm-twisting in support of an administrator's ideas could easily wreck an institution, and characterized presidential leadership as consisting, in large part, of seeking out faculty members with innovative ideas, and giving them encouragement and financial support.[7]

Democratic management

Faculty participation in policy formation and university government is here to stay. In colleges and universities—and in business and industry as well—there is a new emphasis on democratic processes. One of the great spokesmen for humane and democratic management was Douglas McGregor, who served as president of Antioch College and also as professor of industrial management at MIT. It was he who wrote:

The motivation, the potential for development, the capacity for assuming responsibility, the readiness to direct behavior toward organizational goals are all present in people. Management does not put them there. It is a re-

[6] James A. Perkins, *The University in Transition* (Princeton, N.J.: Princeton University Press, 1966), pp. 57, 81.
[7] *Ibid.*, p. 56.

sponsibility of management to make it possible for people to recognize and develop these human characteristics for themselves.

The essential task of management is to arrange organizational conditions and methods of operation so that people can achieve their own goals *best* by directing *their own* efforts toward organizational objectives.[8]

Perhaps among all of the colleges and universities in the United States, Antioch College is best known for its emphasis on community participation and responsibility. Its administrative committee, which is formally only advisory to the President but which actually exercises a strong influence on institutional policy and operation, has long been composed of administrative officers, faculty members, and students. At Antioch, McGregor found a laboratory in which he could test his theories of democratic management. An Antioch faculty member is reported to have said of him that, "If there was anything he was trying to overcome or destroy, it was the institutional habit of talking about the virtues of democracy while running affairs autocratically."[9]

McGregor nevertheless discovered that administrators must make decisions. Just before his resignation at Antioch took effect, he made the following confession:

Before coming to Antioch I had observed and worked with top executives as an adviser in a number of organizations. I thought I knew how they felt about their responsibilities and what led them to behave as they did. I even thought that I could create a role for myself that would enable me to avoid some of the difficulties they encountered. I was wrong! . . .

I believed, for example, that a leader could operate successfully as a kind of adviser to his organization. I thought I could avoid being a "boss." Unconsciously, I suspect, I hoped to duck the unpleasant necessity of making difficult decisions, of taking the responsibility for one course of action among many uncertain alternatives, of making mistakes and taking the consequences. I thought that maybe I could operate so that everyone would like me —that "good human relations" would eliminate all discord

[8] Warren G. Bennis and Edgar H. Schein (eds), *Leadership and Motivation: Essays of Douglas McGregor* (Cambridge: MIT Press, 1966), p. 15.
[9] *Ibid.*, p. 56.

and disagreement. I could not have been more wrong. It took a couple of years, but I finally began to realize that a leader cannot avoid responsibility for what happens to his organization. In fact, it is a major function of the top executive to take on his own shoulders the responsibility for resolving the uncertainties that are always involved in important decisions. Moreover, since no important decision ever pleases everyone in the organization, he must also absorb the displeasure, and sometimes severe hostility, of those who would have taken a different course. A colleague recently summed up what my experience has taught me in these words: "A good leader must be tough enough to kick a man when he is down." This notion is not in the least inconsistent with humane, democratic leadership. Good human relations develop out of strength, not of weakness.[10]

College and university administrators should not act without consulting or fully involving those who may be affected or who will have to carry out a policy or decision in day-to-day operation. Nevertheless, administrators must act. To do so often requires quiet and unpretentious courage.

Many administrators, whether from lack of courage or failure to comprehend their roles, do everything possible to avoid making decisions or taking initiative. Hutchins once observed that many administrators busy themselves with so many activities that they should leave to subordinates that they have no time to do anything important; they conscientiously take their salaries and never administer at all. He referred to these functionaries as mere office holders.[11] A former vice chancellor on one of the University of California campuses has said that:

> At the present time not less than 60 percent of all academics in the universities in this country have so profound a distaste for the classroom and for the pains of genuine scholarship or creative thought that they will seize upon anything—curriculum iconography, faculty politics, bureaucratized research, *anything*—to exempt themselves respectably from each.[12]

[10] *Ibid.*, pp. 67, 68.

[11] Robert M. Huchins, "The Administrator," *Journal of Higher Education*, November 1946 (17), pp. 395-407.

[12] Robert A. Nisbet, "What Is An Intellectual?" *Commentary*, December 1965 (40), pp. 93-101.

The same psychological mechanism, if my observation is correct, characterizes 60 percent, if not more, of all academic administrators.

Administrators must act

One of the most crucial tests of administrative competence is to choose able administrative associates and subordinates and to delegate to them a high degree of authority, responsibility, and discretion. In a memorandum on possible administrative reorganization prepared after the Berkeley student disturbances in the fall of 1964, I wrote as follows:

Although . . . great progress has been made in administrative decentralization, there should be an immediate study of the desirability of still further delegation of responsibility and authority from the President to the heads of the several campuses, which may require further delegation of authority by the Regents to the President himself . . . It would be senseless, of course, to put greater authority in the hands of those incapable of exercising it intelligently and effectively. But the point is that the heads of the campuses should be administrative officers to whom great authority could be delegated *with confidence,* and it will be impossible to persuade highly qualified men to take the chancellorships unless they are assured the privilege of making the decisions which will permit them to administer their campuses efficiently and to secure the confidence and cooperation of their faculties.

Admittedly, there are dangers in such extensive delegation. It will work only when:

1) The president has full confidence in the chancellor.
2) The chancellor is completely loyal to the president.
3) The president feels reasonably certain that the chancellor will consult with him when matters of fundamental policy are in question. This, of course, means that the chancellors must be very clear about agreed upon policies and sensitive to policy implications of particular decision, especially those that raise new policy questions or require new interpretations of previously formulated policies.
4) The president is confident that the chancellors will keep him fully informed concerning the operation of

their campuses and the major decisions that have been made. The same principles should guide internal administration of a particular campus or institution.

The president of a large and complex university or the dean of a large and complicated college will probably, for the most part, have to exercise leadership indirectly through vice presidents, deans, and other administrative officers, as well as through wise and influential members of the faculty. Rourke and Brooks have pointed out that the cabinet system of college and university government has emerged simply because the range of decisions is now so great as to require a division of labor in performing executive functions and a high degree of delegation in the exercise of authority. The president (or dean), becomes, in effect, a prime minister.[13]

Personal interaction

The same authors have described how a large number of routine decisions, that once took up a great deal of administrative time, can now be programed, and many of them can be made by computers. The main reason for programing decisions is to free administrative officers for face-to-face relationships with various participants—for example, with the principal members of their administrative staffs and, especially in colleges and universities, with faculty members themselves at all ranks. Administrators should give far more attention to the intricacies and subtleties of human relationships. And the management of these relationships is a process in which, at least for the foreseeable future, men will retain superiority over machines or routinely administered regulations.[14] In this regard, permit me to quote again from my memorandum on University reorganization:

> I have the impression . . . that face-to-face relationships are seriously lacking at various levels in the University. They have been lacking in meetings of the Academic Senate, in informal relationships between principal administrative officers and members of the faculty, between faculty members and students, and between administrative officers and members of the faculty, between faculty mem-

---

[13] F. E. Rourke and G. E. Brooks, *The Managerial Revolution in Higher Education* (Baltimore, Md.: Johns Hopkins Press, 1966), pp. 110-11.

[14] For further discussion of decision making, see Rourke and Brooks, pp. 32-43 and 113-22.

bers and students, and between administrative officers and students . . . Administration from the office is insufficient to develop the human relationships on which morale and commitment of an organization so heavily depend.

Management and leadership

The importance of face-to-face relationships applies to administration all the way down the line. When, as an academic dean, I was most effective in encouraging fruitful academic enterprises or in promoting curricular innovations, I spent a great deal of time in faculty members' offices and in other informal faculty relationships. As my administrative paper work increased, I spent more and more time at my desk, and less and less time in direct human relationships. I ceased being a leader and became a manager.

The most important distinction an administrator needs to make is that between management and leadership. In a volume which, in a growing literature on the administrative process, is still the most suggestive, Selznick pointed out that the function of leadership is to define the goals of the organization and then "design an enterprise distinctively adapted to these ends, and to see that that design becomes a living reality." Put it another way, the purpose of leadership is to infuse an enterprise with significance beyond the requirements of day-by-day operation. "This institutional leader," said Selznick, "is primarily an expert in the promotion and protection of values."[15]

One of the principal defaults of leadership is the failure to set goals. A second is the failure to test every administrative act, each organizational structure, each educational program, by its relevance to agreed-upon purposes. The failure to chart a university's directions and to stay on course is to expose the institution to cancerous growth from within and to vagrant pressures from without. The function of leadership is to encourage sensitivity to social needs without distorting the university's goals and compromising its inherent values. Similarly, the function of leadership is to respond to internal pressures by encouraging those that embody the institution's purposes and discouraging those that would destroy or compromise its integrity.

The administrator's most important role is to bring to bear on decision making, at all points, the wider reference— the longer

---

[15] Philip Selznick, *Leadership in Administration: A Sociological Interpretation* (Evanston, Ill.: Row, Peterson & Co., 1957), pp. 28, 37.

view. "The university," said Dean Brown of Princeton recently, "is like a corporation with 500 vice presidents and 1,000 products."[16] Said Selznick,

> Members planning different roles, and involved in varying degrees will differ in their ability to understand the reasons behind many decisions. Many members will have only partial views of the organization and only a limited understanding of its objectives and principles, and because of weak or narrowly defined participation, their experience within the organization may offer little opportunity for greater comprehension.[17]

One of the principal purposes of administration is to expand everyone's horizon.

The burden of Selznick's book is, as I said before, the distinction between management and leadership. The manager presumably would be devoted to a certain kind of administrative efficiency. He would be preoccupied with administrative procedures and orderly processes, with lines of authority and channels of communication, with bureaucratic housekeeping, with respect for hierarchies of status and position. The leader, on the other hand, would be concerned with values and the commitment of participants to them; with procedures, regulations, and operations as the embodiment of purpose and not as the manifestations of sacred ritual; with the members as creators of the organization and not its pawns. The leader would consider organization to be expendable because it was merely an instrument for the attainment of shared purposes and values, and new instruments would be necessary from time to time.

But organizations are subject to the law of inertia. After institutionalization has taken place, change becomes difficult. Educational institutions are notoriously conservative. Administrative structures are retained long after they have become dysfunctional. Old knowledge makes way for new reluctantly and belatedly. Schools and colleges train students for jobs that no longer exist or teach them skills no longer used. Professional education lags far behind advanced professional practice. This is the lesson Selznick teaches in the early part of his book.

It is surprising, therefore, to read further on in his volume that "leadership declines in importance as the formal structure

---

16 J. D. Brown, "Organization and Leadership in a Liberal University," *Graduate Journal,* Fall 1964 (6), pp. 333-338.
17 Selznick, p. 98.

approaches complete determination of behavior. Management engineering is then fully adequate to the task."[18]

Fostering instability

I would propose a hypothesis exactly opposite to Selznick's, namely, that after institutionalization, leadership becomes more rather than less essential. The purpose of leadership after a university or college takes on a special character is to appraise ends and means. The leader should challenge and question. He should search for men with new ideas, and help them bring these ideas to fruition. In a word, the most important purpose of leadership in the mature stages of an organization's history is to promote innovation. Earlier, the function of the leader was to foster organizational stability; later, it is to produce at least a certain degree of instability. But perhaps I have misinterpreted the quotation I have just given, for in the last sentence of his volume Selznick wrote as follows:

> If one of the great functions of administration is the exercise of cohesive force in the direction of institutional security, another great function is the creation of conditions that will make possible in the future what is excluded in the present. This requires a strategy of change that looks to the attainment of new capabilities more nearly fulfilling the truly felt needs and aspirations of the institution.[19]

Although there is little research on the process of inducing change in educational organizations—particularly in colleges and universities—we can find some leads in the general literature on organizational and administrative theory. First, an innovative organization is one with a variety of inputs. Diversity in background and experience and a lively interchange of ideas and attitudes is conducive to identification of problems and to ingenuity in suggesting a wide and rich range of alternative solutions. If this is true, academic administrators should resist scholarly and educational inbreeding, and press for diversity both in approaches to a discipline or a specialty and in approaches to the education of undergraduates and graduates.

Likewise, a high degree of *lateral* communication is necessary to stimulate and support change. This suggests that means should be devised to break down departmental insulation, bring

[18] *Ibid.*, p. 92.
[19] *Ibid.*, p. 154.

about greater contact across disciplines, and enable free and inventive minds to find their counterparts in other sections of the university. One of the functions of the administrator is to help an innovator to find allies. As Thompson put it:

> When a new idea is known and supported by groupings beyond the authority grouping, it is not easy to veto it. Multiple group membership helps to overcome the absence of a formal appeal by providing an informal appeal to a free constituency of peers . . . The greater ease of acquiring group membership and the greater legitimacy of groups will reduce the risk of innovation to the individual. Responsibility for new ideas can be shared as can the onus of promoting them.[20]

The recruitment of established and distinguished scholars to the support of educational innovations, especially those promoted by younger faculty, is a highly useful form of support and protection.

Eliminating resentful onlookers

Finally, said Thompson,

> Administrative activities should be dispersed and decentralized down to the level of the innovative area, allowing administrative personnel to become part of integrative problem-solving groups rather than resentful onlookers sharpshooting from the outside.

I take it that this participation should occur, formally and informally, at all levels of the organization. Also, if the faculty excludes central administrators from its major senate committees, as is the case at Berkeley, administrative personnel will have little influence on significant educational decisions. Only by collaboration between faculty and administration can a semblance of coherence be maintained in an institution's affairs.[21]

It is the responsibility of the central administration to stimulate and reward fruitful change in all parts and functions of the university, and to see that these changes move the entire institution more effectively toward a coherent set of goals. This the administration cannot achieve as a group apart from, but only as in-

---

[20] V. A. Thompson, "Bureaucracy and Innovation," *Administrative Science Quarterly,* June 1965 (10), pp. 1-20

[21] Henry J. Wriston, *Academic Procession: Reflections of a College President* (New York: Columbia University Press, 1959), p. 82.

dividuals actively associated with the men and the forces capable of generating progress in the organization. . . .

Although I believe in shared power and shared responsibility, I do not believe an administrator can keep his institution firmly on course and promote fruitful innovation toward desired goals by completely surrendering or even by completely sharing his authority. In discussing the administrator's role as mediator, Kerr seems to say that the administrator himself does not need to possess power. It is presumably sufficient for the administrator to have ready access to each center of power in the institution, to have the opportunity to persuade, to have "a fair chance in each forum of opinion, a chance to paint reality in place of illusion and to argue the cause of reason as he sees it."[22]

I am not ready to accede to this position. My observation, if not my evidence, is that the university president, guided it is true by his academic vice president and academic deans and by appropriate faculty agencies, must retain final authority over the appointment and promotion of faculty and administrative personnel and over the allocation of material resources within the organization. I believe that the president should not hesitate to exercise this power when it is necessary in order to correlate means and ends.

A product of failure

The educational malaise at Berkeley is the product in part of the failure of all concerned—faculty, administrative officers, and regents—to face and resolve the problems of organizational purpose and proportionate emphasis. Protesting students declared that undergraduate curriculum had no coherence, unity, or relevance, and treated students as though they were mere IBM cards. These criticisms were probably too sweeping to be fair. But it is not unjust to say that on the Berkeley campus there is a serious imbalance between research and teaching—an imbalance that has been fostered and perpetuated by senate committees concerned with qualifications for appointment and promotion and an imbalance that needs to be challenged or redressed by administrative leadership and authority. . . .

Student protests and the report in 1966 of the Senate Select Committee on Education have stimulated scattered curricular and instructional innovation on the Berkeley campus. A still more recent report of the Special Committee on Academic Pro-

---

[22] Kerr, p. 40.

gram of the College of Letters and Science, if carried out effectively, would finally bring the College into the twentieth century. It is significant that the latter report says nothing of consequence about the importance of teaching, although the Muscatine Report made the formal recommendation that appointment and promotion committees should require every department to accompany a recommendation for advancement to tenure rank with a formal dossier on the teaching performance of the candidate. No doubt these dossiers could be improved, but I have never been on an appointment committee in which at least perfunctory comments on the candidate's teaching were not included. Neither have I ever been on a promotion committee which worried seriously about the candidate's competence as a teacher or which made a special effort to reward a faculty member for demonstrated excellence in instruction, particularly if time and energy devoted to teaching had curtailed his research publication.

I should expect that under the momentary student pressure, teaching may be taken a little more seriously by the committees, and that an exceptional teacher, here and there, may be promoted without a long bibliography. But I don't expect these cases to be very numerous and I don't expect the concern over teaching to last very long. I doubt that the deficiencies in teaching and undergraduate education at Berkeley will be redressed without decisive administrative intervention, administrative application of relevant sanctions and rewards, and perhaps regential initiative. Administrative and especially regential intervention would probably evoke strong faculty resistance. Administrators would be courageous indeed to open themselves to faculty censure, but the price of significant educational reform may be tension between faculty and administration.

It seems clear that the human resources of an organization must be mobilized toward the attainment of clearly defined goals. These goals need to be widely understood and widely accepted. If there is continuing dialogue about their validity, about the means which are necessary for their attainment, and about the discipline they should impose on the institution's activities, there may be less need for initiative at higher administrative levels and fewer occasions for administrative veto.

A strong hand

If it is true that today a college or university president will

have to exert his leadership primarily through others, it follows
that he must have a strong, if at times indirect, hand in the se-
lection of administrative personnel extending as far as the de-
partment chairmanship, since—at least in large, complex universities—the department chairman is the key administrative officer.
I have always been opposed to the election or rotation of department chairmen. Obviously, the chairman must be acceptable to
the members of the department, and he should be appointed only
after adequate consultation. But appointment is, in my experience, the only way to assure crucial departmental leadership.

In the same way, academic deans and vice presidents must
be acceptable to their constituencies if they are to play an effective role in the collective leadership of the institution.

My conception of administrative roles will be unacceptable
to those who take an extreme position on faculty authority and
control. My attitude, however, seems to me to be consistent
with the statement on the government of colleges and universities recently issued by the American Association of University
Professors, the American Council on Education, and the Association of Governing Boards of Universities and Colleges. What
this statement says concerning the president could be said essentially of other principal academic administrative officers. The
relevant paragraphs are:

> The president, as the chief executive officer of an insti-
> tution of higher education, is measured largely by his capac-
> ity for institutional leadership. He shares responsibility for
> the definition and attainment of goals, for administrative
> action, and for operating the communications system which
> links the components of the academic community. . .As the
> chief planning officer of an institution, the president has a
> special obligation to innovate and initiate. The degree to
> which a president can envision new horizons for his institu-
> tion, and can persuade others to see them and to work
> toward them, will often constitute the chief measure of his
> administration.[23]

The point was put more bluntly, but no less appropriately,
by President Perkins when he wrote:

> *No university can develop in sensible ways unless a*
> *general consensus has been achieved at the heart of its in-*

[23] *AAUP BULLETIN,* Winter 1966 (52), pp. 375-379.

stitutional life among those concerned with its future. But it will be, I suggest, those who spend full time at the business of direction and management who must assure this consensus—who must see to it that educational purpose and institutional interests develop in harmony.[24]

[24] Perkins, p. 59.

PART IV
COMMUNITY CHANGE
AND LEADERSHIP

PART IV
COMMUNITY CHANGE
AND LEADERSHIP

The community in America as we have known it in the past is in deep trouble. The urbanizing trend has created huge urban complexes where face-to-face and geographically distinct groupings of people, traditionally identified as community, are largely lost. On the other hand, rural communities are in many cases becoming "ghost towns" as the small town and farm population migrate to the city. Professionalization, increasing levels of education, and particularly high mobility have led to a loss of commitment to community leadership among a high proportion of our best prepared citizens. This highly mobile and educated type is often more concerned with a "community of interest" related to his profession or organization, than he is with the geographic community.

Within this context, citizens available for community leadership functions are often limited to the more traditional and less educated types who identify with the historical idea of community. They may not be conscious of the inability of many community institutions to meet the needs of the future; they may have too limited perspectives from which to solve the pressing problems that confront them. If this perspective is to be expanded, if community involvement and development are to attract the interest and time of capable people, and if a new kind of "community" adequate to the needs of the future is to emerge, local leadership must become better prepared to solve problems and capitalize on opportunities that appear.

A basic requirement in understanding leadership issues at the local level is a mechanism for discovering who existing leaders are. The first selection, "Locating Leaders in Local Communities," is an excellent summary and critique of some of the most common and thoroughly-tested approaches. Decision-making, social activity, reputation, and positional means of identifying leaders are each analyzed for their adequacy. The authors conclude that each method tends to identify somewhat different kinds of leaders, which emphasizes among other possibilities, the variety of leader roles that occur in most communities. Particularly in urban centers, leaders tend to specialize in interest areas, and relatively few influentials are identified with a variety of issue areas. In small communities there tends to be (as demonstrated by a variety of studies) a much greater involvement of top leaders in a variety of issue areas.

In either small or large communities "reputed" leaders will, to a large degree, be heads or recent heads of major community businesses or other organizations; they will tend also to be the "positional" leaders. However evidence provided by Freeman and his associates suggests that they will not be directly involved in most key decisions that affect the community. Reputation derives largely from position rather than participation.

Participation in decisions appears to rest largely with individuals at subordinate positions in organizations, such as government employees, officials of voluntary organizations, and other "effectors" or functionaries with assigned responsibility for community change (according to Freeman et al.) and decisionmaking. Another category includes the activists who are highly industrious in seeking special interest goals.

The conclusions reached by Freeman and his colleagues emphasize the importance of detailed understanding with respect to the kinds of leadership that exist in varying sizes and types of communities. Each community is somewhat unique and may require careful study to determine which approach to leadership analysis is most appropriate if clear understanding of local power and influence dynamics is to be attained.

The selection by Lassey and Johnson summarizes some of the key issues that must be understood by community development professionals or local leaders if they are to mobilize leadership to accomplish community development. Basic sources of leadership (similar to those defined by Freeman et al.) are described, as are the characteristics or components of an effective local leadership group with community development as a focus.

Since many local communities lack adequate understanding and appreciation of contemporary knowledge about community change, the role of the outside community consultant is discussed at some length. Finally a summary of basic principles of leadership and community development are presented and briefly explained.

Wildavsky conducted a detailed study in the small city of Oberlin, Ohio, to determine the nature of the leadership structure related to a series of major decisions of community-wide relevance. He found that a truly pluralistic system of participation existed, without evidence of "elite" control.

The principle rationale for including this selection is the very carefully description of the process through which a pluralistic community leadership structure operates. If widely shared participation in important community decisions is an ideal to which we would aspire, Wildavsky provides the kind of case study that may stimulate others of us to insist on, and work towards, a similarly democratic and pluralistic leadership structure.

A "strategy for change" in a local institution is described in case study fashion by Cottle. As has Wildavsky, Cottle demonstrates how systematic efforts to attain community participation have produced a new concept of involvement which avoided what could have become a major local crisis. The "strategy" centered on human relations training.

The training involved the entire school community: the superintendent, his administrative staff, the teachers, and lay members of the community. It was focused on personal growth for the specific purpose of *organizational* adaptation to change, with the content of training directly applied to actual problems faced by the organization. Cottle describes the entire process in considerable detail, as an example of how specific training of all members of a single community system can facilitate gradual and systematic change that will accommodate future needs, while avoiding undue crisis and disruption in the process.

One of the key problems and frustrations for any community leader is the difficulty in securing widespread citizen participation. Seaver discusses this dilemma in some detail, with specific reference to the community planning and renewal process.

He emphasizes that citizen participation cannot be systematically programmed merely to gain support for pre-determined goals. Once citizens are truly engaged they are likely to raise serious questions about the adequacy or direction of the goals. This means that any city official or local leader who promotes citizen participation had better be prepared to respond with a commitment to listen and act on clearly articulated citizen demands. This requires two-way communication and two-way education. In any case "the engagement process is unlikely to be orderly, predictable or even rational."

There appears to be no single format or procedure for citizen engagement that applies to all situations, Seaver argues. The sole key element seems to be genuine collaboration between community professionals and citizens. This may require assistance from skilled and specialized staff or consultants to facilitate communication, provide training, and generally serve in a liaison capacity with citizens. However, this kind of professional assistance provides no guarantee of a successful citizen participation process, since ultimately it is the planners and officials who must actually engage and respond. Ultimate success with community change may require the closest possible collaboration between officials and the community, as consultants to the community, rather than as policy-makers apart from direct access by citizens.

The final selection by Wileden describes the role and function of the "professional" leader in working with citizens and citizen leaders. Although he emphasizes the rural community context, many of his definitions of professional leader responsibilities have much broader applicability.

Wileden suggests that the professional leader ought to act primarily in a "helping" capacity: to assist lay groups in more effectively defining goals, adequately devising procedures for attaining them, and then providing support and consultation in the process of implementation. It is of critical importance that the professional leader maintain an objective and somewhat detached stance, so as not to be identified with factions or conflicting ideologies. It is all too easy to get emotionally involved in the issues under discussion to the point where effectiveness as an objective consultant is essentially impossible.

As community complexity increases, partly because of accelerating social change, the utility of highly trained and experienced community consultants is likely to increase substantially. This is a kind of leader role that may provide the citizen leader with the support, training, and objective assistance which will enable local leadership to overcome the frustrating obstacles blocking future-oriented community progress.

LOCATING LEADERS IN LOCAL COMMUNITIES: A COMPARISON OF SOME ALTERNATIVE APPROACHES*

by Linton C. Freeman, Thomas J. Fararo, Warner Bloomberg, Jr., and Morris H. Sunshine

Most investigators would probably agree that leadership refers to a complex process whereby a relatively small number of individuals in a collectivity behave in such a way that they effect (or effectively prevent) a change in the lives of a relatively large number. But agreement on theoretical details of the leadership process or on how it is to be studied is another matter. Much of the recent literature on community leadership has been critical. Gibb has suggested that there are a great many kinds of leadership—many different ways in which changes may be effected. He has proposed that leaders be assigned to various types including "the initiator, energizer, harmonizer, expediter, and the like." Banfield has stressed the importance of the distinction between intended and unintended leadership. And both Dahle and Polsby have called attention to the desirability of considering the extent of the effect a given leader has in expediting a particular change and the range of changes over which his effect holds. It seems evident, then, that although these critics might agree with the minimum definition presented above, they would all like to see some additional factors included within its scope.

Polsby has translated the comments of the critics into a set of operational guides for research. He has suggested that a satisfactory study of community leadership must involve a detailed examination of the whole decision-making process as it is exhibited over a range of issues. Here we should have to specify each issue, the persons involved, their intentions, and the extent and

* Reprinted with permission from the *American Sociological Review*, 1963.

nature of their influence if any. Such a program represents an ideal that might be used to think about the process of community leadership. But as a research strategy, this plan raises many problems.

In the first place, both influence and intention are concepts presenting great difficulty in empirical application. Both require that elaborate observational and interviewing procedures be developed, and both raise reliability problems. May we, for example, take a person's word concerning his intentions, or must they be inferred from his behavior? And even when two persons interact and one subsequently changes his stated position in the direction of the views of the other, it is difficult to prove that influence has taken place. But even if these questions were eliminated, a practical problem would still remain. To follow the prescriptions listed above would be prohibitively expensive, requiring detailed observation of hundreds (or thousands) of individuals over an extended period. To record all interaction relevant to the decisions under study, it would be necessary to observe each person in a large number of varied situations, many of them quite private. Even then it would be difficult to evaluate the impact of the process of observation itself. Given these considerations, Polsby's ideal has never been reached. All existing studies of community leadership represent some compromise.

Most authors of community leadership studies would probably agree that the critics are on the right track. But most have been willing (or perhaps forced by circumstances) to make one or more basic assumptions in order to achieve a workable research design. Four types of compromise have been common. They will be discussed below.

Perhaps the most realistic of the compromise studies are those based on the assumption that active participation in decision making is leadership. Typically, in such studies, one or a series of community decisions are either observed or reconstructed. In so doing, an attempt is made to identify the active participants in the decision-making process. These decision-making studies frequently are restricted to a small number of decisions, and they usually fail to present convincing evidence on the questions of intent and amount of impact. But they do provide a more or less direct index of participation. If they err it is by including individuals who, though present, had little or no impact on the decision. On the face of it this seems preferable to the likelihood of excluding important influentials.

A second compromise approach is to assume that formal authority is leadership. Aside from arbitrarily defining which positions are "on top," these studies underestimate the impact of those not in official positions on the outcomes of the decision-making process.

The third approach assumes that leadership is a necessary consequence of social activity. This assumption leads to studies of social participation. Such studies have used everything from rough indexes of memberships in voluntary associations to carefully constructed scales of activity in such associations, In each case it is reasoned that community leadership results from a high degree of voluntary activity in community affairs. The social participation approach is thus the converse of the study of position. While the former stresses activity, the latter is concerned only with formal authority. But to the extent that activity in voluntary associations leads to having an impact upon community change, activists are leaders.

The final approach assumes that leadership is too complex to be indexed directly. Instead of examining leadership as such, proponents of this approach assess reputation for leadership. Their reasoning suggests that all of the more direct approaches neglect one or another key dimensions of the leadership process. They turn, therefore, to informants from the community itself. Often rather elaborate steps have been taken to insure that the informants are indeed informed. For example, positional leaders may be questioned in order to develop a list of reputed leaders or influentials; then the reported influentials are polled to determine the top influentials. In such cases it is reasonable to suppose that the grossly uninformed are ruled out.

Various critics have condemned the indeterminacy and subjectivity of this procedure. But its defenders reason that the reputational approach is the only way to uncover the subleties of intent, extent of impact, and the like in the leadership process. What, they ask, but a life-long involvement in the activities of a community could possibly yield sophisticated answers to the question "Who are the leaders?" The reputational approach, then, assumes the possibility of locating some individuals who unquestionably meet the criteria of community leadership, and who in turn will be able to name others not so visible to the outside observer.

Currently, the controversy continues. Proponents of one or another of these competing points of view argue for its inherent superiority and the obvious validity of its assumptions. Others take the view that all of these approaches get at leadership. But these are empirical questions; they can be answered only on the basis of comparison, not by faith or by rhetoric. A number of partial contrasts have been published, but so far no systematic overall comparison of these procedures has been reported. The present report represents such an attempt. An effort is made to determine the degree to which these several procedures agree or disagree in locating community leaders.

The data presented here represent a part of a larger study of leadership in the Syracuse, N. Y. metropolitan area. . . .

DECISION-MAKING

The study of participation in the decision-making process was of central concern in the Syracuse study. The first major task of the project team was to select a set of community problems or issues which would provide a point of entry into a pool (or pools) of participants in the decision-making process. Interviews were conducted with 20 local specialists in community study and with 50 informants representing diverse segments of the city's population. Care was taken to include representatives of each group along the total range of interest and institutional commitment. These 70 interviews provided a list of about 250 community issues. The list was reduced to a set of 39 issues according to the following criteria:

1. Each issue must have been at least temporarily resolved by a decision.
2. The decision must be perceived as important by informants representing diverse segments of the community.
3. The decision must pertain to the development, distribution, and utilization of resources and facilities which have an impact on a large segment of the metropolitan population.
4. The decision must involve alternative lines of action. It must entail a certain degree of choice on the part of participants; and the outcome must not be predetermined.
5. The decision must be administered rather than made by individuals in "the market." For the purpose of this study, an administered decision was defined as one made by individuals holding top positions in organizational structures which empower them to make decisions affecting many people.

6. The decision must involve individuals and groups resident in the Syracuse Metropolitan Area. Decisions made outside the Metropolitan Area (e.g., by the state government), were excluded even though they might affect residents of the Metropolitan Area.

7. The decision must fall within the time period 1955-1960.

8. The set of decisions as a whole must affect the entire range of important institutional sectors, such as governmental, economic, political, educational, religious, ethnic, and the like.

The next step in the research process required the determination of positional leaders or formal authorities for each of the set of 39 issues. The study began with those individuals who were formally responsible for the decisions. The element of arbitrary judgment usually involved in the positional approach was thus avoided. Here, the importance of position was derived from its role in determining a choice among alternative lines of action rather than of being the consequence of an arbitrary assumption.

The responsible formal authorities were determined on the basis of documents pertinent to the 39 decisions. In addition, several attorneys were consulted to insure that correct determinations were made. The number of authorities responsible for making each of these decisions ranged from two to 57.

The interviews started with authoritative persons. Respondents were presented with a set of 39 cards, each of which identified a decision. They were asked to sort the cards into two piles: (1) "Those in which you participated; that is, where others involved in this decision would recognize you as being involved," and (2) "Those in which you were not a participant." For those issues in which they claimed participation, individuals were then asked to name all the others who were also involved. Here they were instructed to report on the basis of first-hand knowledge of participation rather than on hearsay. Respondents were also given a questionnaire covering their social backgrounds.

When the interviews with authorities were completed, their responses for those decisions on which they possessed authority were tabulated. Then, any person who had been nominated as a participant by two authorities for the same issue was designated as a first zone influential. Two nominations were deemed necessary in order to avoid bias due to accidental contacts, mistakes of memory, or a tendency to mention personal friends. In the final tabulations this same rule of two nominations was applied to authorities also. Therefore, no person is counted as a participant unless he has two nominations by qualified nominators.

As the next step, all first zone influentials were interviewed using exactly the same procedures as those used for authorities. Their responses were tabulated for the decisions in which they had been involved, and any person nominated by one authority and one first zone influential was also classified as a first zone influential and interviewed. Then any person nominated by two first zone influentials was designated a second zone influential—two steps removed from formal authority but still involved. We did not interview beyond these second zone influentials. We might have continued with third and fourth zone and so on; but on the basis of qualitative data gathered during the interviews, we suspected we were moving well into the periphery of impact on the outcome of decision making.

In all, 628 interviews were completed. Of these, 550 qualified as participants. These participants, then are the leaders as determined by the decision-making phase of the Syracuse study. They were ranked in terms of the number of decisions in which they were involved. For the present analysis the 32 most active participants are considered.

SOCIAL ACTIVITY

Each of the 550 participants uncovered by the decision-making study was asked to complete a questionnaire covering his social background and current activities. These questionnaires were returned to 506 informants. The answers included responses to a set of questions designed to elicit as much information as possible about voluntary association memberships. Specific questions were included to determine memberships in the following areas:

1. Committees formed to deal with community problems.
2. Community service organizations.
3. Business organizations.
4. Professional organizations.
5. Union organizations.
6. Clubs and social organizations.
7. Cultural organizations.
8. Religious organizations.
9. Political parties, organizations and clubs.

10. Veterans' and patriotic organizations.
11. Other clubs and organizations.

Memberships in these organizations were tabulated, and a rough overall index to voluntary activity was calculated by simply summing the number of memberships for each person. The respondents were ranked in terms of number of memberships, and the 32 most active organizational members were included in the present analysis.

REPUTATION

Each questionnaire also invited the respondent to list the most influential leaders in the community. Eight spaces were provided for answers. Nominations were tabulated and, following traditional procedures, the top 41 reputed leaders were listed. The responses of those 41 respondents were then tabulated separately. The top 32 were derived from their rankings. This was done in order to maximize the chances that our nominators would be informed. As it turned out, however, the top 32 nominations of the whole group and the top 32 provided by the top 41 were exactly the same persons and in the same order. For Syracuse these nominations showed remarkable consistency all along the line.

POSITION

In determining the top positional leaders it seemed desirable to avoid as much as possible making the usual arbitrary assumptions. Traditional usage of the positional approach dictated the determination of the titular heads of the major organizations in business, government, the professions, and the like. Within each of these institutional areas choice could be made in terms of size, but it was difficult to determine how many organizations should be selected in each area.

An empirical resolution for this problem was provided in a recent report by D'Antonio et al. These authors provided data on the proportions of reputed leaders representing each of the seven relevant institutional areas in ten previous studies. Since agreement on these relative proportions was reasonably close for the six middle-sized American communities reported, they were used to assign proportions in each institutional area in the present study. The proportions derived from D'Antonio and those used in the present study are reported in Table I. In this case positional leaders are the titular heads of the largest organizations in each of the institutional areas, and each area is represented according to the proportion listed in Table I. Thirty-two organizations were chosen in all. As a check on its validity, the list of organizations was shown to several local experts in community affairs. They were in substantial agreement that the organizations listed seemed consistent with their perceptions of the "top" organizations in Syracuse. The heads of these organizations might be expected to have formal control over much of the institutional system of the community.

TABLE I
Percentage of Leaders in Each Institutional Area

Institution		Six Cities		Syracuse
Business		57		59
Government		8		9
Professions		12		13
Education		5		6
Communications		8		6
Labor		4		3
Religion		5		3
Total		99		99

These, then, are the raw materials of the current study. An attempt was made to determine the degree to which these several procedures would allocate the same persons to the top leadership category.

RESULTS

The several procedures for determining leaders did not converge on a single set of individuals. Top leaders according to one procedure were not necessarily the same as those indicated by another. An index of agreement for each part was constructed by calculating the ratio of the actual number of agreements to their total possible number. Results are listed in Table II.

It is possible that any of the methods used, if modified enough, would have yielded significantly different results.[1] The

TABLE II

Percentage of Agreement in Determining Leaders by Four Traditional Procedures

Participation 25 33 39	Social activity 25 22	Reputation 74	Position

procedures we followed seem in their essentials to be like those followed in most of the studies so far published. (Those who believe they have altered the use of positions, nominations, memberships, or other indexes in such a way as to obtain a major difference in the output of the technique have only to demonstrate this by empirical comparisons.) Our impression is that most versions of each approach represent only vernier adjustments of the same device and thus can have only marginally differing results.

Table II suggests that there is far from perfect agreement in determining leaders by means of these four methods. In only one case do two of these methods concur in more than 50 percent of their nominations. Reputation and position seem to be in substantial agreement in locating leaders. To a large degree, therefore, reputed leaders are the titular heads of major community organizations. They are not, however, themselves active as participants in decision making to any great extent.

Reputation for leadership seems to derive primarily from position, not from participation. But it appears unlikely that position itself constitutes a sufficient basis for reputation. The reputations, however might belong to the organizations and not the individuals. In such a case, when an informant named John Smith as a leader what might have been intended as the fact that

[1] The choice of the top 32 leaders in each category, if, for example, somewhat arbitrary. When another number is used, the absolute percentages of agreement vary, but their standings relative to one another remain stable.

the Smith Snippel Company (of which John Smith was president) is influential in community decisions. Smith would thus have been named only because we had asked for a person's name. Our hypothesis, then, is that reputation should correspond with the participation rate of organizations rather than the participation rates of individuals.

On the basis of this hypothesis, the data on participation were retabulated. Each participant was classified according to his organization or place of employment. Then the head of each organization was credited not only with his own participation, but with the sum of the participation of his employees. In this manner an index of organizational participation was constructed and the top 30 organizational leaders were determined. Individuals so nominated were compared with those introduced by the earlier procedures. The results are shown in Table III.

TABLE III
**Percentage of Agreement Between Organizational
Participation and Four Traditional Procedures**

Traditional Procedure		Percentage of Agreement
Participation		33
Social activity		25
Reputation		67
Position		80

The proportions shown in Table III support our hypothesis. Organizational participation seems to uncover substantially the same leaders as reputation and position. The top reputed leaders, therefore, though not the personnel of these organizations have the highest participation rates.

This result accounts for a great deal of participation in community decision making. Since organizational participation provides a workable index, many participants must be employees of large community organizations. But this does not explain the most active class of individual participants—those who were picked up by the individual participation index. These people seem to be virtually full-time participants in community affairs. We know that they are not organizational heads, but we have not determined who they are.

In view of the sheer amount of their participation, the top participants must be professional participants of some sort. And, as a class, professional participants in community affairs should be government officials and employees of fulltime professional executives of nongovernmental agencies formally and primarily committed to intervention in community affairs. With this as our hypothesis, the individuals nominated as leaders by the four traditional indexes were all classified into either government and professional or non-professional categories. Then percentages of government personnel and professionals were calculated for all four indexes. The results are shown in Table IV.

Again the results support our hypothesis. The most active individual participants are typically government personnel.

TABLE IV

Percentage of Leaders According to Four Traditional Procedures Who Are Government Officials or Employees or Profession Participants

Traditional Procedure		Percentage of Government Personnel or Professional Participants
Participation		66
Social activity		20
Reputation		20
Position		28

The participation index thus gets at personnel quite different from those selected by reputational or positional indexes, or by social activity. These differing cadres of people seem to represent different kinds of leadership behavior with respect to the local community.

SUMMARY AND DISCUSSION OF RESULTS

These results indicate that at least in Syracuse "leadership" is not a homogeneous category. Which "leaders" are uncovered seems in large part to be a function of the mode of study. The several traditional indexes allow us to locate one or another of three basic types of "leaders."

First, there are those who enjoy the reputation for top leadership. These are very frequently the same individuals who are the heads of the largest and most active participating business, industrial, governmental, political, professional, educational, labor and religious organizations in Syracuse. They are uncovered by studies of reputation, position, or organizational participation. In view of their formal command over the institutional structure and the symbolic value of their status as indexed by reputation, these individuals may be called the Institutional Leaders of Syracuse.

These Institutional Leaders, however, are for the most part not active participants in community affairs. There is no evidence that they have any direct impact on most decisions which take place. Their activity may be limited to that of lending prestige to or legitimizing the solutions provided by others. They might conceivably be participating decision makers in secret, but more likely they serve chiefly to provide access to the decision-making structure for their underlings: the Effectors.

The Effectors are located by studying participation. They are the active workers in the actual process of community decision making. Many of the most active Effectors are government personnel and professional participants, and the others are the employees of the large private corporations directed by the Institutional Leaders. In some cases, the Effectors are in touch with their employers, and it seems likely that their activities are frequently guided by what they view as company policy; but judging from our data, they are often pretty much on their own. At any rate, these men carry most of the burden of effecting community change.

The third type of leader might be called the Activists. There people are active—and often hold office—in voluntary organizations, community service organizations, and clubs. Although they are not involved as often as the Effectors, the Activists do participate in decision making. For the most part they seem to lack the positional stature to be Institutional Leaders. Furthermore, they often work for or direct smaller organizations in the community. They lack the power base provided by association with government or one of the major industrial or business firms. Yet, seemingly by sheer commitment of time and effort to community affairs, these Activists do help shape the future of the community.

In conclusion, the various differing approaches to the study of community leadership seem to uncover different types of leaders. The study of reputation, position or organizational participation seems to get at the Institutional Leaders. Studies of participation in decision making, on the other hand, tap the Effectors of community action. And studies of social activity seem to seek out the Activists who gain entry by dint of sheer commitment, time, and energy.

In part, our results are dependent upon the Syracuse situation. It is likely that 25 years ago, when Syracuse was smaller and less diversified, the Institutional Leaders and the Effectors were the same people. And 25 years from now this description will probably no longer hold. Other communities, in other stages of development and diversification will probably show different patterns. But until more comparative studies are done, conclusions of this kind are virtually guesses.

LEADERSHIP AND COMMUNITY DEVELOPMENT*

by William R. Lassey and Hans Johnson

Within most American communities sources of leadership potential may be summarized thus:[1]

(a) *Institutional leaders:* Persons holding office in a community, whether elected, appointed, or otherwise designated to carry out professional leader roles. They perform leadership functions in major part because of positions they occupy. Within the institutional leadership category, various levels of legitimizing influence and functional influence can be defined.[2]

* Adopted from "Community Development Theory and Practice," in *Community Development in Montana: Resources, Methods, Case Studies,* edited by William R. Lassey and Anne S. Williams, Bozeman, Montana: Big Sky Books, 1970.
[1] Derived from various studies of leadership conducted by Lassey and Williams. For example: *Leadership for Community Development: Analysis of an Indian Reservation Area.* Center for Planning and Development, Montana State University, Bozeman, Montana, 1971, and "Pluralistic Leadership and Area Development," Paper presented to the Annual Meetings of the Rural Sociological Society, 1971.
[2] See the preceding selection by Freeman, et al.

(b) *Power leaders:* Leadership of this nature is often found in communities that are characterized by paternalism of old and established families, a political boss, a long term office holder, or the management of a dominant business. Such individual leaders or small leadership groups may occasionally have a complete and often paralyzing control over the life of a community.

(c) *Situational leaders:* Leaders may emerge from within the community to exercise influence in dealing with specific issues, without necessary reference to existing leadership patterns or institutions. Newer residents in the community may have important potential for influence in this context.

(d) *Pluralistic leadership:* This is the ideal of democratic communities. Such leadership allows power to be shared widely and allows authority to be delegated. A broadly based feeling of involvement and influence by many citizens usually prevails from this form of leadership structure.

A community which relies primarily on one or the other of the first two types, limits the possibility for self-determination, and allows a limited number of leaders to make decisions and dictate local action. A mature and developing community usually accepts the responsibility of greater participation implied in the third, and especially the fourth circumstance.

In many communities considerable influence is exercised by individuals who hold no formal positions of leadership. Quite often such people are long-time local residents, relatively wealthy, or control important businesses or organizations; they often hold significant positions in organizations based outside the community. In some instances they work behind the scenes to promote and support change that is resisted by formal leadership. In other situations they are tradition oriented and exercise power largely to stop changes which are viewed as undesirable.

The important point about such legitimizing leadership influence is that it must be recognized and understood if most major community devlopment efforts are to be successful. Legitimizing leaders are often sufficiently influential that a project can be stopped, *or* made successful, as a consequence of their "behind the scenes" role, regardless of widespread citizen participation.

It is a fact of community life that some individuals have a much more powerful role in decision-making than others; democracy is limited by major differences in skill, wealth, intelligence, occupational status, and general prestige. Community development leaders will increase the likelihood of success if they are aware of the power factors, rather than if they operate on the false assumption of uniform distribution of influence within the community.

Elected local officials are often high status individuals in the community, but in many cases simply do not have a great deal of power or influence. In many instances the elected jobs pay relatively poor salaries, and the most competent people in the community will not work for the rate of pay. In other instances the elected jobs simply do not have enough status to attract the most competent individuals. Consequently, it is often a mistake to rely entirely on elected local officials to initiate or lead community development efforts.

Unless local leaders have resided in the community for a considerable period of time, they have trouble exercising significant influence. This may mean they can be very helpful in doing many of the important details within a development program, but must gain the confidence of longer term leaders to significantly affect decision-making associated with major changes in the community.

Components of Effective Community Leadership

Characteristics of an optimal leadership group include:[3]

1. Involvement of the most widely experienced and broadly educated persons in the community;
2. Interest in community affairs springs from firm commitment to community progress, rather than strictly self-interest;
3. Widely representative of socio-economic and ethnic groups within the community;
4. Consists in somewhat equal proportions of (a) individuals who were born in the community, (b) individuals who were born elsewhere but have lived in the community a long time, and (c) persons who have lived in the community a relatively short time;
5. Most leaders have had enough contact with sub-groups of the population to facilitate understanding of varying points of view;
6. Marked by congeniality but not "cliquishness";
7. Leaders realize the importance of personal effort, working through informal and formal organization, in focus-

[3] Summarized from a list of characteristics described by Murray Ross in *Community Organization*. New York, Harper and Row, 1968, p. 120.

ing public attention on community problems and needs. These seven desirable characteristics of a community leadership group are by no means absolutely required but rather constitute an ideal model. To the extent that a community varies from the ideal, or if community leadership resources are limited for other reasons, benefit would quite likely be derived from the assistance of outside help in the form of a consultant or a group of community development specialists.

Role of the Consultant

Community development should be the primary responsibility of local leaders and volunteer citizens. However the process is usually enhanced by the assistance of professional specialists. Several classifications of "consultants" have been delineated: (1) the professionally trained community specialist, who may be a university professor, a chamber of commerce employee, an extension specialist, a church worker, a social welfare worker, a public health worker, etc; (2) the institutional administrator who directs or guides several field workers; (3) the private planning or development consultant, employed by a professional firm; (4) consultants hired full-time by the community to direct planning and development programs, and (5) state or federal consultants assigned to work with a group of communities.[4]

A consultant may help initiate a development program or be called in to assist an effort already underway. Development programs that become vital to the participants should achieve a momentum of their own, and should become increasingly the responsibility of the people involved. An effective consultant can help keep a program operational through periods of crisis and may contribute important knowledge about program content and method of approach to realizing community potential.

Great skill is required of the consultant if he is to strike a proper balance between exerting his influence and encouraging local initiative and participation. The consultant's initiative is usually greater in the early stages, and then tapers off as the local citizens gain confidence and competence.

The consultant's job calls for a combination of capacities:

1. Technical skill in the process and content of community planning and development;

---

[4] For further elaboration on professional leader or consultant roles, see Arthur F. Wileden, *Community Development*, Totowa, N.J.: Bedminister Press, 1970.

2. Belief in the potential for local self-help and effective development programs;
3. Ability to understand and communicate with local leaders and citizens;
4. Understanding of local politics, community power structures, and the dynamics and characteristics of the community;
5. Organizational ability.[5]

The community consultant must be willing to accept other people as fellow human beings with unique wants, beliefs, needs, customs, values, and a sense of worth. This mental attitude leads to openness toward contribution of ideas from individuals in the community. Local citizens are usually much more ready to cooperate with consultants if they are treated as partners in the change process and given the opportunity to do as much as possible for themselves.

Willingness to accept lay citizens unconditionally is not a trivial thing. To accept others as equal human beings, the consultant must relate to them with due respect for their individuality and he must seek to understand and respect their image of themselves, even when this image does not appear to be very realistic.

The consultant cannot hope to remain "unclassified." One of the first things local people will want to know is where to place him in their own stereotypes. Once he has been placed, they will tend to deal with him accordingly and weigh everything he has to say from the point of view their stereotype represents. In this sense, it is better for him to expose his weaknesses and hope to be accepted for what he is.

Consultants must understand the need to elicit cooperation and collaboration within the community, through accepted political and power channels. Failure to effectively communicate with influential citizens and leaders of public opinion can only lead to serious implementation problems.

Since obsolescence of local organizations may be a primary reason for lack of effective development, it is extremely important for the consultant to have a clear understanding of organizational alternatives and possible new organizational designs. In addition he must understand the process through which an organization can be modified or a new organization initiated.

---

[5] Adapted from Ward Hunt Goodenough, *Cooperation in Change*, Russell Sage Foundation, New York, 1963, p. 377.

Clearly, these "requirements" are extremely demanding, and few consultants with this broad capability are available.

A Summary: Some Basic Principles of Leadership and Community Development

Existing principles of community development have been drawn largely from experience and have not always been adequately related to general scientific knowledge. Nevertheless, these principles have proved applicable in a great many community situations. Failure usually occurs not because the principles were inapplicable, but more often because local leaders or consultants do not understand how to apply the concepts:[6]

1. Leaders of community development programs must treat the community and its surrounding environment as an integrated social system. Community development is more likely to be effective when decision and action involve established informal primary groupings as well as formally organized committees, councils, boards, and commissions.

2. The goals of development must be stated in terms that have positive value to the community's members, and must elucidate achievements which citizens seriously want to attain.

3. The organizational structure in any community must be developed according to the characteristics of the local situation. Imposed organization is often inadequate and inappropriate.

4. The community must be an active partner in the development process. Community development consultants may suggest, advise, and propose, but the *decisions must be made by the community members.*

5. Development consultants and citizens should have a thorough knowledge of the main values and principal features of the community's culture. This often requires collection of detailed information about the community. A development program is more likely to be successful when ideas and actions are in tune with the social, political, economic and ecological systems of the community.

6. Initial community deveopment activities—study, research, and planning—are more likely to succeed when they meet the following conditions:

    a. grow out of some strongly felt interest, problem, need;

    b. effectively utilize existing levels of knowledge, skill,

---

[6] We are indebted to Dr. Edward Moe, University of Utah, for many of these principles. For example, see *Current Perspectives on Community Resource Development*, published by the Agricultural Policy Institute, North Carolina State University, 1969.

understanding;

c. offer relatively great return for the amount of effort and work involved.

d. offer the least possibility of conflict with important attitudes, values, status systems, and security systems.

7. The probability, or at least possibility, of conflict is inherent in any community development program. Programs involving change are more likely to be successful when leaders and their consultants are aware of:

a. actual or latent incompatibility in the ideas, attitudes, values, status, and security systems of the people.

b. threats to vested interests which may develop as a result of the differential ability of individuals to achieve goals through the community development program.

8. Community development is essentially educational in nature. It is a process of learning how to positively change the community.

9. Community development should be based primarily on the democratic process; policy determination and action are more likely to be successful and lasting when they are democratically developed and implemented.

10. Leadership is more likely to be successful if it is broadly representative of interests and ideas of the people.

11. Development stages and procedures must make sense to the community's members. People cannot long support what they do not understand.

12. Change through community development programs is facilitated when the many related activities of various public and private agencies are coordinated. Where there are several consultants at work, systematic communication and coordination between them is essential.

13. The change consultant must earn the personal respect of the community's members. He should try to avoid making himself the indispensable man in the development situation.

14. The American community places heavy cultural emphasis on action; a community development program is more likely to succeed when an early emphasis is placed on action, without neglecting research and planning.

15. Community development programs are more likely to be effective when the people participating in them help to constantly evaluate and re-evaluate their objectives, methods, activities, and the total context in which the programs are developed and implemented.

LEADERSHIP IN A SMALL TOWN*

by Aaron B. Wildavsky

The essential purpose of the case histories and role studies presented in the previous chapters was to present evidence which would enable us to decide what kind of political system exists in Oberlin. We have described every major decision . . . during the period from January, 1957, to June, 1961. . . . If we find that the same participants exercise leadership in nearly all significant areas of decision, that they agree, and that they are not responsible to the electorate, we conclude that a power elite rules in Oberlin. If we discover that a majority of citizens are influential in all or most cases, the proper conclusion is that Oberlin is ruled by the people as a mass democracy. And if we find that the leaders vary from one issue area to the other, with such overlap as there is between issue areas concentrated largely in the hands of public officials, we must conclude that there is a pluralist system of rule in Oberlin. Once having arrived at the correct conclusion, it will become possible for us to attempt to explain why this particular power structure exists, to account for such changes as have taken place since the 1930's, and to go into the dynamic aspects of how decisions are made in the Oberlin Community.

Following Dahl's procedure, we set up a Leadership Pool consisting of all those who participated in a particular decision and could conceivably be candidates for leadership. Then we separate out those who lost, who got nothing of what they wanted. This leaves us with a Leadership Elite—those who in some way helped secure an outcome they deemed to be favorable. Within this broad category, we seek to distinguish among those who initiated, vetoed, or gained consent for a policy proposal.

Rarely is it possible to trace the first origins of an idea. To

* Taken from *The Search for Community Power*, edited by Willis D. Hawley and Frederick M. Wirt, Bedminister Press, Columbus, Ohio, 1968.

initiate a policy in our terms means to seize upon an idea, develop a policy proposal, and pursue it to a successful conclusion. To veto a proposal means either to secure its defeat entirely or to modify or reject a part. To gain consent one must secure the assent of others for a favorable policy outcome. These categories are further divided in order to give some idea of the degree of leadership. This is inevitably somewhat arbitrary and we have sought to do as little violence to reality as is possible by restricting ourselves to three broad degrees—high (implying a major role in initiating, vetoing, or gaining consent), low (a discernible but minor role), and moderate (a residual category).

For analytical purposes the case histories are divided into seven issue areas—housing, utilities, welfare, industrial development, zoning, education, and nominations and elections. After describing leadership in these decisions, we shall compare them to discover the extent of overlap between issue areas and the kind of individuals who exercise influence in more than one area. . . .

We find a clear outline of a pluralist system in accordance with the theory stated in the first chapter. There is no person or group which exerts leadership in all issue areas. To the extent that overlap between issue areas exists, it is held predominantly by public officials—the City Manager, Mayor Long, City Council—who owe their positions directly or (in the case of the Manager) indirectly to expressions of the democratic process through a free ballot with universal suffrage. The one exception is Don Pease, co-editor of the News-Tribune, who owes his prominence in the light plant issue to membership in the Public Utilities Commission, who has the kind of dispensible occupation which permits time for leadership, and whose job encourages, if it does not demand, rather wide participation in community affairs. . . .

Although men like Long, Dunn and Comings, who combine public office with unusual activity, are clearly outstanding leaders, none of them has all the influence there is to have in any case. They all require the consent of others. . . .

The number of citizens and outside participants who exercise leadership in most cases is an infinitesimal part of the community. This is necessarily the case since the total number of all those who participate at all in any way is quite small. Meteors who participate in only one or two cases (and that sporadically), and specialists, who confine their participation to one or two issue areas, make up the bulk of influentials. The ability of citizens who devote much time and effort to a single case or issue area to become leaders is clearly indicated as is the initiative and support provided by generalist public officials. . . .

Although leadership is diffused in Oberlin, the outcomes of community decisions are not merely random occurrences but fall instead into a rather well-defined pattern. From inspection of the leaders in the cases we have described it appears that a rather broad coalition of interests, though its members occasionally disagree and suffer defeats, has been victorious on most issues of importance. This combination of the Co-op, some college people, out-of-town businessmen, and Negro leaders has, for the sake of convenience, been called "the planners."

The major analytic tasks confronting us are, first, to account for the success of the planning coalition and, second, to explain why the more oligarchic power structure of the thirties gave way to the pluralist system we have found today. The explanatory factors we shall employ include differential rates of participation, the structural conditions created by the non-partisan ballot, the existence of several independent centers of influence, and, most important, the more active and skillful exploitation of key bases of influence by the planners.

The planning coalition was in part consciously created— Long, Dunn, Hellmuth, Comings, Blanchard and Ellis set out to recruit commuting businessmen, Negroes, and college people— and partly the result of engaging in conflict and discovering who was on what side. As the various planning policies were debated it became obvious that the cost involved and the constant use of government had led to a split among the activists. Many of the local businessmen were directly affected by the increased water rates, threatened by the possible influx of competing enterprises, and generally fearful of change which might upset the accustomed patterns of affairs in the community. From conversations it appears that some felt that their middle class status was threatened by increased costs which might compel them to become wage earners and reduce their hard-won standard of living. Others objected to changes in the community introduced without their consent, changes which foreshadowed a deprivation of their customary influence and the deference they felt to be their due. At the same time, the commuting businessmen and college people welcomed policies which had the magic label of "planning" and which showed promise of improving community services. The taxes they paid on their houses did not seem onerous to them and they were more than willing to sacrifice a little cash for rewards in terms of better schools, and more attractive housing areas and streets. Negro activists like Wade Ellis made common cause with the planners not only because of a general sympathy with them but also because they saw new industry and a housing code as means of improving the conditions of their race in Oberlin. Their eminence within the Negro sector enabled them to overcome some opposition from Negro homeowners who had low incomes and objected to higher costs. Skill in coalition building was exercised by Dunn and Long as they proposed policies meeting widespread preferences, recruited personnel to promote them, provided a rationale for those who chose to agree, and modified opposition where necessary without giving up essential elements of their program.

If its members had to run together as Republicans or Democrats however, the planning coalition probably would have been impossible. Take the case of Charles Mosher, publisher of the News-Tribune. He was a Republican State Senator, a career legislator, a person who worked hard at his job and looked forward to advancement within the party. He would have found it exceedingly difficult, if not impossible, to justify supporting Democrats as Democrats in Oberlin city elections. His allegiance to the party and the expectations of party officials would have been violated by such an action. Under a non-partisan system, however, Mosher could and did support Bill Long and other Democrats on the ground that their party affiliation was not relevant to local affairs. Men like Eric Nord and Homer Blanchard and other commuting businessmen, most of them Republicans, would also have felt uncomfortable at being formally allied with Democrats. Moreover, as is common among middle and upper class individuals, they tend to shy away from active participation as partisans, preferring to avoid the tones of political hostility associated with party strife. They were much more easily recruited under the banner of non-partisan good citizenship than they would have been under party labels.

Central leadership for the planners was provided by tandem, cooperative arrangements between Councilman Bill Long and City Manager Richard Dunn. They helped set the general direction, provided huge amounts of energy, initiated proposals of their own, vetoed some they did not like, and helped gain support for the policies of others with which they agreed. Allied with them on the basis of shared perspectives and mutual agreement were active out-of-town businessmen, the editors of the local paper, some college faculty, a few Negro leaders, members of the Co-op, and a sprinkling of others. The point is not that all people falling within these categories gave their support, but that they provided a corps of activists, mostly specialists, who shared the task of developing policies and gaining public approval. It is doubtful, for example, that the category of out-of-town business-men numbers more than one hundred individuals. But they pro-vided two-sevenths of the 1959 Council (Nord and Blanchard), four of the eleven candidates for City Council in 1961 (Nord, Blanchard, Griswold, Johnson), and a vastly disproportionate share of commission and committee memberships appointed by the Council.

College people like Ken Roose, George Simpson, and David Anderson performed similar functions. It is probably true that the traditionalists had a substantial minority of support in the faculty, but except for a brief flurry in the 1959 election, these people were not especially active.

Why was the planning coalition successful in getting most of what it wanted? One answer could be that it possessed resources which were superior to those of its opponents. Another answer could be that resources were employed more actively and with greater skill. A third possibility is that it met with no appreciable resistance because others agreed or did not feel strongly enough to bother to challenge the coalition. Let us, then, survey the ma-jor resources (bases of influence) which were employed to con-trol decisions in Oberlin and appraise their degree of dominance over others and the rate and skill with which they were em-ployed. We will see that the planning coalition was superior in its possession and use of time, energy, official position, knowl-edge, persuasion and political skill. And that resources com-monly thought to be dominant, such as money, control of credit, jobs, social standing, and the like were not crucial or were mainly in the losers. . . .

Most of the wealth that exists in Oberlin is not used for any political purpose at all. Hence, those who have little but use what they have are not necessarily disadvantaged. And since all par-ticipants (except those at the barest margin of financial exis-tence) have a little cash to spare, wealth is not terribly important. No doubt the existence of financial obligations may help in get-ting a few signatures on a petition or in obligating an individual to do some work. But these are effects easily obtained by other means. In the secrecy of the ballot box, no one need fear reprisal. There may be some who fear to participate actively lest they in-cur the displeasure of the wealthy. Yet we know of no such cases and, if they exist, they have not prevented blatant opposition to policies favored by presidents of both banks and wealthy merchants. The victorious planners are in no position to exert financial sanctions over anyone (College faculty and commuting businessmen hire few townspeople, lend no money) unless it be a few employees of the Co-ops who are not noticeably active in town politics.

Social standing appears to be an insignificant base of influence in Oberlin. No doubt there are deference relationships in Oberlin but these do not appear to translate themselves into the political realm. There are some families who frequent a Country Club in Elyria and who hold dances in auspicious surroundings. But most of them are not active at all in the community and the few who do take part are rather equally divided between the opposing factions. Eric Nord and Robert Fauver may gain something from high social standing, but Bill Long, Richard Dunn, Ira Porter or John Cochran do not. If these activists receive deference, it is due to something other than their social position. To be sure, high social standing may predispose individuals toward activity but no one political group has anything like a monopoly of that resource.

Friendship is a valuable resource which is widespread in the community. . . . While it is difficult to say that anyone made much better use of friendship than others, it does appear that the planners had more success in getting their acquaintances to become active in civic affairs than did the traditionalists, with the exception of the 1959 election.

One reason for the greater activity of people identified with the planners is a consequence of another resource at their disposal—officiality, the holding of elected or appointed public office. This enabled the planners to recruit kindred spirits for positions on the many city commissions and special committees formed to promote policies like the housing ordinance. As these people began to participate, conversations with many of them reveal that they became more interested and engaged in additional activity. They came to know what was going on, developed new friendships, a taste for political "gossip," and even saw some positive results now and then which further solidified their interest.

The most obvious advantage which officiality brings to a Councilman is his vote and to the City Manager, his formal authority. There being few or no effective means of coercion in Oberlin (such as patronage), Councilmen are relatively free agents and can dispose of their votes to secure their preferences.

This is evident in the many votes establishing and enforcing housing and zoning ordinances, a new water system, continuing and expanding the light plant, and also in internal bargaining whereby individual members receive concessions, such as modifications of the housing code, in return for their votes. The many examples of the City Manager's use of his office include blocking the Gibson apartments, exercising discretion in enforcing the housing code, and presenting information unfavorable to the Elyria offer to supply water. Officiality is limited, of course, by the official's perception of community sentiment and by desire for re-election and reappointment. Indeed, it would be extremely difficult for any faction to secure its preferences in most areas of community policy unless they were able to occupy public office and they are sensitive to the need for popularity which this entails. Nevertheless, in regard to the general run of decisions which do not occasion much interest, officiality is a crucial resource. This is all the more true when it is recognized that officiality provides access to other resources—knowledge and information, popularity, friendship, development of skills, the expectation of activity and the legitimization of attempting to exercise influence.

In a democratic political system, officiality is largely dependent on popularity with the voters as the 1959 election demonstrates. The planners proved to be more popular. But why was this so? Although this question cannot be answered conclusively, it does appear that the traditionalists were considerably less skillful, and less continuously active. Their decision to run as a group concentrated their popularity and enabled Long to tar them all with the same brush as hidebound and against progress. Time after time they were caught with less than full knowledge of a particular issue and made to appear uninformed. They did not foresee their weakness among college people and Negroes and did little to appeal to these sections of the population. The major difficulty here, it seems, was that they started too late. Their burst of activity at election time could not make up for the continuous activity among the planners to pursue policies which would appeal to college people and Negroes, and, possibly more important, to recruit leaders from among these groups. The opinion leaders in the two communities were overwhelmingly for the planners long before the election, a circumstance which may have made it extremely difficult for the traditionalists to make an impact at election time, as their precinct workers discovered. By contrast, the program of the planners appeared to be considerably more positive and received favorable notice from activists in college and Negro quarters. The slate which the planners put forward was deliberately chosen to make a broader appeal through inclusion of Blanchard and Nord who were known to be conservative businessmen. As the election returns show, the planners appealed to a much wider section of the community than did their opponents.

As the planners were more popular, so were they more persuasive in a context where ability to persuade others is perhaps the chief resource available to anyone who wishes to influence a community decision. . . .

In part, the greater knowledge of the planners was a function of their officiality—the City Manager, Councilmen and Commission members had a right to demand information, were in an advantageous position to receive it, and were required by their positions to be knowledgeable. The advantages this knowledge confers are evident in virtually all the cases under discussion from the water and light plant decisions, where members of the PUC had little difficulty in showing that opposing proposals were illinformed, to the City Manager's ability to help block the Gibson apartment and to further recreation goals by knowing what was happening. To a considerable extent, however, the superior knowledge which the planners possessed was a product of their greater effort to inform themselves. . . .

It would be wrong, however, to think of skill as something esoteric or a composition of various tricks. For the most part, in Oberlin, it consists of rather simple kinds of actions. First, the collection of information so that one is better informed than others. Second, the development of a rationale for approaching those who make the decision. Third, the use of citizens committees and Council Commissions to test community sentiment, to gather support, and to ward-off opposition. Fourth, open meetings to give opponents a chance to vent grievances, to convince the doubtful, and to comply with feeling of procedural due process so that no one can accurately say that he was not given a chance to present his views. Fifth, ceaseless persuasion through personal contact, the newspaper, and official bodies. Finally, and this is perhaps most subtle, an appreciation of group dynamics and a general sense of strategy which includes pinpointing the crucial individuals and persuading opinion leaders of important groups. . . .

The point is not that this general approach reveals the presence of some mastermind but rather that the opponents of the planners had nothing to match it. The traditionalists never quite found a way to combat the use of committees and commissions as strategic instruments. To do so would have required a recognition of the danger they posed and the recruitment of a corps of specialists to compete with them. Only by matching the interest and activity of the planners could they have competed with them on the level of knowledge and persuasion. They did not do so, it appears, partly because they did not think the effort was worthwhile and partly because they could not adjust their thinking to a new type of situation in which participation in public affairs, however limited it might appear, had been significantly enlarged. The planners had pyramided their resources by using officiality, knowledge, skill, time and energy to gain popularity, using this popularity to promote policies expanding their base of support, using this increased support to win an election, using the additional personnel to promote new policies, using time in office to develop more knowledge and skill, and so on. . . .

What emerges most clearly from this discussion of resources is the accessibility of the most effective ones. Most people have time and energy if they care to use it, most can obtain knowledge if they work at it, all have a vote to help determine who holds public office, and virtually anyone who feels he can get support is in a position to run for office. Only a small number take advantage of these opportunities but they are there. Presumably, if sufficient numbers of people felt sufficiently unhappy about the existing state of affairs they would find these resources available to them and could quickly increase the rate at which they were being employed. True, there are some whose socio-economic position or low education have not provided life experiences which would predispose them toward effective participation. There is reason to believe, for example, that members of the Negro community could benefit themselves if they expanded their participation, even though their responses to the questionnaire do not show that there are issues they would like to promote which are not being debated in town. It is true also that interests they have are being promoted by a few of their leaders and by white people who identify with them so that the benefits they receive are greater than their participation per se would justify. Should a number of new leaders—men who would help formulate and interpret their demands and explain the connections between what they want and what happens in community affairs—arise from within the Negro community, the disabilities they may suffer today might be lessened.

The basic answer to the question of why the planning coalition was successful is that it utilized commonly available resources at a much greater rate and with considerably more skill than its opponents. Time, energy, knowledge, persuasion and skill were all available to others in quantity. The only resource the planners came near to monopolizing was officiality and that for only a limited two-year period, subject to approval by the electorate.

What about "other factors" in the situation which may have been significant but which we have not mentioned? It is hardly possible to exhaust the total range of conceivable explanations. But it is desirable to consider at least three others: rule by businessmen, social changes, and the presence of a "great man" who molded local history in his own image.

Regardless of our previous analysis, it may be said, the fact remains that most of the influential planners were businessmen and this alone may account for their victory in a capitalist society. Yet as we observe the opposing forces over a wide range of decisions in Oberlin, several issues splitting the community from top to bottom, it becomes strikingly evident that the term businessman is woefully inadequate as a predictor of common interests, complementary strategies, or mutual support. The fact is that men who can all properly be called businessmen have taken opposing sides on most of the controversies in Oberlin. Otherwise, it would be exceedingly difficult to account for the conflicts over the past several years, since most of the activists (with the exception of the City Manager and a few college people) are businessmen of one kind or another. . . .

In an attempt to show whether the change in power structure between the 1930's and the later 1950's could be related to changes in the social composition of Oberlin, an investigation was made on census returns since the turn of the century. What they reveal is that Oberlin appears to be a remarkably stable community. . . . The safest conclusion would appear to be that although social changes may in some degree be responsible for the success of the planners, the available evidence does not suggest that we can lean too heavily on this kind of explanation.

The role of the individual in history has long been the subject of inconclusive debate. Is he a true maker of history or is he merely a manifestation of deeper social currents? The case of Lenin's relationship to the Bolshevik Revolution is instructive on this point. Lenin did not and could not have accomplished the first October Revolution which was a result of such factors as mass upheaval due to a bloody war, breakdown in the Czarist system, and the work of many revolutionaires not including the Bolsheviks. Yet it can be said that without Lenin there would have been no Bolshevik (November) Revolution. For he was the only prominent Bolshevik who was in favor of making the attempt and it was he who convinced his fellow conspirators to go ahead. It can be said, then, that while Lenin could not have created the conditions for Revolution, he was able to seize the strategic moment in a vast cataclysm and turn it to his own advantage. Probably the best that can be done in this famous "chicken-and-egg" controversy is to look upon the conditions of the time as setting broad limits within which the remarkable individual can move, that is, to look upon the remarkable individual as thwarted or assisted in varying degrees by these circumstances.

Had Bill Long come to Oberlin in the 1930's he probably would not have been as successful in community affairs as he was at a later date when his opportunities for gaining allies and pursuing change through planning were greater. . . . To say this, however, may be no more than to suggest that Long might not have tried to do in the thirties what he found feasible in the fifties.

Yet it does appear that if Long had not moved to Oberlin, a number of developments . . . might not have taken place. At least, and this seems to be a safer statement, the changes that he helped bring about might well have been delayed. It is true that [some issues] had been discussed before he came to Oberlin and became active. Yet if he had not participated in hiring a person like City Manager Dunn, nor used great quantities of energy, knowledge and skill in bringing these items up for decision, nor persisted where other men might have stopped, much less would have been done. Of course, Long could not and did not do it alone. But he seized upon and created opportunities which might otherwise have come to naught. Without his presence, Oberlin's political system probably would have been much more fragmented; the existing central direction might have given way to relatively autonomous specialists.

BRISTOL TOWNSHIP SCHOOLS: STRATEGY FOR CHANGE*

by Thomas J. Cottle

The civil rights movement, in recent years, has sparked many efforts to improve school programs and to change the learning environment for both white and black students. Most of these attempts have failed, or have succeeded only marginally. It has become increasingly clear that promoting change in the schools, as in other social institutions, is a far more difficult task than anticipated. The enormous inertia of "the system" seems to defeat all but the most determined and ingenious efforts. A strong commitment to change by a few teachers or administrators in a school system is rarely enough. Rather, it appears that before fundamental reform can take place, all school personnel must be involved in a concentrated effort to remove both personal and institutional resistance to change. One such program that holds high promise for success is taking place in Pennsylvania, just north of Philadelphia.

For the majority of travelers, Bristol Township is merely the inevitable town adjoining the toll booth on the Pennsylvania Turnpike just before entering or immediately after leaving New Jersey. But to the people who live there it is much more.

This sprawling bedroom community contains most of Levittown's 17,000 homes and a population of more than 67,000. Many of the community's husbands and fathers commute to Philadelphia, twenty-one miles to the south, or to Trenton, roughly the same distance to the north. Of the township's 21,000 children, 14,000 attend the public schools, and, therefore, come under the watchful eye of Superintendent Knute Larson and his associates in the Harry S. Truman School Administration Building. About 7 per cent of these students are black, but more sig-

* Reprinted with permission from the *Saturday Review*, September 20, 1969, pp. 70-82.
© Copyright 1969 Saturday Review, Inc.

nificantly, enough of the township's families live at a level of poverty to entitle the district to aid under Title I of the Elementary and Secondary Education Act, which provides federal funds for the education of the disadvantaged. Bristol Township—not to be confused with the town of Bristol —remains essentially a working-class community. Its racial and ethnic tensions are heightened by its proximity to Philadelphia and Trenton with their larger and more militant groups. It is a community that many people point to as "backlash prone"—the kind where racial problems can explode at any moment. The township made nationwide headlines in 1957 when families bitterly swarmed around the first Levittown home to be occupied by a black family while other neighbors stationed themselves on the front lawn pledging protection to the family inside. But the township is fortunate that its educational leaders are aware of the need for social and educational change if the tensions of contemporary society are to be lessened. Superintendent Larson, a large, raw-boned, pragmatic man, is skeptical of fashionable panaceas in education, but he is also sensitively aware of the community's problems. As a result, a number of fundamental actions have been taken to make the schools more responsive to all elements in the community.

First, the township built fifteen public schools (as well as four parochial schools) during a seven-year period. It also established an "opportunity class" for students who were disciplinary problems in an effort to return them to their regular classes, and launched a community-school program offering a wide variety of activities for both children and adults in a school that remained open from 8 a.m. to 10 p.m., six days a week, twelve months a year.

Second, it reassigned students in some schools when it became obvious that the overcrowding of black students in two schools was intolerable to both parents and teachers because of increasing disciplinary problems and generalized hostility. Black students were bussed, without significant opposition, to less crowded, predominantly white schools. Indeed, the board of education was unwilling to perpetuate institutions where the disadvantaged grew nowhere together.

Third, the school district formed an Intergroup Education Committee that worked on curriculum changes, and then turned to an examination of the racial conflict in the community that gradually had grown to dangerous proportions. These tensions

weren't omni-present, but they were persistent and troubling.
There was talk, for example, of militant community organizing
going on in one black neighborhood, night fights between police
and students, and an invasion of activists from Philadelphia and
Trenton "stirring up unrest" in the three areas where Negro con-
centration is highest. Then came the action.

The story at Franklin Delano Roosevelt Junior High School
began on a date few whites could remember. Blacks, however,
recall the day as the anniversary of Malcolm X's death. On that
day thirteen students refused to attend their homerooms. They
proclaimed it a holiday and insisted that their parents wanted
them home. Phone calls revealed that some mothers were confused, but all wanted their children at school. The students perse-
vered, the principal gave them a choice, and they left, their
strength and support growing. Temporary suspensions were issued immediately, but within a few days the students had returned, and the social temperature of Bristol Township climbed.

The second eruption came some months later in the second
week of May 1968, soon after Martin Luther King's assassina-
tion. A black girl "bucked the line" in the cafeteria. A white
teacher ordered her to go back, and—wham! She hit the teacher.
Two other girls rushed to the student's defense. The three were
suspended, one for the entire year. The black community was
aroused. "To hear the black leaders, you'd think the teacher hit
the girl with her chin," someone recalled. A group of Hell's
Black Cobras, young adults, eighteen to twenty-five, snarled
about the school grounds. Eventually the police entered the
school grounds, and black leaders, too, intervened. Everyone
was tense.

In the main, the police seemed unhappy with their charge of
admitting only "proper personnel" to the schools, the teachers
ambivalent about the presence of outsiders, the black community
upset over the perceived Uncle Tomness of their leaders who
seemed to be selling them out. The black students were explod-
ing with demands for reinstatement of their sisters, more black
teachers and counselors, and changes in the dress code.

The situation was bad, but it could have been far worse.
What helped was the sensitivity and understanding shown by administrators and teachers in their negotiating with students, parents, and community leaders. Somehow, punishment seemed far
less important to them than communication, and somehow, too,
these administrators and teachers seemed humanly prepared for
the situation.

Behind their preparation was a valuable experience with a human relations training program from which the Intergroup Education Committee was an offshoot. The education leaders of Bristol Township had discovered the efficacy of this kind of training and during the winter of 1967-68 had asked Professor Max Birnbaum of the Boston University Human Relations Laboratory in New York City to develop a human relations training program for the school district.

Public attention has focused increasingly, in recent months, on various approaches to "sensitivity training," and as public interest has grown, so has the confusion over just what such training is all about. There are, in fact, a number of different brands of sensitivity training, each with its own objectives, techniques, and outcomes in personal and institutional change. Professors Robert Chin and Kenneth D. Benne in their study, *The Planning of Change*, identify three different approaches. The first, based on the now traditional T-group (Training-group) experience, is designed to produce personal growth, understanding through radical confrontations in which members of hostile groups express their feelings, often in violent fashion, in an effort to encourage mutual understanding.

In contrast to an emphasis on personal growth and development, the third approach stresses interpersonal understanding aimed at improving work efficiency among employees or colleagues. It is this latter approach that Professor Birnbaum and his staff at the Boston University Lab employ.

The training program Birnbaum and his colleagues developed for Bristol Township's schools was based on several clearly defined assumptions about the nature of change and the ways in which resistance to change—both personal and institutional—can be overcome. First, the training program must be strongly and consistently supported by the district's educational leaders—the superintendent and his top staff. Second, the program must include the entire school community. The superintendent, his staff, and the entire teaching force must participate; ideally the program should include important lay members of the community as well. Piecemeal efforts at reform addressed to small groups within the educational system—a limited number of teachers, for instance—cannot be effective. As Birnbaum has written, "no institutional change will occur until all, or nearly all, of the individuals who must implement change have accepted the need for innovation." Third, training must be focused on personal growth *for organizational adaptation to change*, rather than on personal growth alone. This is a program of applied human relations training that seeks simultaneously to remove both institutional and personal resistance to change. It is focused, therefore, on actual problems faced by individuals in their respective schools rather than on a therapeutic approach to individual development. In this way, participants not only become more conscious of the sources of their own attitudes and actions on the job but also come to appreciate more fully the pressures—both personal and institutional—that influence the actions of their colleagues.

Unlike some sensitivity training, the questions and problems to be explored become highly specific. The group experiences emphasizing interpersonal sensitivity and personal growth do not pretend to deal with educational change in socially charged areas. The currently fashionable "touching and feeling groups," for example, or the more traditional T-groups in which issues of authority and intimacy are "explored" and "worked through," are not necessarily dysfunctional, but seem less suitable for the needs of most school systems requiring change. It is Birnbaum's belief, moreover, that, at this point in our history, "confrontation sessions" where angry blacks intimidate whites are no longer as functional as they may have been two or three years ago. The growing resistance of whites to the black challenge today tends to reinforce the natural defensiveness induced by such sessions, and makes participants even less willing to accept change or to see the confrontation in the context of daily school relationships.

It is for these reasons that a complete school system approach is stressed, and emphasis is placed on specific professional problems. The overarching strategy is to work on major resistances to change in all school personnel. Where prejudices reinforce the status quo, they must be gently exposed, and then examined as part of the normal human condition to reduce the defensiveness, the fear of exposure, and the feeling of guilt. They can then be dealt with in terms that will make some change possible. The major goal of the laboratory sessions, therefore, is to help administrators and teachers reduce their fears of (and resistance to) "appropriate" and "needed" changes in teacher-administrator, teacher-student, and administrator-student relationships.

The plan for Bristol Township called for each of approximately 800 people (700 staff and 100 community representatives) to participate in one of two kinds of training groups. For selected school administrators, teachers, and principals, five-day workshops centered on skills in leadership and special sensitivities for handling so-called minority group problems. According to the plan, these people would return to their schools where they would act as trained cadres working "actively to create a climate of mutual respect and good will (and also make) themselves available to staff, students, and the school community when problems arise in the human relations areas." These cadres were to be the nucleus to which teachers subsequently going through training sessions would orient themselves. The cadre members were chosen in part because they were neither ultra conservative nor excessively liberal in their racial attitudes. Their job is a difficult one, for as one teacher suggested in laughing over the seeming impossibility of modeling himself after his instructor, "we were supposed to be miniatures of Birnbaum, 'mini-Maxes,' as it were."

Two-day workshops were designed for all other school personnel as well as selected parents and community leaders, including members of the police force. Ideally, even these quickie sessions would "heighten staff awareness of human relations problems," and increase the individual's capacity "for dealing with tensions and incidents that arise from majority-minority relations."

Here then lay not only a plan for dealing with unrest but a rather representative example of the majority of American schools' reaction to it and a circumscribed philosophy for treating it. Presently, the name of the game is to reduce racial incidents, avoid police intervention, keep schools open, and ameliorate as best as one can situations where "overly angry" demands result in harsh disciplining. Some argue that modern techniques such as group sessions maintain the status quo, and hence merely lessen the frequency of beatings and expulsions. Others feel that perhaps these techniques are a first step in real change, change that might mean the birth of new programs, new curriculums, new life. Still others can't see any connection between the techniques, as elaborate as they may appear, and radical community change that ultimately would render violent protestations obsolete and human relations training laboratories comically anachronistic.

A two-day workshop last April, which the author attended as an observer, was typical of the abbreviated training sessions. No one could tell for sure just what thoughts entered the minds of the thirty people who assembled that Thursday morning in the large dining room on the second floor of a Bristol motel. About

9 o'clock in the morning they came, a bit nervous, to commence whatever it was they were about to commence. The group consisted of sixteen teachers, one principal, eight district education specialists such as librarians and music teachers, and five laymen from the community. It was a group with mixed backgrounds and experience. For instance, there were teachers for whom Negroes, and Jews, and the very concept of welfare were totally foreign before their arrival in Bristol not so many years earlier. Others had lived their whole lives in the community.

Slowly they chose chairs placed around tables arranged in a large rectangle with the center open. In front of them were name cards, and at one end, in casual dress, sat their two leaders, Birnbaum and his associate, Jim Small. Along one side of the room a waitress arranged coffee, tea, and sweet rolls on a small table. This observer sat removed from the group, but still in full view.

To describe in detail what transpired in the course of the next two days would be a violation of ethics, a disclosure of materials that are confidential. Without breaking a trust, however, some things may be reported.

Max and Jim, as they were instantly called, spent the entire first day, from 9 in the morning until 10 at night, interviewing all thirty people, one by one. The purpose of the interviews was twofold: to offer the participants an opportunity to introduce themselves to the group and give some idea of their background, and to start building a group agenda by identifying those problems and issues in the school and community that each felt to be important. The individual interviews within the group setting, as all the others listen, make it easier to speak of ethnic and racial differences and attitudes without some of the tensions normally felt in everyday social intercourse. They also help the participants to understand how influential their own religious and ethnic backgrounds have been in shaping their attitudes and actions—and how diverse these backgrounds are. And, finally, the interviews bring out personal information that helps to generate mutual trust among individuals, and contributes to the growing cohesiveness of the group.

Reluctant, at first, to reveal much of themselves, the participants were influenced, persuaded, and sometimes prodded into speaking more freely. Occasionally an important aspect of the interviewing technique would involve "role-modeling," in which the leaders honestly admitted to their own prejudices, ambivalences, and insecurities, and thereby helped participants admit to their failings and uncertainties. Gradually, as trust developed and the leaders revealed so much of themselves, the others could not help but speak of the poverty they had experienced, their anger at being called a wop or a kraut, the brittle tensions between people of hard and soft coal mining regions, their ambivalence toward blacks, or toward young people generally. They spoke too, in these interviews, of trying to be fair with all students, taking and treating them one by one as they came along, and of their assurance that prejudice is learned in the home, rarely in the school.

Ideally, group interviewing brings out the singular identity of each participant, only to have these identities merge into a web of enduring trust and promise for change. A delicate technique, group interviewing requires a special skill in encouraging openness while avoiding psychotherapeutic kinds of intervention. The personalities and temperaments of the leaders, perhaps even their charisma, may be essential energy that ignites and maintains the force of such a procedure. But the energy is clearly wasted if for even a moment the objective of change within the context of school is lost or submerged. For the goal is not sensitivity training for personal growth, but is always problem oriented.

As the participants' confidence in each other increased, others joined in the interviewing, reacting, probing, asking, seeking new understanding. Gradually the discussion turned to the inevitable tensions of black and white, rich and poor, old and young, male and female, teacher and student, parent and child, single and married, and always the leaders seeking the sources of conflict, without opening personal scars. Just enough so that by the next day one could ask about such matters as inter-racial dancing and dating, or could describe one's own experience with prejudice. Just enough persuasive joking and nagging, advancing and receding, to make it almost possible to imagine what it is like to be the single black person in a classroom, the boy called kike, or the girl not asked for a date. Just enough to permit people to tell why regulations mean so much, and why manners and order often overshadow human expansiveness, creativity, and adventure in the classroom.

A noticeable relief spills into the room when the leaders consent to a coffee break or lunch time or Coke time. Somehow the group, the all-of-them-together, has been born. The hours since the morning now mean history, the medium for recollection and trust. The hours in the future mean the moment when the interviewing radar will get to oneself. In the afternoon, television and newspapers are blamed for exacerbating racial tensions, which now, like a theme or irrepressible melody, dance in and out of the discussion, returning unexpectedly under topics like athletics or the meaning of manhood.

Just before dinner, members of the group turn to speak of their home towns where prejudice rarely existed, or at least was unrecognized. They also speak of a town's Jew Hill or its Italian ghetto. Then the undercurrent of blackness-whiteness returns. It comes back in terms of social mobility, ethnic groupings, patronage systems, rural-urban comparisons, and status inconsistencies, and the leaders spend a moment lecturing on the multiplicity of values endemic in a pluralistic society.

During the evening session, as the men and women in the motel bar below sip drinks and speak of themselves, and perhaps the world, discussion in the group upstairs returns to racial tensions. The group is just now starting to label differences and "get these differences out on the table." The leaders move with special prudence, abiding by their own sense of where one can push and where one cannot. They hunt focal persons, all the while watching for others who listen more to one member than to another. Aware of the resistances, they work to pump the bubbles of energy and understanding out from the wells of self-consciousness. For the moment, however, the group moves slowly. People are tired, anxious to leave, forgetting momentarily that tomorrow means resuming.

Fresh the next morning, "old friends" convene, some seeking new seating arrangements almost as if their identities might somehow be strengthened in a different location. They are quickly at work, the discussions more open, more penetrating, their anger and defiance direct and exposed, their resistance melting a bit around the edges. The focus is on immediate problems, with the long and revealing experience of the previous day providing understanding and a context for specific issues. They are back at a brand of work they had never known, with an energy and drive that seems to them almost magical. Soon it is afternoon. Participants seem to be sensing the end, the pieces begin to fit together. Abruptly, a discussion of prayer in the public schools explodes. Everyone's talking. They've caught on. They've gotten it. It has taken many hours and four coffee breaks, but suddenly they are appreciating human differences and needs and the fact that while some men will kill to eliminate these differences, others might kill just to preserve them. They're listening, laughing, making sure they don't forget certain special phrases. Then it is over. Some are glad to leave. Max and Jim have shaken hands and departed. Everyone moves out, trying to figure out just what has happened in these upstairs rooms—and whether the future will be altered by these two days.

To speak later with teachers is to learn that for some the impact of the experience doesn't diminish even months afterward. For the cadres, the effect remains uncertain and the feeling of inadequacy endures. "But still we've got to do something. At least things have been put on the table, and we can speak openly of black and white issues." Although their immediate concerns lie primarily with race, the effect of social class, religion, and ethnic differentiations are also more clearly understood.

Reactions to these groups are yet to be studied systematically. On the basis of a few conversations, it seems that some find the experience too blunt, wasteful, and irrelevant. Others find it valuable, useful, morale building, though anxiety provoking. Many teachers argue that the training groups have been instrumental in bringing some schools over a hump of racial unrest And many, too, point to the dramatic example of Joe Ruane as one "who got a lot out of the group."

Joseph John Ruane, the principal of FDR Junior High School, did indeed get a lot out of the group. The story of the change in "Karate Joe," as he once was called, is far from typical; it almost borders on the apocryphal, and no one treasures this more than Joe. It was in his office that the suspension of the three girls took place. It was in his schoolyard that police stalked about keeping the Cobras away from an already "too tense situation."

Years ago, Joe Ruane was a tough man, a man who'd just as soon shove a kid up against a locker as speak with him. There were no discussions, no negotiations with Karate Joe in those days. The door to his office stayed tightly shut, opening only for disciplinary problems. Then a teacher would come in, complain or cry, and Joe would storm out to settle the matter. But no more. Discipline problems persist naturally, but Joe Ruane has changed. His door stays open, and when he cannot negotiate with tolerance, he's likely to turn to an assistant principal "who'll inevitably be seen by the kids as 'Mr. Nasty'."

More often, however, Joe will turn over discipline problems to his Inter-group Advisory Council, a group of· twenty-two thoughtful ninth-graders. Several times this past year, this group of black and white students has had to make serious decisions regarding school disruptions. Once it was about fighting in the halls, another time skirmishes after basketball games. In both cases, the council, given full control by Ruane and teacher Arnold Hillman, who sits as faculty representative, devised disciplinary procedures that worked.

To generate the council, Ruane, Hillman, and science teacher Albert Ulbinsky—all graduates of the five-day leadership workshop—aided several student leaders in planning a general student election, replete with area redistricting in order to achieve greater black representation. In the end, fifteen whites and eight blacks were elected. The actions of the council, their deliberations over drug taking, racial unrest, smoking, quality of teaching, and physical discipline have been their own, not their advisers'. A highly respected group, it remains eager to tackle any school problem, from the Cobras to filth in the cafeteria.

"No one used to be more bullheaded than I," Joe will announce publicly. "The muscle worked. Now I see it's bad. I can deck 'em, but it isn't going to prove anything except that the kids are right about the Establishment." Apparently others agree. When flareups occurred at a neighborhood school last spring, the principal asked Ruane to speak with the parents. Quite a tribute from one principal to another.

The story of Karate Joe is told with relish in Bristol Township as dramatic proof of the effectiveness of the human relations program, but Birnbaum demurs. "Obviously," he says, "such a miraculous conversion was a long time in preparation. Joe Ruane just happened to be ready for change, and his training group showed him how. There's nothing magical in human relations training—if there were, we would have to be suspicious of it."

As dramatic as the story of Joe Ruane is, another event provides better evidence of the social efficacy of the program. During a 1969 football game between archrivals Woodrow Wilson and Bishop Egan, several black youths were arrested for stealing. Presumably they had snatched purses and then had been seen "walking mysteriously" through the parking lot. The police arrived and seven persons were arrested. Five of these, juveniles, were released in custody of their parents. Another two were given disorderly conduct charges; in addition, one was charged with resisting arrest and threatening a police officer. Bail for him, originally set at $2,000, was reduced substantially after black leaders intervened.

The incident, however, was handled gently and compassionately by teachers and administrators. They were able to "hang-loose" and let "the kids" handle their own behavioral reactions within the schools. After a fretful weekend in which adult activists tried to stir up action in the black community, it was the students, on Monday morning, who resolved the problem. They ran closed meetings to discuss the issues, inviting school and community officials as they saw fit. The situation was touch and go, but it never did erupt. A sufficient number of students had developed faith in the fairness of some administrators and teachers to resist the call for militant action.

Despite these promising results, for Knute Larson the Bristol Township experiment can never be totally successful. "The training groups," he says, "can do just so much." Many problems do remain. The cadres are constrained by their lack of experience in human relations work and by other teachers' natural resentment of being "guided by their colleagues."

Larson doesn't fear dress styles, music fads, beads, granny glasses, underground newspapers, long hair, or even Students for a Democratic Society. He's proud of the 35 per cent of Woodrow Wilson High School graduating seniors who go on to some form of higher education, and the fact that Bristol Township is willing and able to hire good teachers, black and white. The content of his apprehension is predictable: "Things are bad, let's face it. Nobody is doing anything about the cities, and if they go down, we will all go with them. At least we're trying to do something about our problems."

More generally, results of programs like the one in Bristol Township are always tentative, always in balance. As they say on almost every campus, "things could blow next week." So far the approach taken has worked, racial tensions have not erupted even in areas where hostilities and anger lurk almost everywhere, but no one can yet claim that the training groups significantly reduce individual prejudice, though they do seem to increase awareness and get the problems "out in the open" where they can be seen and discussed. Hopefully, this means that little understood attitudes and feelings will not continue to control individual behavior and organizational decisions. One must ask whether political and social institutions will reinforce these changes, or will work to maintain that status quo the groups have sought to challenge. Social change is difficult to bring about, but it just may be occurring in Bristol Township.

THE DILEMMA OF CITIZEN PARTICIPATION*

by Robert C. Seaver

In the broadest sense, citizen participation in public affairs, particularly at the local level, is a fact of political life that applies no more and no less to urban renewal and city planning than it does to any other function of government. At the ballot box, in public hearings, and through all the other less formal avenues that our system provides, the people will make their views known and their interest felt. This phenomenon is intensified today by the growing expectations and militancy of groups not formerly recognized in the traditional urban power structure. So in a way it is misleading to speak of a dilemma of citizen participation for it implies some choice, however equivocal.

Yet in a more limited sense there is a dilemma. It is not whether to have citizen participation in the broad sense—that is taken for granted—but whether to incorporate as a part of official process a more positive form of citizen engagement. In this limited sense, the dilemma goes this way: Experience shows that failure to get across to the people the rationale of a given proposal may evoke opposition based more on emotion than on the merits of the case, and therefore far more virulent. Yet in some cases, efforts to bring the community into the process early enough to create understanding has seemed to do more to forearm the opposition than to win support. So arises the argument that the best citizen participation is the least citizen participation.

This argument is superficial and probably frivolous. There

* Taken from Selected Readings Series Seven, *Citizen Participation in Urban Development*, Volume 1, Edited by Hans B. C. Spiegel, NTL Institute for Applied Behavioral Science, 1968. Reproduced by special permission of the author and the publisher from Pratt Planning Papers, 4, The Pratt Institute, New York City. Written when the author was Chief of the Bureau of Community Affairs, City of New York Housing and Redevelopment Board, 1960-65.

are too many instances—regrettably eclipsed by the horror stories
—to indicate that it is possible to work with the community with
benefit to both sides. The critical question seems to be whether
or not the conditions necessary to successful citizen engagement
are tolerable to the administrative, political, and professional
establishment in whose hands the initiative lies. Some of these
will be suggested later. They do not necessarily imply the sur-
render of integrity or the abdication of responsibility. But they do
imply some sharing of the decisions in the process. So to many
responsible people in the field the question—whether to accept
the conditions will accomplish more than to reject them—is very
real.

It will become more real. A new body of thought in the social
welfare field—the client as partner rather than recipient, the poor
as abused rather than delinquent—has been given a firm shove
forward by the statutory requirement of "maximum feasible participation" by the poor in community programs under the federal
war on poverty.

Congress has, in effect, set a new national standard of citizen interest and involvement that, however hazy, goes far beyond anything ever contemplated in more than a few localities
prior to the antipoverty program. The two chief features of this
standard are that it recognizes the vested interest and certain
corollary if unspecified rights of the people who are directly affected by public programs, and that it places at least a part of the
power to shape or respond to such programs in their hands. This
standard is being established in the very communities where renewal is most likely to be needed, and long-range planning finds
its maneuvering room. Even if it were not, the tide of events is
such as to sweep the underlying philosophy into such areas. Ad-
vent of these ideas has already led to instances where community
residents were mobilized by personnel paid with antipoverty
funds by one local agency, to oppose the renewal or planning
proposals of another agency. Some renewal and planning veterans, looking ahead, wonder if it will be possible to live with this
standard. They are far from sure that the answer is yes, but fearful of the implications if it is no.

One reason the question is so opaque is that within the urban renewal field, and to an even lesser degree in city planning,
there never has been an adequate resolution in policy or practice
of what citizen participation is, can, or should be or do. Indeed,
the central difficulty in discussing it is that almost everyone has
a different view based on unspoken assumptions and perspec-

tives that in turn spring from differing personal imperatives, political philosophy, social understanding, and other variables. The basic idea that somehow the parties in interest should have some voice in the process commands almost everybody's assent. But who the parties are, what kind of a voice they should have, about what aspect of the process, and with what degree of influence, are questions that evoke the most diverse array of strongly—even combatively—held opinions.

Policies and practices in citizen participation reflect this diversity from one locality to another. More importantly, they reflect it in the quality of the engagement effort in any given locality. That is, the substance of the exchange between citizen and agency in any community is much more likely to be the result of a functional compromise among the respective views of the various people responsible for action than it is to reflect the abstract principles of participation espoused by policy-makers. Beyond a certain point, this descrepancy is one practical measure of how productive or destructive the exchange will be.

These gaps are not merely semantic. They reflect real differences over the proper scope and nature of social welfare efforts, whether renewal and planning are properly concerned with these, and the proper relationship between profession and lay opinions in public affairs. Detailing these is beyond the scope of this short paper. The point is that the dilemma of citizen participation arises from these differences and not from some inherent quality of the process itself. The more they can be resolved or at least made explicit the clearer the substantive issues become, and the brighter the prospects for honest and even productive collaboration between city and citizen.

Nobody can claim a magic formula to insure such a happy outcome. Probably none exists. But it is possible to suggest some commonsense steps in a more rational approach to communication between citizen and agency.

One is to recognize that there are formidable obstacles to productive citizen-agency exchange, acknowledge them and ventilate them as freely as possible in discussion. If in the course of this some of them disappear, so much the better. At least they are in the open and can be taken into account.

First of all, virtually everyone who is a party to the renewal or planning process operates from a different set of imperatives. With the certainty of oversimplification, the situation may be typified this way: The elected executive hopes if possible to offend no one—the voters directly affected, their legislators, the

"responsible" elements of the community, various other segments of the local power structure; he may also hope to satisfy
some secondary aims or commitments in the process of getting
something constructive done. So he proclaims his administration's willingness to listen to all views in its pursuit of progress
and betterment, and hope for the best. The appointed administrator may be more or less sensitized to the web of interests surrounding the matter, and have greater or less skill in coping
with it. But he is most likely to respond to the need for tangible
achievement. So he listens, but subordinates what he hears to
what he has been told—or himself believes—is the most important objective. Under him, the bureaucrats will fit what remains
of the message into the iron maiden of procedures and programs
at their disposal, and the technicians will further select what they
are capable of responding to in light of their own professional
disciplines and personal capacities. The result of this process
may be a response that comes as a shock to the citizens who are
unaware of the hazards of transmission loss and filtration that
beset their original statements. This model presupposes good
faith on all sides. It does not take into account attempts to exploit the issues for ulterior purposes—though the situation offers
fertile ground for such tactics.

Secondly, there is gross disparity between the actual capabilities of renewal and planning programs as such, and the results citizens expect of them, or have been led to expect. This is
a manifestation of the more general disparity between the global
manner in which citizens perceive community wants and needs,
and the compartmentalized structure of public programs designed to meet them. The bureaucrat or technician is frustrated at the citizen's apparent inability to understand that he
cannot solve all problems because they are not all his responsibility. The citizen is frustrated at the bureaucrat's apparent indifference to the richness and diversity of his wants and needs.
This is particularly true of renewal, which may be the first public
program to touch intensively a deprived area with a dreary history of neglect. It will unleash a flood of complaints, resentments, and demands which far outreach the limited tools of the
program itself. Yet the far-reaching power of those tools to
change the makeup of a neighborhood somehow lures planners
and politicians alike into a grandiosity of expression that only
serves to reinforce the popular misconception that renewal is a
panacea. Essentially an instrument of physical change, it is spoken of as if it could solve all social and economic problems as

well. The people, dazzled at the prospect of so much so soon, are naturally disappointed and hostile when the bulldozer (or some lesser form of displacement) issues forth instead of milk and honey. The long-range prospects offered by planning are sometimes even more disillusioning in their short-term product. To gloss over the realistic limits of what renewal and planning can accomplish directly, and what they must leave to coordinated efforts through other forms of public action, can only lead to misunderstanding and bitterness. So, too, however, will refusal to discuss concerns outside their immediate scope.

Thirdly, but related, is that within their direct scope, renewal and planning are beset by goal conflicts which must be balanced out in the development of specific proposals. To cite a few: tax base preservation vs. housing the poor; minimum cost vs. maximum amenities; minimum disruption and relocation vs. maximum housing improvement and production. Some of these are products of renewal's split personality; its conception as an instrument of physical and economic betterment, with social benefits important but indirect aims, vs. growing efforts to satisfy immediate social needs directly. Others spring from conflicts within the social goals: integration vs. neighborhood preservation (especially in ghetto areas) for example.

Turning from these general observations, a second step is to recognize certain realities about the process of citizen engagement that may seem self-evident to many, but are often ignored or forgotten in practice. Officials at all levels often seem to fail to understand what they are setting in motion when they undertake to engage the community. This failure, more than any real threat in the process, seems to produce most of the disfunctions and bad experiences, which are exacerbated when the foregoing obstacles are encountered. One of these realities has already been noted. It is that the engagement process cannot be neatly confined to an agenda of pure planning or renewal questions. Once engaged, the community will not be patient with the procedural niceties and delays of renewal, nor will it be satisfied with simply discussing a roster of future benefits and satisfactions. A city that undertakes to engage the community in the renewal and planning processes must anticipate the likelihood that supplemental services and interim activities will be required. It should be prepared to see the community, once engaged, steadily press its concern with immediate problems—with special emphasis on social and community services—even while discussing more remote solutions. Another reality is that, once begun, engagement is not something that can readily be turned off or manipulated to some predetermined end. Its initiation represents a commitment on the part of local government and its professional establishment to let the people have their say and to respond reasonably to their expressions. Failure to fulfill the commitment will not end the process, only escalate it via other channels. Sometimes when the community begins to ask hard or embarrassing questions, professionals retire beneath a mantle of experience and qualifications to demand that their judgments be accepted as revealed truth; administrators retreat behind a smoke screen of procedural objectives. Neither satisfies the community, who see the process as directed toward their welfare (and why not—that was what they were told, wasn't it?) not toward the observance of rules or standards that seem to them arbitrary or artificial. The inevitable result of such a failure to fulfill the commitment is a continuing miasma of hostility and mistrust that communicates to other neighborhoods as well, and other areas of government activity.

So in addition to flexibility and responsiveness to concerns outside the scope of renewal and planning, the engagement process must entail a continuing two-way communication rich with education as well as information. This is the only way that emergent proposals can be shown as reasonable to the lay people on the other side of the table, and the procedural requirements made understandable.

It will not take long, either, for at least some in the community to sense it if the process of participations is not genuine. To attempt a pro forma engagement process with the idea of obtaining sanction without giving some options is to risk a schism that may well wreck sound and basically acceptable plans. The community must have a chance to make some contribution, exercise some real choice. Fortunately, situations are rare where there is one and only one technically, economically, and politically acceptable solution to a given set of problems. But among the choices may be one that is more acceptable to the community for reasons that may appear completely irrelevant to the official or professional. To learn which it is should be a primary goal of the engagement process. The bare minimum of reality should be an opportunity for the community to choose among sound options.

In no reasonably diverse community is there likely to be found a single "voice" that may be engaged with assurance that its sanction will mean sanction of the whole community or even a majority within it. There are in most communities many interests, usually advancing demands which are at cross purposes or mutually exclusive. To elicit as many as possible of these is essential if the community is to be presented with choices among possible options that are meaningful as proposals are developed. More important, if these diverse positions are not made explicit in full view of all factions, it will be impossible to arrive at compromise or choice among them through community consensus, and agency decisions about them are likely to appear—and be branded—capricious or arbitrary. To try and keep diverse interests separate or under wraps is to invite all factions to turn their fire on the agency.

Furthermore, it is a virtual certainty that the "organized" community as it is first encountered does not represent the full range of interest which will be affected by the ultimate proposals. Even the most assiduous engagement efforts will probably leave some of these untouched, only to later awake to the implications of formulated proposals, and come forward to state their interest—at a time when it is least possible to accommodate them.

Even if late-blooming demands are kept to a minimum, the engagement process is unlikely to be orderly, predictable or even rational. The subject is inherently volatile and explosive—charged with profound implications for the lives and fortunes of many, and hence with emotion. Social and economic factors influence the citizen's ability to understand and respond to information provided to him, and the level at which he may engage in dialogue about it and his own wants and needs. They will also influence the individual and community view of the trustworthiness and good faith of the source, whether it be official, community leader, community worker, or other. Communities themselves vary widely in structure and composition, problems and available solutions. So just as there is no single renewal plan or technique which will meet the needs of all communities everywhere, there is no single format or procedure for citizen engagement that applies to all. The dole key element seems to be genuine collaboration. Without it, nothing is mobilized but opposition.

The importance of skilled, specialized staff in dealing with these realities has already been discovered by most cities with experience in citizen participation. Their experience indicates that a wide range of skills and backgrounds can work effectively in the process, and that procedures can vary widely with good results. But only in relatively small communities with relatively simple problems and structures—in effect, where the administrator is at the project manager level—is it possible for him as principal official to handle all community relations single-handed. Even then, the degree of continuing personal contact required, the sustained nature of the education, information, and service activities necessary to a productive dialogue, is likely to be burdensome. When the burden is underestimated at the outset, or let fall somewhere along the line, problems are certain to arise.

However, no number of specialized community liaison staff, or degree of skill among them, will guarantee a successful engagement process. The community worker can only facilitate communication. Planners and officials who are responsible for the formulation of substantive proposals are the ones who must actually engage, for they are the ones with the power to respond in practical fashion to community views and demands. If they take no part in it, the engagement process will lack the essential element which is required for any prospect of success.

Some will ask, why bother? For planners at least, one answer suggests itself. Among the pervasive inconsistencies and conflicts that characterize renewal and planning as public programs is one between the technical operations themselves and the medium of their implementation—politics. The former are abstract, usually long-range, anti-crisis, and contingent. The latter is concrete, immediate, crisis-oriented, and definitive. Thus many planners see cherished concepts and objectives lost in the ordeal of compromise and accommodation through which their work must pass on the way to realization. Sometimes they may feel that the end product bears little important resemblance to their original concept.

Is it possible that the reason lies somewhere in a failure of planners to build a constituency for their competence? That instead of identifying their efforts with some consensus in the battle, they have remained aloof and let their efforts fall among the factions, to be torn apart? If so, perhaps planners should insist on working in the closest possible collaboration with the community, not apart from it—in effect making themselves consultants to the community rather than prescribers for it. There have been instances where planners, working within the entire context of stresses, limitations, and conflicts of a given situation, have helped a community arrive at a viable solution which was implemented by the political and administrative authorities. But such advocate planning, whether done from within or outside the official establishment, imposes some grave responsibilities. Where these attempts have led to professional and political conflicts, little has been accomplished without the most painful kind of controversy and furor. Where they have led to community demands for solutions which are beyond the capacity of available economic, administrative, or political resources, nothing has been accomplished. There is nevertheless a good deal to suggest that planners— and others in the renewal and planning fields—have more to gain than to lose in embracing the action horn of the citizen participation dilemma. Like all sharp objects, it needs to be treated with respect. But it need not gore. And there may be no choice. The waves of community action and citizen interest that are building on the entire local government front may force the choice unless it is made with good grace and skill first. It is worth thinking about.

THE PROFESSIONAL LEADER*

This is not a treatise on the professional leader. Volumes of materials approaching the subject from many points of view have dealt in detail with his job and training. He is, of course, much more than just a paid employee. He is presumed to be a person of competence in his field, and it is presumed that his competence is recognized. But what we are basically concerned with here is the role of the professional in the field of community development and the ways in which his competence in the field of community development is developed.

The Role of the Professional Leader. It is only rarely that the professional leader, as we think of him here, is a member of the local primary group. In a democratic society he is essentially a paid expert, be he a teacher, preacher, organizer, or extension agent. And, of course, these are just a few of many possible fields of professional leadership. Take the minister of a church, for example. He may know more about his church than anyone else in it and he may be officially a member of it. But his position in it

* Reprinted with permission from *Community Development*, by Arthur F. Wileden, The Bedminister Press, Totowa, N. J., 1970.

is only temporary. Try as he may to the contrary, he is always looked upon as an outsider. When his position as a professional worker in the church ceases, he is, with very rare exceptions, no longer a member of the local church group. He may even be prohibited from being a member. So it is with almost all professional leaders.

What then is the role of a professional? Let us take a look at the reasons for a person's employment as a professional. For one thing it is assumed that he has a competence to bring to the organization or agency that will help it to define more clearly its functions and to carry on those functions in society. It is also assumed that he will strengthen the agency or organization and make it more effective in carrying on its functions. His success as a professional will be measured in terms of his success in achieving these objectives.

In what way is the role of a professional different from that of the volunteer leader in the same organization? Is he, like the volunteer, a spokesman for the group? Yes, when he is sure he is speaking for the group, but it would be better if he had a volunteer take over the spokesman's job. Of course, there are times when he must speak for the group, but he had better be sure that he does accurately represent what it stands for. State and national professional leaders are today often accused of not accurately understanding, or of misrepresenting, the attitudes and objectives of the groups they propose to represent. This leads to a questioning of the honesty and integrity of the professional.

Is he a group planner? Often, probably too often, he tries to serve in this role. It is easy for him to yield to the temptation of developing the plans and outlining the program for the organization. It often seems quicker and easier to do it this way. Certainly he should be in on the planning, and certainly he should be expected to make suggestions and present evidence relative to the merits of different plans. He should even express his judgment, when called for, as to what seems best for the organization. But he is definitely not the planner, his role being only to facilitate the planning.

Is he a group executive? The answer is yes, when properly authorized to speak and act as the group's executive, but not until then. The determination of who should carry out the decisions is the group's to make. The group is his constituency and he is employed by it to do its will. When he can no longer do this to the satisfaction of both himself and the group, he should either resign from his position or leave the executive role to someone else.

Is he a group educator? If we interpret the role of "educator" in its true sense, this appears to be the role in which the professional community leader should excel, and where he should reflect his greatest competence. After all, he is a professionally educated man working for the group. His education, as we will discuss later, should not be limited to the narrow field of his assigned leadership but should be in terms of society as a whole. He should help his organization to see and to take its place in the broader scheme of things. His constituency is both his organization and the general public.

It is in this regard that we agree with Sanderson and Polson[1] and with Ross[2] that the professional leader has his most valuable duty to perform. Sanderson and Polson write that it is his duty to "inspire, stimulate, discover, develop, and train" voluntary leaders. Ross defines his role as guide, enabler, expert, and therapist. His success as a professional leader will in no small degree depend upon his success in performing these roles. His most beneficial roles are those of the careful observer, of the educator, of the group advisor, and of the group interpreter.

His Preparation and Training. It is his preparation and training that qualify the individual for his job as a professional leader. The nature of that training is therefore very important. It needs to be sufficiently specialized to qualify him to serve properly the organization or agency that will employ him. At the same time it needs to be sufficiently comprehensive in orientation so that he may view his particular professional field in its broader relationship to society. These requisites are met in varying degrees from one profession to another and from one training program to another.

The training itself, as we think of it today, takes roughly three forms. We have come to call them pre-service training, in-service training, and on-the-job training. Most of pre-service training is at the college level. The developing standards within the various professions seem to require such training to an ever greater extent. As a matter of fact, in most professions today there is a trend toward more and more training at the graduate level or its equivalent. This is the case in most fields of professional community leadership. The trend is for undergraduate

[1] Sanderson and Polson, *Rural Community Organization.*

[2] Ross, Murray G., *Community Organization—Theory and Principles.*

training to be of the broadening nature and for graduate training to provide more specialized professional training. In the various fields of community leadership basic training in the social sciences is becoming increasingly recognized as essential. Because of the rapidly advancing and changing fields of knowledge, various types of in-service training are also becoming recognized as essential if a professional worker is to keep up to date. This is particularly true of some of the newer professions that started with relatively untrained personnel, and of those professions where the standards are being raised. These seem to include practically all types of community leadership. A far-reaching illustration of recent efforts in in-service training is that now being offered at selected agricultural colleges in the United States for the training of cooperative extension personnel. Each year several hundred extension people from all over the United States attend these summer schools. The training offered is both of a general and specialized nature and carries credit at the graduate level.

Another type of in-service training is aimed directly at the field of community leadership itself. It is basically for professional leaders, but is planned to include professionals representing all phases of community life: schools, churches, public health, welfare, organizations, and various phases of adult education. It may encompass a period of several days or several weeks. Its purpose is to enable professional leaders, sharing a common background of subject matter material, to consider together at the theoretical level the problems which they and their volunteer leaders need to work out at the community level. It is with this purpose in mind that this author, for more than a decade, has been encouraging a very successful series of annual Workshops for Professional Community Leaders.[3] Topics of central concern in recent years have been Situation Analysis—A Method for Identification of the Major Problems of the Emerging Community; Automation and Human Values; Guiding Social Change—Criteria for Decision Making; and the Changing City—Problems and Opportunities.

We probably are indebted to the Veterans Administration following World War II for the popularity of the idea of on-the-job training. Even though it was not designed as a leader training

---

[3] Wileden, A. F. (ed.)—The following reports are available: *Situation Analysis—A Method for Identification of the Major Problems of the Emerging Community* (1965); *Automation and Human Values* (1963); *The Changing City—Problems and Opportunities* (1962).

program, it has demonstrated its possibilities on a large scale. Just as we have pointed to the possibility of training volunteer leaders through supervision by professionals, there is the possibility of training professionals by other professionals, and this method is gaining in acceptance. Probably in no agency is it being done on a larger scale than in the Extension Service, where the approximately 8000 county extension agents in the United States are being supervised and serviced by about one-fourth that number of supervisors and specialists. The job of these state and federal supervisors and specialists is more and more being recognized as that of servicing the county personnel with the latest information and of training this personnel in adult education and extension methods. This is done while they are on the job and in terms of the actual situations and problems that arise.

A WORKING RELATIONSHIP

One of the most perplexing aspects of the community development process is the working relationship between the local community and the outside professional. The natural tendency for the professional worker is either to absolve himself from any responsibility for action, or to be impatient with the slowness or seeming inability of local people to arrive at their believed "right" decisions. On the other hand, the tendency on the part of local people is to fail to understand the point of view of the outside professional. This is due, at least in part, to failure in the communication process, but its roots are much deeper than that. We refer to the value system of the professional as contrasted with the value system of the local people. Local people want to preserve those things which have become important to them, and they want to be sure that the new does not jeopardize the old. This goes to the heart of the relationship between the local community and the outside professional.

Let us take a look at the local aspects of the situation. In spite of many changes, the local community, variously conceived, is a very important place to the people who live there. It is where they own property and pay taxes. It is where most of them find their employment. It is where their children go to school and where they and their family go to church and experience most of their family living. It is really the most important place in the world to them. They have much at stake in the future of their community.

At the same time, the future of the local community as a community is today being challenged to its very foundations, and local people know it. They recognize that they are increasingly interrelated with other communities like themselves, or different from themselves, and that they are increasingly dependent on the broader society. This makes the local community increasingly receptive to outside ideas and to outside influences. It is a major reason why community development is increasingly popular today.

Just what are the responsibilities that might properly be assumed by the local community in this community adjustment-development process? Let us briefly hypothesize:

1) The people in the local community have a responsibility for keeping informed on the situation and changes in their community and in the world about them. This is basically a matter of education, and they should be free to call on and expect help from professional researchers and educators, both inside and outside the community, in this educational process.

2) The people in the local community have the responsibility for determining the kind of community they want to live in. This is essentially a matter of objectives and goals, and involves comparative value systems and the making of value judgments. Maybe this is where the church has an important function to perform.

3) The people in the local community have the responsibility for determining how they propose to achieve their agreed-upon objectives and goals. This involves the study-discussion-decision making process, and again, educational understanding both in subject matter content and group process is important.

4) The people in the local community have the responsibility for putting their decisions into action or for seeing that they are put into action. Again, they should feel free to call on and expect help from both public and private agencies outside the community for technical advice and occasionally for assistance.

Let us also look at the other side of this picture—the role of the outside professional in relation to the local community. It is very difficult to generalize on this matter because of the varied backgrounds and institutional assignments of the workers involved. But again, let us hypothesize essentially from the point of view of the worker who views himself as a community development professional.

1) The major role of the outside professional is that of the educator, presumably as either or both a researcher and/or adult educator. As already indicated, this research and education needs to be concerned with an understanding of situations both within and outside the local community and with an understanding of changes that are taking place and their implications. It also needs to be concerned with the organization methods and group processes essential to local decision making and local group action.

2) The outside professional needs be concerned with the application of his knowledge to local action situations. His role here is basically that of an adviser/consultant, which from his point of view may well be considered as work in experimental or pilot situations. This is essential not only to especially critical local situations, but also as a basis for developing an adequately tested body of knowledge in community development.

2) The outside professional may also properly take responsibility for recording and publicizing various types of experiences in community development. This is essential to the educational process in that people learn not only from their own experience but also from the experiences of others, and these experiences need to be recorded, analyzed, and interpreted. This can only be done in perspective by the trained professional worker.

4) The outside professional needs to be familiar with and, if possible, in constant contact with top-level agency professionals who are in any way related to the field of community development. He needs to know "who may be called on for what" and relay this information as needed to local communities. Furthermore, he should concern himself with developing an understanding on the part of the agency people as to the essential characterists of community development, and should attempt to bring the organizations and agencies together in some sort of working relationship

PART V
THE STUDY OF LEADERSHIP
IN SMALL GROUPS AND
ORGANIZATIONS

PART V
THE STUDY OF LEADERSHIP
IN SMALL GROUPS AND
ORGANIZATIONS

As the foregoing selections indicate, leadership research has been undertaken from a variety of academic viewpoints, principally psychology, sociology, political science, communication science and management science. Each discipline has offered a somewhat unique contribution, but few persistent efforts to integrate the findings from alternate viewpoints have occured.

In the selection immediately following, Spotts does a rather thorough job of summarizing and integrating studies of leadership up to approximately 1964. He summarizes research based conclusions from psychology, sociology and management, while suggesting some of the gaps in knowledge to which further research might be applied.

The early research centered primarily on two approaches: (1) the study of "traits" which seemed to characterize effective leaders and (2) study of the situation or environment which gave rise to leadership behavior. The examination of traits or characteristics of leaders helped to refine the list of ideal types but failed to be very scientifically productive in defining essential requirements for leadership. The situational studies generally concluded that leadership requirements depend heavily on the context in which leader acts are to be performed. The kind of leader behavior required rests in part upon the group of people involved, in part on the task to be accomplished, in part on the work environment, and in part on other "functions" which leaders are expected to perform.

The functional approach to leadership studies was generated from situation research and concentrated on the kinds of behaviors required for a group or organization to survive and achieve defined goals. The required behaviors could be performed by a variety of individuals rather than designated leaders only. It was in these studies that the task and maintenance functions were delineated; the effects of various leadership styles were also clarified. Generally the functional research has been highly productive and has helped substantially to lay the groundwork for "interactionist" studies: the most current and highly refined approach to the study of leadership.

This fourth approach stresses the "quality" of the interaction between the leader and his subordinates and relates this quality (or qualities) to productivity, motivation and other variables related to group or organizational performance. Results of these studies lead to the conclusion that the most effective leaders concentrate primary attention upon helping to improve "group" or "team" functioning, rather than emphasizing the technical details of the task to be accomplished. More attention is given to providing a productive climate or environment for task accomplishment, as opposed to closely supervising the activities of group members.

It seems quite clear that success as a leader depends primarily on the ability to enlist and maintain follower commitment and collaboration in the achievement of defined goals, which implies a need for aspiring leaders to understand principles of individual and group behavior as these principles apply to the practical goal-oriented situation.

In the second selection Fiedler describes some of the conclusions of his own research over the past several years. He distinguishes between the "style" of the leader and character of the group or organizational "circumstance" as it contributes to leadership effectiveness. The central factors studied include position power of the leader, task structure, and leader-member interpersonal relations.

He concludes that there are circumstances in which task-oriented leaders perform more effectively than relationship-oriented leaders and vice versa. Nearly anyone can become a "leader" if he carefully chooses the circumstance favorable to his leadership style; or, in other terms, it is less problematical to change a leader's work environment than it is to change his personality. A leader can more easily learn the circumstances in which his style is effective than he can learn to change his style. This means, among other implications, that the success of an organization may depend more on the ability of the organization to adapt to the styles of its leaders than it does on the ability of the leaders to perform leadership functions as defined by the organization.

Any "summary" of research is out-dated ever more quickly as a consequence of expanding behavioral science studies and the extremely rapid alteration in organizational, community and general socio-economic structure. However, the research summaries presented by Spotts and Fiedler outline most of the basic approaches and conclusions of leadership study until the mid 1960's. Since that time a variety of experimental and field studies have been undertaken, from which new results are rapidly becoming available.

The very nature of socio-economic-technological changes demand close attention to new leadership approaches if we are to deal effectively with changed circumstances. Probably the greatest current gap in knowledge revolves around how to adapt social institutions, at the local, area, state and national levels, to the emerging conditions of the future. Leaders must be developed who are capable of understanding these conditions, creating the institutions to meet the new opportunities and solving the multiplicity of problems. There is no clear outline of the specific knowledge and skills required for these tasks.

The very mobility and professionalization of educated manpower tremendously complicates the issue. The individuals with highest potential tend also to be those most heavily involved in activities which do not allow direct attention to institutional adaptation, particularly at the local level. The reward system, in terms of salary levels and working conditions, tends to be most inadequate at the local, area, and state level. Hence, high potential leadership is drawn into business, government, or voluntary organizations with national or even international scope.

The great leadership research need therefore seems to center on studies that will help define how leaders can better perform at the local level, how the reward system can be restructured to attract highly capable talent, and how local social institutions must be altered to effectively capitalize on the opportunities which the future holds. At the same time we must discover how to apply the findings of existing and developing knowledge to practical leadership situations at the local, area and state level.

The alternative may be to lose capability for effective functioning as a localized society, thereby allowing the huge organizations of regional, national or international dimension to dominate and overpower the very idea of local community. This may very well be the appropriate operational mode of the future, but we had better understand the potential consequences adequately enough to make deliberate choices, rather than allowing local loss of responsibility by default.

THE PROBLEM OF LEADERSHIP: A LOOK AT SOME RECENT FINDINGS OF BEHAVIORAL SCIENCE RESEARCH*

by James V. Spotts

. . . . Although literally hundreds of leadership studies have been conducted during the last two decades, there is, at present, no universally accepted theory of leadership. In fact, many divergent and contradictory theories have been proposed. However, during the last few years, research has reached a point where some consistent findings have begun to emerge. This paper will examine some of the past discoveries that are relevant for understanding leadership phenomena and will provide one assessment of the current status of research in this field. . . .

. . . . The mixed and conflicting assumptions about leadership . . . are, frankly, remarkably similar to ideas held, at one time or another, by investigators who have attempted to study and understand leadership from a scientific point of view. Cartwright and Zander (1953) assert that two major problems seemed to have caused behavioral scientists the most trouble. The first is that it has been extremely difficult for investigators to separate and disentangle their assumptions about what leadership *should* be from the straightforward research on the question of *what consequences follow specific leadership practices.* That is, the scientific investigation of problems like leadership is a difficult task; particularly, because it involves value judg-

* Reprinted with permission of the *Kansas Business Review*, School of Business, University of Kansas, Vol. 17, No. 6, June 1964, pp. 3-13.

ments or statements implying that something is "good" or "bad." Scientists are notoriously poor at dealing with questions of value, and it has been difficult for them to separate their own armchair assumptions about what constitutes "good" or "poor" leadership from the variables they are attempting to study. It is only in recent years that investigators have begun to deal with the value question in empirical terms. Thus, leadership is increasingly being defined in operational terms such as behavior that increases production and employee morale or decreases turnover, absenteeism, and so on.

The second, and perhaps more complex, problem has been that of trying to find acceptable scientific definitions for terms like leader and leadership. For some investigators, leadership is viewed as a *characteristic of the individual;* for others, it is seen as a *property of the group.* Some workers define leadership as anyone who performs leadership *acts;* while others define it in terms of *prestige, status, or ability to influence others.* The complexity of the definitional problem is reflected by the fact that in a recent review one investigator compiled a list of 130 different definitions of leadership in a sampling of research literature prior to 1949.[2]

THE STUDY OF LEADERSHIP

Many of the scientist's conceptions about man have their historical roots in philosophical assumptions and ideas that have been a part of the cultural heritage for some time. These philosophical notions are sometimes very valuable in that they sharpen the scientist's conceptions of the phenomena under investigation and help him take into account factors that might otherwise be ignored. However, such ideas can just as easily blind him to other scientific data.

During the eighteenth and nineteenth centuries, philosophers were engaged in heated arguments as to the relative importance of *great men* versus the *situation* these men found themselves in. One group of philosophers believed that the personal characteristics of the great men—men of destiny, such as Napoleon, Caesar, Churchill, and the like—determined the course of history. Some exponents of this view were Thomas Carlyle, Friedrich Nietzsche, Francis Galton, and William James. For example, Carlyle argued vehemently that a true ge-

[2] Bentz, V. J., "Leadership: A Study of Social Interaction." An unpublished manuscript.

nius would contribute no matter where he was found, and James asserted that the great men were the major forces behind the creative mutations and innovations in society.

Opposed to this group were the environmentalists, a group of thinkers who boldly asserted that it was the *Zeitgeist* or situation rather than the great man that determined the course of history. These philosophers declared that the great man was nothing more than an expression of the needs of his time; if one man did not fill this need, another would step forward to do so. This group contended that no man could change society and that any changes wrought by a great man were illusory in that they were only another expression of the needs of the period.

There are concrete parallels to these two kinds of thinking and speculation in current leadership research. That is, much of the early work aimed at discovering the *traits* of the leader is a logical outgrowth and development from the philosopher's *great man* theme. Similarly, the modern exponents of the environmentalist position may be reflected in the work of the investigators who have attempted to study the effects of *situational* factors upon leadership behavior.

The Trait-Oriented Approach

One major vein of early research focused upon isolating the physical, intellectual, or personality traits that distinguished a leader from his followers. Such studies have found that leaders tend to be somewhat bigger than their followers (but not much). Well-accepted leaders also evidence somewhat better adjustment than do followers (but, again, not much).

In one early study, Tead (1935) reported that the traits of the effective leader were nervous and physical energy, a sense of purpose and direction, enthusiasm, friendliness, integrity, technical mastery, decisiveness, intelligence, teaching skills, and faith! In another study, Barnard (1948) stated that the significant traits that distinguished leaders from their followers were physique, technical skill, perception, knowledge, memory, imagination, persistence, endurance, and courage! Other investigators have asserted that the "successful" leader has an above average education, is active in social organizations, and has high moral and ethical standards. (Wald and Doty, 1954) Characteristics such as adjustment, good appearance, need for achievement, assertiveness, and fear of failure have also been reported as necessary leadership traits. (Henry, 1948) While these qualities would be desirable in a leader, none of them seem essential. In this context, Solomon aptly stated:

> The world has seen numerous great leaders who could hardly lay claim to any kind of formal education. History is replete with non-trained, non-academic Fords, Edisons and Carnegies who could not even claim a grammar school education yet managed to become leaders whose influence was felt around the globe.
>
> As for appearance or robust health, need we mention more than the delicate Ghandi, or George Washington Carver, the frail, shriveled, insignificant little Negro who was one of America's greatest scientists, and so many more like them. As for high ideals, fine character, etc. where would Hitler, Capone or Attila the Hun rate here?[3]

While Solomon characterized some of the exceptions to trait-oriented leadership research, a casual examination of the studies cited above quickly reveals one of the major shortcomings of this kind of approach; namely, that rarely, if ever, do two lists agree on the *essential* characteristics of the effective leader. Bird (1940) and Stogdill (1948) have surveyed well over one hundred studies in this area. The discouraging finding was that less than five per cent of the traits reported as characteristic of the effective leader were common in four or more of the studies surveyed. Secondly, there was some evidence to suggest that the leaders, in fact, cannot be markedly different from their followers. Thus, while the leader must be intelligent he cannot be—or appear to be—too much more intelligent that the other group members. Extremes in personality are not usually associated with leadership, if for no other reason than they make the person too different from the other members of his group.

Investigators appear to be generally coming to the conclusion that certain minimal abilities may be required of all leaders. However, these same traits will probably be widely distributed among the non-leaders as well. Moreover, there seems to be an increasing recognition of wide variations in the characteristics of individuals who become leaders in similar situations and of even greater divergence in the traits of leaders working in different situations. (Jenkins, 1947)

The Situational Approach

General dissatisfaction with the failure to isolate leadership traits led some investigators to focus their research efforts more upon the problem of the situation in which leadership occurs. These workers share the assumption that the traits and skills that characterize a "good" leader will vary from group to group and from situation to situation. Associated with this assumption is the notion of *emergent* leadership, which postulates that temporary or situational leaders will arise in groups when necessary to meet the demands of new situations.

The notion that "new" leaders will emerge when groups are in periods of stress or crisis is well documented. Crockett (1955) found that, when a designated leader failed to provide the leadership functions he was supposed to perform, other members provided them, so there would be a minimal loss in group effectiveness. Similar results were reported by Kahn and Katz (1956) in the work situation. These investigators found that, when foremen failed to provide adequate leadership, informal leaders arose in the work groups and provided the needed functions.

Situation-oriented research has assumed that it is unreasonable to expect one leader to always be able to do everything better than anyone else. In out terms, the question might be posed as follows: Is it reasonable to expect a successful businessman to be equally as "effective" in other types of leadership, such as the president of General Motors, a commander of a B-52, the president of a local P.T.A., or a leader of a Special Forces platoon in the jungles of Viet Nam? Obviously, the situation has much to do with determining what leadership skills will be required. Stogdill cogently stated the problem (pp. 64-65).

It is not especially difficult to find persons who are leaders. It is quite another thing to place these people in different situations where they will be able to function as leaders. Thus, any adequate analysis of leadership involves not only a study of the leaders but also of the situation in which leadership acts occur.

There are many studies in the literature that support the notion of situational leadership. For example, Thrasher (1927) in a study of street gangs reported that the particular activity of the group was a major factor in determining who would be the gang leader. In a similar study, Whyte (1943) found that the leaders of these informal gangs actively manipulated their group's activities so as to maintain their leadership. The leader tended to involve his group in activities where he knew he would excel and avoided those situations and activities where his leadership might be threatened.

In a study of the leadership patterns of navy enlisted men on ships during wartime discussed by Burke (1943), it was found that three different patterns of leadership emerged depending upon the situation. In combat, the officers were the effective leaders of the enlisted group. However, during the periods of rest and boredom between battles, it was the "jokesters" and entertainers who seemed to occupy major leadership roles. Finally, when the ships were returning to port the men with previous shore "contacts" emerged as leaders. Similarly, Dunkerly's study (1940) of leadership patterns among college women points to the significance of situational factors. Those girls chosen as *intellectual leaders*, such as house president and the like, were found to be superior to their peers in judgment, initiative, and intellectual ability. Those girls selected as *social leaders* were generally superior to others in dress and appearance. Finally, girls selected as religious leaders were reported as being less "neurotic" than the others. Surprisingly enough, or perhaps not so surprisingly, the social leaders were found to be most "neurotic."

Bass (1960) reports that cross-cultural studies by anthropologists also support the importance of situational leadership factors. He notes that among the Samoans, where there was a highly developed sensitivity to position and social rank, quite different patterns of leadership were evidenced than were found in the individualistic Eskimo society where no man's importance was considered relative to another. Again, leadership among the Iroquois Indians was attained through acts of generosity, hospitality, and cooperation, but, among the Kwakiutls of the Northwest, leadership was established through one's ability to compete financially with others.

Clearly then, there is a wealth of scientific evidence pointing to the significance of situational factors as determinants of leadership behavior. However, this has been found to be only one facet of the leadership problem.

The Functional Approach

A third approach to the study of leadership developed from a functional orientation to the problem. This approach developed under the influence of Kurt Lewin, founder of field-theory in social science, from subsequent theorizing and research in group dynamics and, to some extent, from the human relations movement.

With the Functional Approach, emphasis in research shifted from the study of the leader as a person to the study of the group. One major aim here has been to discover the kinds of behavior that are necessary for a group to survive and attain its goals. In this context leadership is defined as all those member acts that aid in the development of the group and accomplishment of the group's task. Thus, leadership may be performed by one or many members of the group. It is viewed as a quality that a person may display in varying degrees rather than as something he possesses entirely or not at all. Consequently, leadership may be "possessed" to some degree by any member of a group, regardless of his formally designated office or position.

The Functional Approach considers both the individual and the situation in which leadership occurs. This approach assumes that groups (and leaders) are continually faced with two interrelated tasks. The first is that groups must find ways to deal with problems associated with attainment of agreed-upon goals, i.e., resolve task problems. Secondly, group members must find ways to improve and strengthen the group itself, i.e., resolve internal maintenance problems, to achieve its goals.

Benne & Sheats (1948), Bales (1950), and others have attempted to isolate some of the major task and maintenance behaviors that appear in well-functioning groups. Those member (or leader) functions that seem to be effective in moving groups toward resolution of task problems include such acts as asking for clarification of issues at hand, summarizing the contributions of others, proposing new ideas and courses of action, giving and receiving information, coordinating the ideas and suggestions made by others, and so on. Members or leader functions that seem to aid in the resolution of internal problems and maintenance of the group include giving minority views a chance to be heard, mediating and harmonizing conflict within the group, maintaining open channels of communication, ventilating feelings for the group and so on.

There are a number of studies to suggest that the behavior of the leader varies considerably depending upon the task at hand. For example, Carter and his associates (1950) studied the activities of leaders on three different tasks; reasoning, mechanical assembly, and group discussion. In the reasoning tasks, the leaders more frequently asked for information or facts. When confronted with the mechanical assembly task, the leader most frequently expressed the need for action and worked actively with his men. Finally, in the group discussion situation, he was most likely to give information and ask for expression of opinions. The results of the Carter study were based upon data obtained with artificially created laboratory groups. However, similar results have been reported from studies of real-life work groups. Stogdill (1951), in a study of leadership patterns of officers in 46 naval organizations, found that the relative emphasis placed upon particular leadership functions was highly influenced by the task situation. While all officers did some coordinating, this function was most frequently stressed in the work of the executive officer. The function of exercising administrative control was most prominent in the activities of the district medical officer; technical supervision was most frequently observed with the electrical officer; and consultation was practiced most often by the legal officer.

Two other classic studies are worthy of mention in this area. The first, by White and Lippitt (1956), investigated the effects of three different styles of leadership, which these workers designated as Democratic, Autocratic, and Laissez-Faire, on productivity and member morale.

Democratic leaders generally tended to encourage their members to participate in the decision making, did not give rigid rules as to how things were to be done, and gave suggestions, information, and praise to the groups as a whole rather than to individuals. Autocratic leaders, on the other hand, made all final decisions for the groups, told them how to do things, supervised members closely, and praised and punished individual members. The Laissez-Faire leaders gave no suggestions unless specifically requested to do so. They performed a minimum of leader functions and neither praised nor punished group members.

The results of this investigation show clearly that the behavior of the group members differed markedly under the different pattern of leadership. The following was found in this study.

Democratic leadership resulted in greater productivity (measured by the amount of work done) than did Laissez-Faire leadership. On the other hand, Autocratic leadership led to greater productivity than did Democratic leadership. However, the quality of work was consistently better in the Democratic than Autocratic groups.

There was more direct and indirect discontent expressed in the Autocratic groups than in Democratic ones. When the Autocratic leaders were absent, their groups collapsed. In Democratic groups, there was only a slight drop in work involvement during "leader-out" periods.

Members of the Democratic groups expressed greater cohesiveness and satisfaction with their group experience than did either the Autocratic or Laissez-Faire group members. In this respect, the Autocratic groups were characterized by two patterns of member behavior: either the greatest amount of hostility, aggressiveness, and scapegoating among members or the greatest apathy.

Democratic groups showed the least absenteeism and dropouts while Autocratic groups evidenced the most absenteeism and terminations.

Group members evidenced more submissive and dependent behavior in the Autocratic groups than in the other two and showed unsurprisingly less "talking back" to leaders.

While the findings reported in this study were based upon data gathered from youth groups, subsequent investigations (Baumgartel, 1957; Bovard, 1951; Hare, 1953; Preston & Heintz, 1949) with a variety of adult work groups yielded highly similar results. Taken together, these studies suggest that the "style" of the leader can have marked effects upon group member performance.

The second classic leadership study is by Coch and French, (1948). In the factory studied, changes in products and methods of doing jobs were a necessary result of existing competitive conditions in the field. In addition, a marked increase in absenteeism and turnover in recent years had resulted in unbalanced production lines and had made frequent shifting of individuals from job to job necessary. Job changes were, therefore, frequent and were nearly always accompanied by sharp drops in employee productivity. One serious problem that had developed out of this situation was an intense resistance by the production workers to the necessary changes in methods and jobs. This resistance was expressed in frequent grievances to the union about the piece rates that accompanied the new methods and in high turnover, low efficiency, restriction of output, and marked hostility and aggression towards management.

After an initial survey, the experimenters felt that the reactions described above resulted not from the objective difficulties of changing to a new job but from the difficulty of getting people to accept the need for change and to aid actively in creating change. The investigators, therefore, set up a study based upon the idea that participation in the planning and carrying out of change would be helpful. A total of four different work groups were set up; three, the experimental groups, were allowed to participate in the change in different ways, and the fourth, the control group, was treated the same as the groups had been treated in the past.

The control group went through the usual factory routine when jobs were changed. They were told that a change was necessary and that a new piece rate had been set. In this group, there was *no participation* by employees in planning the change though an explanation was given them. The first experimental group involved *participation through representation* in designing the changes to be made; that is, the group elected representatives who met with management to work out the new methods and piece rates. The third variation, used in the other two experimental groups, involved *total participation* by all of the workers in the designing of the new jobs and establishment of the new rates.

Exhibit I shows rather clearly what happened. The control group showed the usual drop in productivity and did not return to its previous level during the period shown. This group continued to carry grievances to the union about the new rates and showed increased absenteeism, job terminations, deliberate restriction of work output, and hostility towards the foremen and management. The first experimental group, with participation through representation, evidenced an initial drop with fairly rapid recovery. The last two experimental groups (combined in the exhibit), in which total participation was allowed, showed practically no drop and then went to a higher level of productivity than before the change.

Two months after the original study, the control group was involved in a new job transfer using the total participation method. With the total participation procedure, this group quickly recovered its previous efficiency rating and, like the other groups, continued on to new production levels. There was no aggression and turnover in the group for 19 days, a fact that contrasted sharply with its previous behavior after the transfer. From the second experiment, the investigators concluded that the obtained results depended upon the experimental procedures

EXHIBIT I
THE EFFECT OF PARTICIPATION ON PRODUCTIVITY

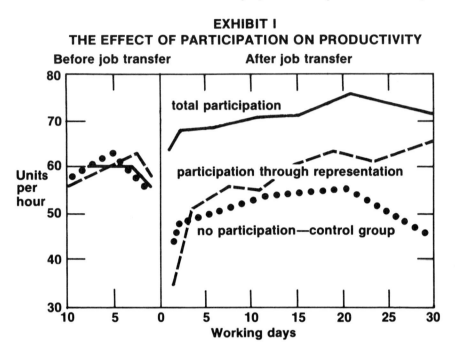

Reproduced by permission from John R. P. French, Jr., C. H. Lawshe, and Floyd C. Mann, "Training for Effective Leadership," *Planning and Training for Effective Leadership* (Ann Arbor, Mich.: The Foundation for Research on Human Behavior, 1956), p. 11.

rather than personality factors, such as skill or aggression, since the same individuals evidenced markedly different behavior in the no-participation treatment as contrasted with the total-participation one.

This particular study gives a striking picture of the effects that participatory leadership may have upon productivity. Other data in this study indicated that the morale of the experimental groups was better than that of the control group. Thus, high production apparently was not obtained at the cost of employee morale or satisfaction; in fact, quite the contrary appeared to be true.

It has been argued by some that research developing out of the Functional Approach fosters "group-think," group decision making, and management methods that encourage the supervisor or manager to give his decision-making function to subordinates. For example, W. H. Whyte in his book *The Organization Man* asserts that the current focus upon groups only encourages in leaders a loss of individuality, conformity, and mediocrity. However, it should be noted that this approach makes no value judgments as to whether a leader should or should not practice a particular leadership pattern. It only asks the question of what consequences are associated with different leadership behavior, and it then leaves the problem of deciding what particular leadership practices will be most effective in a given situation to the practitioner.

Actually, results from studies that have attempted to answer the question of whether leadership should be widely distributed in a group or concentrated in the hands of a few have generally been mixed. For example, Bavelas (1942) found that concentrated leadership resulted in both more efficient performance and lower morale. Similarly, Kahn and Katz (1956), in a study of a variety of high- and low-producing groups in business and industry, found that the supervisors of high-producing group units tended to take clear control of several leadership functions such as planning, coordinating, and so on. However, these supervisors were also more inclined to delegate responsibilities to others, encourage subordinates to make decisions, and take initiative in many activities.

The Interactionistic Approach

Finally, consideration should be given to what may be defined, for lack of a better term, as an Interactionistic Approach to the study of leadership. In many respects, this approach is a logical outgrowth and extension of the Functional Approach. However, there is value in distinguishing the two approaches, if for no other reason than to examine the interactionist's methodology. This approach also has a certain uniqueness in that it stresses the quality of the leader-subordinate relationship as an important determinant of productivity, morale, and other goals seen as "good" or desirable by organizations.

One basic assumption of this approach is that leadership cannot be studied in isolation, because it represents an *interaction* between members of a group. One argument leveled at some of the functional studies was that the results were based upon experimentally constituted laboratory groups that were transitory and divorced from the "real-life" conditions in which leadership occurs. Such complaints can hardly be leveled at interactionistic research, since these investigations characteristically have been field studies in all kinds of work groups and organizations.

A favorite methodology in this kind of research is to select "high-productive" and "low-productive" or "effective" and "ineffective" work groups doing the same tasks in an organization and then study the leader-follower interactions. The answer to the question—Are there significant differences in the superior-subordinate relationships of "productive" and "nonproductive" work groups?—seems to be basically "Yes." Evidence from field studies with B-52 bomber crews, factory assembly lines, public utility companies, infantry combat squads, insurance companies, government agencies, petroleum companies, and so on would suggest that the leader-follower interaction may differ quite markedly in "productive" and "nonproductive" groups (Likert, 1961).

Contrary to what one might suspect, the leaders or supervisors of highly productive units—crews, departments, or divisions—do not appear to devote their greatest time and efforts to technical or job-oriented functions with subordinates. Rather, supervisors or leaders with the best records of performance focus their primary attention upon the human aspects of their subordinate relationships and attempt to build effective work groups with high-performance goals.

High-productive leaders—supervisors and managers—tend to spend more time than low-productive supervisors in motivating their subordinates, providing structure, and keeping them informed as to what is going on, getting their ideas and suggestions on important matters before going ahead, training their subordinates for more responsibilities, trying out new ideas with them, and, in general, showing consideration for the follower and his needs.

At the other extreme, the ineffective or low-production leader frequently demands more from his subordinate than can be done, criticizes them in front of others, treats subordinates without respect for their feelings, rides them for making mistakes, initiates actions without consulting them, and refuses to accept their ideas and suggestions or even explain the actions he has taken.

High- and low-production leaders differ not only in their relationships with their subordinates but also in their relationships with their supervisors. Pelz (1951) found that high-production leaders tended to have much greater influence upon their own superiors on matters relating to subordinates' pay, working conditions, promotions, and so on, than did low-production leaders. In this study, it was also found that, when leaders who had above average influence with their own bosses followed "good" supervisory practices, the subordinates tended to react favorably. However, when supervisors who were below average in the amount of influence they had with their supervisors practiced these same desirable supervisory procedures, they usually failed to obtain a favorable reaction and not infrequently obtained adverse reactions from their subordinates. Apparently, if the leader is to influence his followers effectively, he must also be able to influence his own supervisor as well.

Interactionistic research findings constitute perhaps the closest thing to what might be regarded as leadership "principles" in the whole literature. Although the maxims are fairly well documented by research and experience, they do not form any kind of compact "cookbook" or guide to effective leadership. None of the findings is universally applicable; in fact, one may sometimes obtain similar results with almost opposite leadership practices. Some representative leadership "principles" that are frequently reported in the research literature are as follows:

1. Supervisors of high-productive units spend a greater amount of time developing their work groups into "close," highly cohesive teams than do supervisors or managers of low-productive units.

One assumption here is that a supervisor or leader cannot treat his subordinates with full effectiveness unless he recognizes the work group as a source of morale and motivation. Seashore's study (1954) of high- and low-"cohesive" work groups in a large manufacturing company indicates clearly the powerful influences a small group can exert upon a member's behavior and adjustment. This investigator found that members of high-cohesive groups exhibited much less anxiety than low-pressure to achieve higher productivity, and feeling a lack of support from the company were used as measures of anxiety. Seashore concluded that membership in a cohesive group provides the worker with effective support in his encounters with work-associated anxiety and provides direct satisfactions that are anxiety reducing.

Similarly, research by Trist and Bamforth (1951) with English coal miners supports the importance of the group as a determinant of worker effectiveness and morale. As a part of a program of increasing the mechanization and "efficiency" of mining operations, management broke up the miner's small, face-to-face work groups and assigned the workers to more isolated tasks. The reorganization of the small work groups led to serious problems of absenteeism, turnover, and sickness (including psychosomatic disorders.) This problem became so acute that it was necessary to alter attempts at increased mechanization and restore the small work groups, even though, from an outsider's point of view, this seemed "inefficient."

While the principle of utilization of group factors such as loyalty and group cohesiveness appears to be one of the most firmly established finds in the literature, highly cohesive groups are *not always* the most productive. In Seashore's study, high productivity among cohesive groups was found *only* if the group members saw the company as a supportive and secure situation. Among crews who saw the company as threatening, high cohesiveness was associated with low productivity.

2. General rather than close supervision is more often associated with a high rather than a low level of productivity.

A number of investigators have found that high-production supervisors and managers supervise their employees less closely than low-production supervisors. High-production supervisors make clear to their subordinates what needs to be done then let these subordinates use their own ideas and experience to do the job in the way they find best. Low-production supervisors frequently spend more time with their subordinates than do high-production ones, but the time is broken up into short periods because the supervisors give specific instructions such as "Do this," "Don't do that."

An interesting parallel to this proposition is that leaders tend to supervise their subordinates as they themselves are supervised. (Pfiffner, 1955) Thus, if a department head utilizes general or close supervision, his foremen tend to follow similar practices. It would appear reasonable to assume that low-production subordinates might require more close supervision; however, on the other hand, there is some evidence to suggest that close supervision may actually *cause* poor performance in that it emphasizes precise rules and procedures, at the expense of long-range goals, subordinate morale, and job satisfaction (Likert, 1961).

While general rather than close supervision practices are often more characteristic of high-producing managers than of low ones, research findings *do not* show that all high-producing managers adhere to this pattern. Some technically competent, job-centered, intensive, and tough managers have achieved impressive levels of productivity. However, the members of these groups showed unfavorable attitudes towards their work and supervisors, hostility and resentment towards management, a high number of grievances that went to arbitration, frequent slow-downs, work stoppages, waste, and high job turnover. Likert and Kahn (1956) reported a study that attempted to evaluate the effects of (1) tighter controls and direction and (2) greater employee autonomy and participation as alternative ways to achieve high productivity and employee satisfaction in the same organization! In some sections of the company, results were sought through closer supervision, more detailed work procedures, and other forms of tighter control and direction. In other sections, a program of encouraging more autonomy and participation in decision making was followed. Responsibility for decisions was pushed down to lower levels of the organization and greater freedom was given employees. *In both situations, productivity was increased about 15-20 percent.* Thus, contradictory leadership practices were effective in increasing productivity; however, employee morale changed for the worse in units where tighter controls were imposed and changed for the better in those units where greater autonomy was instituted.

3. The greater the amount of unreasonable pressure toward production that men feel from their supervisors, the lower the productivity and the less confidence and trust they have in their supervisors.

Even this finding must be tempered by situational factors; that is, increasing management pressures toward productivity may have different results depending upon the initial level of pressure. At initially low levels of pressure, an increase in emphasis upon productivity by supervisors not only results in higher productivity but also increases the satisfaction of the men with their supervisor. However, at higher levels of pressure, further increases in emphasis upon productivity by supervisors frequently tend to result in lower productivity and adverse reactions toward the supervisor.

SUMMARY

The studies surveyed represent a fair sampling of more than two decades of leadership research, and, on the basis of these findings, some general conclusions can be drawn.

The available evidence seems to indicate that there are probably no personality traits or characteristics that consistently distinguish the leader from his followers. There is some evidence, however, to suggest that the leader probably cannot be markedly different from his subordinates if he is to be followed. The results of a number of studies indicate that leadership does not occur in a vacuum but at a particular time and place and under a particular set of circumstances. Therefore, the situation determines to some degree the kinds of leadership skills and behavior that may be required. One reassuring finding that has emerged from these studies has been the "discovery" that, when formal or designated leadership fails to provide its required functions, there is a tendency for other members of the group to step in and perform the "needed" functions so that there will be a minimal loss in group effectiveness.

Some workers have investigated the effects of differing kinds of leadership styles and have begun the process of explicating what kinds of leadership acts or behavior helps groups "move forward" and function effectively. Some of these studies suggest that there is a tendency for democratic or participatory leadership behavior to be associated with productivity, increased worker morale, and a number of other factors. Directive leadership has been found to lead to equally high productivity but often results in low morale and commitment to work. However, the relationship between leadership styles and job performance is much too complex to be explained simply by "democratic" or "authoritarian" leadership practices. Different leadership practices seem appropriate for different situations. Thus, under certain conditions, participative leadership may be most effective. Under other conditions, a more directive leadership may be required. Again, the personality characteristics and expectations of subordinates will influence the kinds of leadership practices that are most effective. An increase in the degree of follower participation will often have favorable effects if the subordinates have relatively high needs for independence, a readiness to assume responsibility, the necessary knowledge and experience to deal with problems, and an identification with the goals of the organization. (Tannenbaum & Schmidt, 1958) However, the use of participatory practices with workers who lack these attributes might have highly adverse and undesirable effects.

There is a growing body of research indicating rather clear differences between the behavior of high- and low-production workers in real-life work situations. These studies suggest that high-production supervisors tend to supervise their subordinates less closely, spend more time consulting with their workers, and give them more opportunities to participate in decisions that affect them than do low-production leaders. The quality of the leader-subordinate relationship—the degree of genuine respect and consideration that the leader shows for the follower's needs—appears to be a crucial factor here. This is perhaps another way of saying that employee-centered leadership tends to be more closely associated with subordinate productivity, morale, and job satisfaction than does production-centered leadership.

On the basis of the research surveyed in this presentation, it would seem clear that leaders accomplish their work through other people and their success as leaders depends upon their ability to enlist and maintain follower commitment and collaboration for the attainment of group or organizational goals. In this respect, some of the research considered here may provide ideas that may be worth considering in the concrete work situation. However, at the present time, there is no straight-forward set of supervisory practices that will always yield the best results. Research reported in this presentation suggests that a leader's objectives may be reached through multiple and sometimes even contradictory means. At this point, it would appear that the choice of alternative leadership practices for a given individual will depend upon a number of factors, such as the following:

The leader's personal preference or "style."

The leader's skill in applying various leadership practices.

The leader's confidence in his subordinates.

The leader's value system or the importance that he attaches to organizational efficiency, personal growth of subordinates, company profits, et cetera.

The leader's assessment of the "situation" of his subordinates.

The leader's evaluation of possible undesirable side effects of a particular practice.

Viewed from a historical point of view, the studies considered indicate that behavioral scientists are making progress in understanding the phenomena of leadership. Research has come a long way from the early study of leadership traits, and investigators can now state with some certainty what they know and do not know. Moreover, they are in a position to begin to specify some of the conditions under which given leadership practices may be effective. However, while behavioral scientists may be able to provide managers and supervisors with some tentative "guidelines," leadership research can never specify the "proper" practices for all situations. *In the concrete leadership situation, the final choice and responsibility for specific action must always fall back upon the judgment and good common sense of frail human beings, and, in all due respects to the "leader," this is as it should be.*

REFERENCES

Bales, R. F., *Interaction Process Analysis: A Method for the Study of Small Groups* (Cambridge, Mass.: Addison-Wesley Press, 1950).

Barnard, C. J., *The Function of the Executive* (Cambridge, Mass.: Harvard University Press, 1948).

Bass, B., *Leadership, Psychology and Organizational Behavior* (New York: Harper, 1960).

Baumgartel, Howard, "Leadership Style as a Variable in Research Administration," *Administrative Science Quarterly*, Vol. II (1957).

Bavelas, A., "Morale and Training of Leaders," *Civilian Morale*, G. Watson, ed. (Boston, Mass.: Houghton-Mifflin, 1942).

Benne, K. D. and P. Sheats, "Functional Roles of Group Members," *Journal of Social Issues*, Vol. IV (1948).

Bird, C., *Social Psychology* (New York: Appleton-Century, 1940).

Bovard, E. W., Jr., "Group Structure and Perception," *Journal of Abnormal & Social Psychology*, Vol. XLVI (1951).

Burke, R., "Approaches to Understanding Leadership" (an unpublished manuscript).

Carter, L., Beatrice Haythorn & J. Lanzatta, "The Behavior of Leaders and Other Members," *Journal of Abnormal & Social Psychology*, Vol. XLV (1950).

Cartwright, D. and A. F. Zander (eds.), *Group Dynamics: Research and Theory* (Evanston, Ill.: Row, Peterson, 1953).

Coch, L. and J. French, Jr., "Overcoming Resistances to Change," *Human Relations*, Vol. I (1948).

Crockett, W., "Emergent Leadership in Small, Decision-Making Groups," *Journal of Abnormal & Social Psychology*, Vol. LI (1955).

Dunkerly, M. D., "A Statistical Study of Leadership Among College Women," *Studies in Psychology and Psychiatry*, Vol. IV (Washington, D. C.: Catholic University of America, 1940).

Hare, A. P., "Small Discussions with Participatory and Supervisory Leadership," *Journal of Abnormal & Psychology*, Vol. LVIII (1953).

Henry, W. E., "Executive Personality and Job Success," *American Management Association*, Personnel Series, No. 120 (1948).

Jenkins, W. O., "A Review of Leadership Studies with Particular Reference to Military Problems," *Psychological Bulletin*, Vol. ILIV (1947).

Kahn, R. and D. Katz, "Leadership Practices in Relation to Productivity and Morale," *Group Dynamics: Research and Theory*, Cartwright and Zander, eds. (Evanston, Ill.: Row, Peterson, 1953).

Likert, R., *New Patterns of Management* (New York: McGraw-Hill, 1961).

Likert, R. and R. L. Kahn, "Planning for Effective Leadership," *Planning and Training for Effective Leadership*, S. Seashore, ed. (Ann Arbor, Mich.: Foundation for Research on Human Behavior, 1956).

Pelz, D. C., "Leadership Within a Heirarchical Organization," *Journal of Social Issues*, Vol. VII (1951).

Pfiffner, J. M., "The Effective Supervisor: An Organization Research Study," *Personnel*, Vol. XXXI (1955).

Preston, M. G. and R K. Heintz, "Effects of Participatory Versus Supervisory Leadership on Group Judgment," *Journal of Abnormal & Social Psychology*, Vol. XLIV (1949).

Seashore, Stanley, *Group Cohesiveness in the Industrial Work Group* (Ann Arbor, Mich.: Institute for Social Research, 1954).

Stanton, E. S., "Company Policies and Supervisors' Attitudes

Toward Supervision," *Journal of Applied Psychology*, Vol. XLIV (1960).

Stogdill, R. M., "Personal Factors Associated with Leadership: A Survey of the Literature," *Journal of Psychology*, Vol. XXV (1948).

Stogdill, R. M., "Studies in Naval Leadership, Part II," *Groups, Leadership and Men*, H. Buetzkow, ed. (Pittsburgh, Pa.: Carnegie Press, 1951).

Tannenbaum, R. and W. H. Schmidt, "How to Choose a Leadership Pattern" *Harvard Business Review*, Vol. XXXVI (1958).

Tead, O., *The Art of Leadership* (New York: McGraw-Hill, 1935).

Thrasher, F. M., *The Gang* (Chicago: University of Chicago Press, 1927).

Trist, E. L. and K. W. Bamforth, "Some Social and Pshchological Consequences of the Long-wall Method of Goal Getting," Human Relations, Vol. IV (1951).

Wald, R. M. and R. A. Doty, "The Top Executive: A Firsthand Profile," *Harvard Business Review*, Vol. XXXII (1954).

White, R. and R L. Lippitt, "Leadership Behavior and Member Reaction in Three Social Climates" *Group Dynamics*, D. Cartwright and A. Zander, eds. (New York: Row, Peterson, 1956).

Whyte, W. H., *The Organization Man* (New York: Simon & Schuster, 1956).

Whyte, W. F., *Street Corner Society* (Chicago: University of Chicago Press, 1943).

STYLE OR CIRCUMSTANCES: THE LEADERSHIP ENIGMA*

by Fred E. Fiedler

What is it that makes a person an effective leader?

We take it for granted that good leadership is essential to business, to government and to all the myriad groups and organizations that shape the way we live, work and play.

We spend at least several billions of dollars a year on leadership development and executive recruitment in the United States. Leaders are paid 10, 20 and 30 times the salary of ordinary workers. Thousands of books and articles on leadership have been published. Yet, we still know relatively little about the factors that determine a leader's success or failure.

Psychologists have been concerned with two major questions in their research on leadership: How does a man become a leader? What kind of personality traits or behavior makes a person an *effective* leader? For the past 15 years, my own work at the University of Illinois Group-Effectiveness Research Laboratory has concentrated on the latter question.

Psychologists used to think that special personality traits would distinguish leaders from followers. Several hundred research studies have been conducted to identify these special traits. But the search has been futile.

People who become leaders tend to be somewhat more intelligent, bigger, more assertive, more talkative than other members of their group. But these traits are far less important than most people think. What most frequently distinguishes the leader from his co-workers is that he knows more about the group task or that he can do it better. A bowling team is likely to

* Reprinted from *Psychology Today* Magazine March, 1969. Copyright Communications/Research/Machines/Inc.

choose its captain from good rather than poor bowlers, and the foreman of a machine shop is more likely to be a good machinist than a poor one.

In many organizations, one only has to live long in order to gain experience and seniority, and with these a position of leadership.

In business and industry today, the men who attain a leadership position must have the requisite education and talent. Of course, as W. Lloyd Warner and James C. Abegglen of the University of Chicago have shown, it has been most useful to come from or marry into a family that owns a large slice of the company's stock.

Becoming a leader, then, depends on personality only to a limited extent. A person can become a leader by happenstance, simply by being in the right place at the right time, or because of such various factors as age, education, experience, family background and wealth.

Almost any person in a group may be capable of rising to a leadership position if he is rewarded for actively participating in the group discussion, as Alex Bavelas and his colleagues at Stanford University have demonstrated. They used light signals to reward low-status group members for supposedly "doing the right thing." However, unknown to the people being encouraged, the light signal was turned on and off at random. Rewarded in this unspecified, undefined manner, the low-status member came to regard himself as a leader and the rest of the group accepted him in his new position.

It is commonly observed that personality and circumstances interact to determine whether a person will become a leader. While this statement is undoubtedly true, its usefulness is rather limited unless one also can specify how a personality trait will interact with a specific situation. We are as yet unable to make such predictions.

Having become a leader, how does one get to be an effective leader? Given a dozen or more similar groups and tasks, what makes one leader succeed and another fail? The answer to this question is likely to determine the philosophy of leader-training programs and the way in which men are selected for executive positions.

There are a limited number of ways in which one person can influence others to work together toward a common goal. He can coerce them or he can coax them. He can tell people what to do and how to do it, or he can share the decision-making and concentrate on his relationship with his men rather than on the execution of the job.

Of course, these two types of leadership behavior are gross oversimplifications. Most research by psychologists on leadership has focused on two clusters of behavior and attitudes, one labeled autocratic, authoritarian and task-oriented, and the other as democratic, equalitarian, permissive and group-oriented. The first type of leadership behavior, frequently advocated in conventional supervisory and military systems, has its philosophical roots in Frank W. Taylor's *Principles of Scientific Management* and other early 20th Century industrial engineering studies. The authoritarian, task-oriented leader takes all responsibility for making decisions and directing the group members. His rationale is simple: "I do the thinking and you carry out the orders."

The second type of leadership is typical of the "New Look" method of management advocated by men like Douglas McGregor of M.I.T. and Rensis Likert of the University of Michigan. The democratic, group-oriented leader provides general rather than close supervision and his concern is the effective use of human resources through participation. In the late 1940s, a related method of leadership training was developed based on confrontation in unstructured group situations where each participant can explore his own motivations and reactions. Some excellent studies on this method, called T-group, sensitivity or laboratory training, have been made by Chris Argyris of Yale, Warren Bennis of State University of New York at Buffalo and Edgar Schein of M.I.T.

Experiments comparing the performance of both types of leaders have shown that each is successful in some situations and not in others. No one has been able to show that one kind of leader is always superior or more effective.

A number of researchers point out that different tasks require different kinds of leadership. But what kind of situation requires what kind of leader? To answer this question, I shall present a theory of leadership effectiveness that spells out the specific circumstances under which various leadership styles are most effective.

We must first of all distinguish between leadership style and leader behavior. Leader behavior refers to the specific acts in which a leader engages while directing or coordinating the work of his group. For example, the leader can praise or criticize, make helpful suggestions, show consideration for the welfare and feelings of members of his group.

Leadership style refers to the underlying needs of the leader that motivate his behavior. In other words, in addition to performing the task, what personal needs is the leader attempting to satisfy? We have found that a leader's actions or behavior sometimes does change as the situation or group changes, but his basic needs appear to remain constant.

To classify leadership styles, my colleagues and I have developed a simple questionnaire that asks the leader to describe the person with whom he can work least well:

LPC—Least-Preferred Co-worker

Think of the person with whom you can work least well. He may be someone you work with now, or he may be someone you knew in the past. Use an X to describe this person as he appears to you.

helpful :—:—:—:—:—:—:—:—: frustrating
8 7 6 5 4 3 2 1

unenthusiastic :—:—:—:—:—:—:—:—: enthusiastic
1 2 3 4 5 6 7 8

efficient :—:—:—:—:—:—:—:—: inefficient
8 7 6 5 4 3 2 1

From the replies, a Least-Preferred-Co-worker (LPC) score is obtained by simply summing the item scores. The LPC score does not measure perceptual accuracy, but rather reveals a person's emotional reaction to the people with whom he cannot work well.

In general, the high-scoring leader describes his least-preferred co-worker in favorable terms. The high-LPC leader tends to be "relationship-oriented." He gets his major satisfaction from establishing close personal relations with his group members. He uses the group task to gain the position of prominence he seeks.

The leader with a low score describes his least-preferred co-worker in unfavorable terms. The low-LPC leader is primarily "task-oriented." He obtains his major satisfaction by successfully completing the task, even at the risk of poor interpersonal relations with his workers.

Since a leader cannot function without a group, we must also know something about the group that the leader directs. There are many types of groups, for example, social groups which promote the enjoyment of individuals and "counteracting" groups such as labor and management at the negotiating table. But here we shall concentrate on groups that exist for the purpose of performing a task.

From our research, my associates and I have identified three major factors that can be used to classify group situations: (1) position power of the leader, (2) task structure, and (3) leader-member personal relationships. Basically, these classifications measure the kind of power and influence the group gives its leader.

We ranked group situations according to their favorableness for the leader. Favorableness here is defined as the degree to which the situation enables the leader to exert influence over the group.

Based on several studies, leader-member relations emerged as the most important factor in determining the leader's influence over the group. Task structure is rated as second in importance, and position power as third. (*See illustration.*)

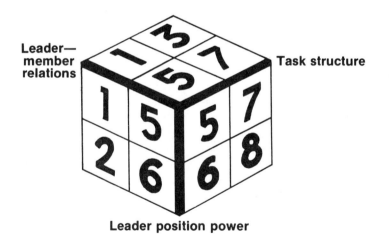

GROUP SITUATION MODEL. Task-oriented groups are classified in a three-dimensional model using the three major factors affecting group performance.

Under most circumstances, the leader who is liked by his group and has a clear-cut task and high position power obviously has everything in his favor. The leader who has poor relationships with his group members, an unstructured task and weak position power likely will be unable to exert much influence over the group.

The personal relationships that the leader establishes with his group members depend at least in part upon the leader's personality. The leader who is loved, admired and trusted can influence the group regardless of his position power. The leader who is not liked or trusted cannot influence the group except through his vested authority. It should be noted that a leader's assessment of how much he is liked often differs markedly from the group's evaluation.

Task structure refers to the degree the group's assignment can be programmed and specified in a step-by-step fashion. A highly structured task does not need a leader with much position power because the leader's role is detailed by the job specifications. With a highly structured task, the leader clearly knows what to do and how to do it, and the organization can back him up at each step. Unstructured tasks tend to have more than one correct solution that may be reached by any of a variety of methods. Since there is no step-by-step method that can be programmed in advance, the leader cannot influence the group's success by ordering them to vote "right" or be creative. Tasks of committees, creative groups and policy-making groups are typically unstructured.

Position power is the authority vested in the leader's position. It can be readily measured in most situations. An army general obviously has more power than a lieutenant, just as a department head has more power than an office manager. But our concern here is the effect this position power has on group performance. Although one would think that a leader with great power will get better performance from his group, our studies do not bear out this assumption.

However, it must be emphasized that in some situations position power may supersede task structure (the military). Or a very highly structured task (launching a moon probe) may outweigh the effects of interpersonal relations. The organization determines both the task structure and the position power of the leader.

In our search for the most effective leadership style, we went back to the studies that we had been conducting for more than a decade. These studies investigated a wide variety of groups and leadership situations, including basketball teams, business management, military units, boards of directors, creative groups and scientists engaged in pure research. In all of these groups that had performed their tasks successfully or unsuccessfully and then correlated the effectiveness of group performance with leadership style.

Now by plotting these correlations of leadership style against our scale of group situations, we could, for the first time, find what leadership style works best in each situation. When we connected the median points on each column, the result was a bell-shaped curve. *(See illustration.)*

Group Situation

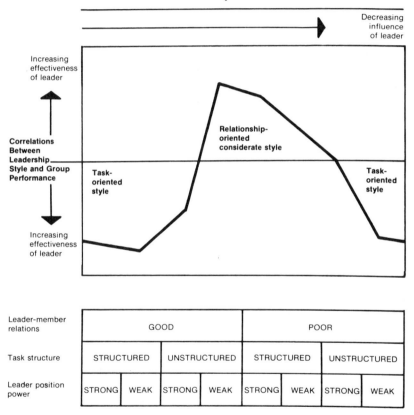

Leader-member relations	GOOD				POOR			
Task structure	STRUCTURED		UNSTRUCTURED		STRUCTURED		UNSTRUCTURED	
Leader position power	STRONG	WEAK	STRONG	WEAK	STRONG	WEAK	STRONG	WEAK

THE EFFECTIVE LEADER. Directive leaders perform best in very favorable or in unfavorable situations. Permissive leaders are best in moxed situations. Graph is based on studies of over 800 groups.

The results show that a task-oriented leader performs best in situations at both extremes—those in which he has a great deal of influence and power, and also in situations where he has no influence and power over the group members.

Relationship-oriented leaders tend to perform best in mixed situations where they have only moderate influence over the group. A number of subsequent studies by us and others have confirmed these findings.

The results show that we cannot talk about simply good leaders or poor leaders. A leader who is effective in one situation may or may not be effective in another. Therefore, we must specify the situations in which a leader performs well or badly.

This theory of leadership effectiveness by and large fits our everyday experience. Group situations in which the leader is liked, where he has a clearly defined task and a powerful position, may make attempts at nondirective, democratic leadership detrimental or superfluous. For example, the captain of an airliner can hardly call a committee meeting of the crew to share in the decision-making during a difficult landing approach. On the other hand, the chairman of a voluntary committee cannot ask with impunity that the group members vote or act according to his instructions.

Our studies also have shown that factors such as group-member abilities, cultural heterogeneity and stressfulness of the task affect the degree to which the leader can influence members of the group. But the important finding and the consistent finding in these studies has been that mixed situations require relationship-oriented leadership while very favorable and very unfavorable job situations require task-oriented leaders.

Perhaps the most important implication of this theory of leadership is that the organization for which the leader works is as responsible for his success or failure as is the leader himself.

The chances are that *anyone* who wants to become a leader can become one if he carefully chooses the situations that are favorable to his leadership style.

The notion that a man is a "born" leader, capable of leading in all circumstances, appears to be nothing more than a myth. If there are leaders who excel under all conditions, I have not found them in my 18 years of research.

When we think of improving leadership performance, we tend to think first of training the leader. Personnel psychologists and managers typically view the executive's position as fixed and unchangeable and the applicant as highly plastic and trainable. A man's basic style of leadership depends upon his personality. Changing a man's leadership style means trying to change his personality. As we know from experiences in psychotherapy, it may take from one to several years to effect lasting changes in a personality structure. A leader's personality is not likely to change becuase of a few lectures or even a few weeks of intensive training.

It is doubtful that intensive training techniques can change an individual's style of leadership. However, training programs could be designed to provide the opportunity for a leader to learn in which situations he can perform well and in which he is likely to fail. Laboratory training also may provide the leader with some insights into his personal relationships with group members.

Our theory of leadership effectiveness predicts that a leader's performance can be improved by engineering or fitting the job to the leader. This is based, at least in part, on the belief that it is almost always easier to change a leader's work environment than to change his personality. The leader's authority, his task and even his interpersonal relations within his group members can be altered, sometimes without making the leader aware that this has been done.

For example, we can change the leader's position power in either direction. He can be given a higher rank if this seems necessary. Or he can be given subordinates who are equal or nearly equal to him in rank. His assistants can be two or three ranks below him, or we can assign him men who are expert in their specialties. The leader can have sole authority for a job, or he may be required to consult with his group. All communications to group members may be channeled through the leader, making him the source of all the inside information, or all members of the group can be given the information directly, thus reducing the leader's influence.

The task structure also can be changed to suit the leader's style. Depending upon the group situation, we can give the leader explicit instructions or we can deliberately give him a vague and nebulous goal.

Finally, we can change the leader-member relations. In some situations it may be desirable to improve leader-member relations by making the group homogeneous in culture and language or in technical and educational background. Interdisciplinary groups are notoriously difficult to handle, and it is even more difficult to lead a group that is racially or culturally mixed. Likewise, we can affect leader-member relations by giving a leader subordinates who get along well with their supervisor or assign a leader to a group with a history of trouble or conflict.

It may seem that often we are proposing the sabotaging of the leader's influence over his group. Although common sense might make it seem that weakening the leader's influence will lower performance, in actuality our studies show that this rarely happens. The average group performance (in other words, the leader's effectiveness) correlates poorly with the degree of the leader's influence over the group.

In fact, the findings from several studies suggest that a particular leader's effectiveness may be improved even though the situation is made less favorable for him.

The leader himself can be taught to recognize the situations that best fit his style. A man who is able to avoid situations in which he is likely to fail, and seek out situations that fit his leadership style, will probably become a highly successful and effective leader. Also, if he is aware of his strengths and weaknesses, the leader can try to change his group situation to match his leadership style.

However, we must remember that good leadership performance depends as much upon the organization as it does upon the leader. This means that we must learn not only how to train men to be leaders, but how to build organizations in which specific types of leaders can perform well.

In view of the increasing scarcity of competent executives, it is to an organization's advantage to design jobs to fit leaders instead of attempting merely to fit a leader to the job.